Money Unmade

Money Unmade

Barter and the Fate of Russian Capitalism

DAVID WOODRUFF

CORNELL UNIVERSITY PRESS ITHACA AND LONDON

First published 1999 by Cornell University Press

Printed in the United States of America

Cornell University Press strives to use
environmentally responsible suppliers and materials
to the fullest extent possible in the publishing of its
books. Such materials include vegetable-based, low-
VOC inks and acid-free papers that are recycled,
totally chlorine-free, or partly composed of
nonwood fibers.

Library of Congress Cataloging-in-Publication Data

Woodruff, David, 1940–
Money unmade : barter and the fate of Russian
capitalism / David Woodruff.
p.   cm.
Includes index.
ISBN 0-8014-3660-5 (cloth : alk. paper)
1. Monetary policy—Russia (Federation)
2. Barter—Russia (Federation)
3. Financial crises—Russia (Federation)
4. Russia (Federation)—Economic conditions—1991–
I. Title.
HG1080.2.W66   1999
332.4'6'0947—dc21   99-21491

Cloth printing
10 9 8 7 6 5 4 3 2 1

To Yuliya
for life

The world is full of money-talk; economists are our new wise men. . . . Never trust them; trust only the novelists, those deeper bankers who spend their time trying to turn pieces of printed paper into value, but never pretend that the result is anything more than a useful fiction.

—Malcom Bradbury, *Rates of Exchange,* 1983

Contents

Figures and Tables

Preface

On August 14, 1998, as the ruble sank on the currency markets, Boris Yeltsin arrived in the Russian city of Novgorod. Standing on the runway in front of his helicopter, Yeltsin assured reporters that there would be no devaluation of the ruble.

An unremarkable tableau, typical of any country in the midst of a currency crisis. Take a closer look, though, and it becomes remarkable indeed. The helicopter in the background was an ordinary government helicopter, not Yeltsin's special presidential one. That helicopter was in the shop. Maintenance work had long since been finished, but the government could find no rubles to pay for it. All that the president's staff could offer the mechanics was a less desirable means of payment—trainloads of coal.

The only thing unusual about this story is that the mechanics did not agree to the deal. Beyond the realm of money, to which Yeltsin's words were addressed, lay a vast and complicated world of nonmonetary exchange. Six years after the collapse of the Soviet Union, Russia had built an economy in which rubles were valued and universally accepted. But alternate means of payment such as barter and privately issued quasi monies were extraordinarily common. These exchange practices were not a carryover from the Soviet economy; they had new causes and new consequences. And they spread rapidly. By 1998, industry collected as much as 70 percent of its receipts in nonmonetary form, leaving many firms with too little cash to pay salaries and taxes. Many taxes could be collected only in kind. To the denizens of lands where money is taken for granted, the situation seemed absurd, incomprehensible, or laughable. An eminent British business weekly titillated its readers with the news that employees of a tire factory in Volgograd had received their wages in dildos. An American talk-show host, amused by similar reports about the humiliations the nonmonetary economy inflicts on Russian workers, went to the trouble of constructing a mock automated teller, trying to maintain a deadpan expression as he "withdrew" rolls of toilet paper.

What was farce to those outside of Russia was tragedy to those within it. In some industries, wage delays reached over a year. Hunger strikes and the blocking of rail lines were only the most visible manifestations of the suffering that such delays brought on. More quietly and significantly, as many as 60 percent of Russians made a complete or partial retreat from the division of labor, using subsistence farming to minimize their need for the cash their regular jobs as doctors, engineers, or mine workers could not be counted on to generate. Provincial governments, reluctantly taking as taxes what local industry produced, struggled with the problem of how to trade the steel (or fish, or cars) they did not need for the medicines (or electricity, or bricks) they most urgently did. In Moscow, meanwhile, bureaucrats launched series after series of increasingly desperate measures to sweep what cash was available into federal coffers, struggling to avoid financial collapse and make payments on debts swelled by the fiscal failures stemming from nonmonetary exchange.

That the emergence of barter in Russia came as such a surprise and appeared so absurd reflected a profound failure of historical perspective. For most outside observers, Russia's primary challenge after the collapse of the Soviet Union lay in implementing market-oriented measures, such as privatization, or reducing inflation through a tight monetary policy. Since these measures were destined to be unpopular, Russia needed leaders able to ignore short-term discontent in favor of the long-term public good, which would be guaranteed by private ownership, competition, and the stability of the currency. Complaints about these policies were inevitable, but also invariably self-serving.

And so the story was told, over and over. New faces appeared in government, new issues arose on the policy agenda, but for too many, these were changes of actors and scenery in a play with a timeless script. Whether Russia had sufficiently committed reformers to enact the necessary tough measures—this was the unending drama, the longest-running show on the world stage. When barter exchange achieved astounding dimensions and finally began to be noticed, it was just the latest set change. Barter, our familiar means of understanding told us, could only be a version of some known threat to market reforms: a means of tax evasion, a nefarious scheme to facilitate graft, or a system of hidden subsidies. In any event, unflinching reformers needed to take tough measures and get rid of it, as soon as possible. But barter was not just another example of the unending resistance to market reform its advocates were proud to ignore. It was a sign that entirely different issues were at stake.

At the center of the political and economic maelstrom engulfing the Russian Federation in the 1990s is the government's unsuccessful attempt to gain a monopoly over the definition of the generally accepted means of payment. This project of monetary consolidation is not something forced on Russia's leaders by peculiar circumstances. It is a critical but neglected aspect of state building elsewhere. In the developed countries, a monopoly on money is the cornerstone of the economic sovereignty of the national state. We take it so much for granted that only an unusual event, such as the effort to introduce a single European currency, prompts the recollection that the nation-state's monetary powers even have a history. Despite its centrality to economic state building, monetary consolidation has provoked virtually nothing in the way of studies. Yet even a cursory historical investigation of how developed countries achieved monetary consolidation reveals that it is an enormously difficult project of enduring political significance. A unified monetary system is a complicated institution that has vast implications for social actors. Monetary consolidation demands substantial administrative capacities and provokes high-stakes political battles that shape state and society in lasting ways. National integration, and the historic political alliances on which it rests, take on institutional form in the struggle for sovereignty over money.

In the final years of the Soviet Union, the importance of money for national integration became manifest as the creaky financial machinery that had served the country since the 1930s broke down. A spiraling expansion of barter promoted a political and economic fragmentation intimately linked to the breakup of the USSR. When the leadership of the new Russia took power in late 1991, eliminating barter was at the top of its agenda. Yet initial successes were quickly and surprisingly reversed. A new Russian barter emerged in 1994, as changed economic conditions threatened industry with wholesale destruction. Local authorities, in particular, were in no position to tolerate this destruction. They promoted barter to make it possible for industry to continue operation. The result was ongoing monetary disarray and a spread of surrogate monies that federal authorities could do little to stop.

By 1998, Russia's efforts at monetary consolidation were at an impasse. Disagreement between local and national authorities over how to pursue monetary consolidation grew into a stalemate when each proved to have the ability to block the other's preferred solutions in decisive arenas. Instead of an integrated money based on a national political resolution, Russia developed a profusion of barter and quasi-monetary circuits penetrating both the economy and the fiscal system, imperfectly insulated from one another, reflecting local political accommodations among their participants.

Three days after Yeltsin's confident runway assertion, Russia announced a devaluation. Within two weeks, the ruble had sunk by half against the dollar. The banking system, heavily dependent on foreign borrowing, teetered on the edge of collapse. A political crisis of enormous dimensions and uncertain outcome paralyzed policy making. It was unclear under whose leadership the weakened Russian state would return to the dilemma of monetary consolidation. But return it would. The political impasse over monetary consolidation did not promise to be eternal. Before the crisis, political forces with a stake in the national integration that monetary consolidation would promote had begun to coalesce. They proposed different resolutions to the impasse, offering the national state a chance to choose its allies in the battle for sovereignty over money.

The crisis weakened some of these forces and strengthened others. It did not change the underlying political realities. By 1998, six years of the new Russian history had demonstrated what was clear from a long record of world history: sovereignty over money cannot simply be imposed by an ambitious state on a recalcitrant society. Even less is it an automatic by-product of sufficiently disciplined policies aimed at "market reform." Monetary consolidation is a political achievement. It requires political support.

My research on barter has been founded on too many unequal exchanges. To the Russian officials and businesspeople who somehow found time in their hectic schedules to answer my questions and solve my organizational problems, I offer the inadequate recompense of my thanks, without expecting it to cancel the debt.

I would never have written this book if Kiren Chaudhry had not taught me what it might mean to listen for the thunder of world history. My gratitude for her friendship, encouragement, advice, and example is profound.

Other colleagues and friends offered indispensable and deeply appreciated help in this endeavor. Gail Lapidus argued me off some cherished ideas, freeing me to start again. To Ken Jowitt, I offer apologies for all the wechsels in this book (it's really not my fault) and thanks for pointing me to the eternal. Neil Fligstein taught me how to look for how the future gets built. Michael Burawoy was unfailingly generous in sharing his own work and his intellectual excitement. Suzanne Berger and Richard Locke were both kind enough to read the manuscript at a time when their sympathy for my analytic aims and advice on how to realize them were exceptionally valuable to me. Conversations with Steve Holmes—starting with his memorable exegesis of Simmel at the Drunken Boat at some indeterminate date in the early 1990s—have invariably been intellectually bracing. Robin Einhorn gave us Schumpeter. Although he was not directly involved in this project, it would mean a great deal to me if Andrew Janos could see his influence on it.

I also thank Ron Michener for taking the trouble to find an old article in his computer and put it in readable format for me; it made a big difference. Andrea Graziosi gave helpful comments on Chapter 2, and he and A. Kvashonkin kindly made available the Piatakov letter cited there. Gregory Grossman, Oleg Kharkhordin, Robert Powell, and Jeff Robbins made valuable comments on earlier versions of Chapter 4. Rory MacFarquhar shared his hard-won expertise (and data) on Russian nonmonetary tax receipts. Roger Haydon of Cornell University Press managed the astounding feat of being absolutely unsparing without being the least discouraging. Two anonymous readers for the press gave stimulating suggestions. Pamela Clements graciously made my emergencies her own.

I am grateful for permission to reprint material from my essay, "Barter of the Bankrupt: The Politics of Demonetization in Russia's Federal State," in *Uncertain Transition: Ethnographies of Change in a Post-Socialist World,* edited by Michael Burawoy and Katherine Verdery (Boulder: Rowman and Littlefield, 1998). This material appears in Chapters 3 and 4 in substantially revised form.

To all who have helped me, the usual caveat applies with more than the usual force, for my struggles to incorporate their insightful and pertinent advice have met with success far less often than I would have liked. I must be held doubly responsible for all remaining errors.

And now, finally, the dizzying transition across the supposed divide between the professional and the personal, and the end of a long road. At the start of that road I had the enormous good fortune of Peter Blitstein's intellectual companionship, and I would have been permanently diminished without it. Erik Seeman helped me with Shays, and so much else. Oleg Kharkhordin's intellectual and social alchemy have been constantly enriching. Irina Boiko, Vitalii Ivanov, Natalia Kigai, and Igor Sanachev helped me feel at home far from home as I researched this book. I feel a particular sense of gratitude to my mother, father, and brother, with whom I first started to argue.

Five years ago, the kindest of fates took me to a city to which fate has not been kind: Vladivostok, perhaps the most distressing example of the consequences of Russia's monetary fragmentation. Vladivostok did much to inspire this project—and also gave me the person without whom I could never have finished it. To her this book is dedicated.

DAVID WOODRUFF

St. Petersburg

Note on Transliteration

In footnotes, I have transliterated Russian words with the Library of Congress system. In the body of the text, I generally follow the same system, though with some concessions to reader comfort: Yeltsin, not El'tsin; Primorye, not Primor'e. Unless otherwise specified, all translations from Russian are my own.

Money Unmade

INTRODUCTION

Making Money

> Money becomes increasingly a public institution in the strict sense of the word; it consists more and more of what public authorities, public institutions, and the various forms of intercourse and guarantees of the general public make of money, and the extent to which they legitimize it.
>
> —Georg Simmel

The new Russia was born in the hard autumn of 1991. In August, an abortive coup against Soviet president Mikhail Gorbachev collapsed. In its aftermath, Boris Yeltsin and his allies in the leadership of the Russian Republic quickly seized control of key bureaucracies and dismantled the decaying structures of the Communist Party. When the Soviet Union finally disappeared at the end of 1991, this was a fact of more historical than administrative significance. Russia's leadership had already had time to survey its depressing inheritance: an ephemeral authority over the crumbling remnants of the Soviet command economy. Central control over the allocation of production had all but evaporated, replaced by decentralized barter and regional fragmentation. As nearly ninety provinces claimed control over local resources, it began to appear that the new Russia might only be a way station on the path to further disintegration. Shortages of food and other goods in large cities reached a level unprecedented in decades. The structures ensuring the provision in a tolerable fashion of an industrial society's most basic needs were breaking down. The new government's sovereignty appeared evanescent. In these desperate circumstances, Russia's leaders embarked on twin projects: to create a new basis for economic order and a new foundation for state power.

These two projects met at a single point: money. In the new economic order, the desire to make money would set production in motion and ensure the livelihood of both individuals and society as a whole. In the new political order, effective sovereignty would rest on control of the monetary system mediating the sale of goods and the collection and spending of taxes. The ambition to directive control of the physical output of production through imperative commands would be abandoned. Russian life would revolve around money, generating, in the strange physics of politics, new centripetal forces to draw the country together.

Politicians assumed that making money work would be a simple matter that could be accomplished at a single stroke. On January 2, 1992, a sweeping price liberalization allowed most sellers to name the price of their goods. No longer would they be compelled to insist on barter as compensation for the inadequate prices the command economy permitted them to charge. Freeing prices would promote voluntary, money-motivated, and decentralized transactions—but it was not a program for the devolution of political power. Quite the opposite. In contemporary market economies the voluntary transaction is an exchange for money, and money is defined and managed by national authorities. When politics is focused on the management of a national currency—how much of it to print, how to maintain its value, how to set its exchange rate—it is inevitably national politics. Making money work would give the politics of the new Russian state a solid center.[1] When the ruble became czar, all roads would lead to Moscow.

Yet seven years after the fateful August that spelled the end of the Soviet Union, the project of refounding the state on a new money-driven market economy was very far from accomplished. Initially, barter retreated rapidly. The ruble had achieved universal purchasing power in Russia within months after price liberalization. But its power to command resources never became exclusive. New forms of barter began to spread in the first half of 1994, even as inflation dropped with tighter fiscal and monetary policy. Thenceforth barter became ever more prevalent, taking on new and more ramified forms. Firms and local governments issued their own surrogate monies, closely linked to the barter trade. By 1998, estimates for the share of sales in industry that did not rely on state-authorized money ranged from 50 to 70 percent. For all levels of the Russian state, the consequences were enormous. Caught in a profound fiscal crisis, first provincial governments and then the national government began increasingly to tax in kind. By 1996, on the order of 60 percent of local tax receipts and some 40 percent of federal tax receipts were in kind or in surrogate monies, and efforts

---

[1] Jacques Sapir, "Marchés régionaux ou régionalisation du marché?" in *La fin de l'URSS*, ed. Robert Berton-Hogge (Paris: La Documentation Française, 1992), 67–84, at 78–79, has made a parallel argument regarding the economic intent of price liberalization.

to switch to exclusively monetary taxation in the subsequent two years were thoroughly unsuccessful.[2] The move to money had stalled.

Russia's experience provides an exceptional opportunity to investigate an important and yet little studied aspect of state building. Alongside the monopoly on legitimate violence, monopolistic control over the definition and creation of money has become one of the powers we take for granted when we speak of the sovereign nation-state. But Russia's descent into barter reminds us that the powers of today's states are the ambitions of state builders of the past. Like any worthy ambition, the consolidation of monetary control is a difficult yet enduring achievement. Only in the second half of the nineteenth century can the central authorities of the most-developed countries be said to have achieved the thorough dominion in the monetary sphere they continue to maintain. This dominion was hard-won, the culmination of a process of organized coercion and political negotiation similar to those that resulted in the other powers defining the modern nation-state.[3]

This book is a study of the politics of Russia's economic transformation as an example of the politics of monetary consolidation. Monetary consolidation is state building in the monetary realm—the process whereby a state acquires a monopoly over the means of payment that is used across the territory it rules. States have good reasons to pursue such a monopoly. A unified monetary system helps a national state to extract and transmit resources, and so represents an enormous fiscal and administrative convenience. Building such a system is a difficult project that cannot be achieved by bureaucrats alone. Money does not just affect the relationship of a state to its citizens: it also affects the relationship of these citizens to one another. Successful monetary consolidation creates an infrastructure of exchange that is attractive not only to agents of the state. A nationally unified money is the paramount instrument of a nationally unified market, and so it speaks to the business interests of those who feel they can flourish in such a market. One can therefore argue, as I do in this book, that monetary consolidation will be completed when a national state's administrative and fiscal

[2] Estimated from OECD data given in Seija Lainela, "Money Surrogates and Regional Financial Markets in Russia" (paper presented at the 29th National Convention of the American Association for the Advancement of Slavic Studies, Seattle, November 21–23 1997). "In kind" is here a shorthand, as these figures include receipts in various sorts of so-called money surrogates that in essence serviced barter circuits. See chapter 5.

[3] On the place of state-defined money in modernity and in the nation-state, I have drawn above all on Georg Simmel, *The Philosophy of Money*, trans. Tom Bottomore and David Frisby from a first draft by Kaethe Mengelberg, 2d enlarged ed. (London: Routledge, 1990) and Karl Polanyi, *The Great Transformation: The Political and Economic Origins of Our Time* (Boston: Beacon Press, 1965). The relatively recent monopolization of money by the state is also stressed by Max Weber, *Economy and Society: An Outline of Interpretive Sociology*, ed. Guenther Roth and Claus Wittich, 2 vols. (Berkeley: University of California Press, 1978), 1:166–167.

interest coincides with business efforts to shape an institutional environment congenial to its commercial interests. Any state's monetary institutions bear the marks of the political accommodation that gave birth to them.

The politics of monetary consolidation is at base a politics of sovereignty. Through establishment of a monopoly on the definition of money, a state asserts its sovereignty vis-à-vis society, replacing societal self-regulation with state regulation in matters of monetary exchange. In Georg Simmel's characteristically beautiful formulation, when two people use money to facilitate exchange, "the pivotal point in the interaction . . . recedes from the direct line of contact between them, and moves to the relationship which each of them, through his interest in money, has with the economic community that accepts the money, and demonstrates this fact by having money minted by its highest representative."[4] Monetary consolidation also involves determination of the territorial locus of monetary authority. National states seeking to monopolize the definition and issue of money have often had to face down, co-opt, or compromise with subnational authorities asserting their own claims to sovereignty in this realm.

Center-regional conflicts over monetary consolidation have been critically important in Russia. They largely explain the explosion in barter and surrogate monies two years after price liberalization. In seeking the fundamental political roots of the failure of Russia's monetary consolidation, my point of departure is Karl Polanyi's classic, *The Great Transformation*. Polanyi focuses on the role of the national state, especially in England, in both making possible the transition to a self-regulating market and ameliorating its effects. On Polanyi's account, the prelude to the effort to create self-regulating markets was the prior concentration of economic power with the national state, which eliminated subnational authorities' ability to control entry to local markets. The national state was then in a position to remove the remaining barriers to the application of the market mechanism to money, labor, and land. However, trying to treat these "fictitious commodities" as if they were any other commodity, governed solely by the price mechanism, resulted in indiscriminate social destruction. As various social groups sought rescue from the devastation caused by self-regulated markets, they looked to the national state, which controlled monetary and customs policy. Market transformation, launched by a national state that had effectively destroyed the powers of subnational governments, wound up confirming the emergence of the national arena as the critical political forum.[5]

---

[4] Simmel, *Philosophy of Money*, 177. Compare Weber, *Economy and Society*, 636.
[5] My reading of Polanyi has been greatly influenced by the vigorous interpretation in Maurice Glasman, "The Great Deformation: Polanyi, Poland and the Terrors of Planned Spon-

Russia, by contrast, embarked on its market transformation before the groundwork of a unified internal market had been laid and with relatively weak institutional representation of federal authorities in its nearly ninety regional jurisdictions.[6] In particular, the central government was unable to block local creation of alternate means of payment. When the price mechanism threatened to wreak indiscriminate social destruction, the social reaction focused on local authorities, who used nonmonetary exchange to protect industry and maintain critical services. The desperate efforts of local authorities to protect local economies and the weakness of the deliquescing central-planning state inherited by Moscow combined to produce a dynamic unlike that described by Polanyi. The national government launched a market transformation, leading to demands for protection from the price mechanism. But these demands weakened central state institutions, including money, rather than consolidating them.

This dynamic highlighted the intimate connection between forms of exchange and the territorial patterns of economic and political life. Where money promotes national integration and subnational disintegration, barter promotes national disintegration and subnational integration. A national currency knits together a polity and economy national in scope for which the decisions of central authorities are critical. Yet money exchange promotes subnational disintegration as participants in existing organizational structures discover differential opportunities in the world of money. Barter, by contrast, spurs the creation of new coordinating structures on a regional or cross-regional level, due to the organizational difficulties involved in ensuring a "double coincidence of wants" (required since each barter sale must also be a satisfactory purchase). The drive to subnational integration created by barter is accompanied by strains on national integration stemming from both the weak capacity of central authorities to tax in kind and the limited ability of barter exchange to sustain a national market.

How to break through the impasse in monetary consolidation was the central issue of politics in Russia through the second half of the 1990s. It was one whose resolution promised to have a lasting impact on the coalitional basis of the Russian state. Because of money's role in mediating voluntary exchanges, the attainment of monetary consolidation can never and nowhere be a lonely triumph of technocratic political will. As contention

---

taneity," in *The New Great Transformation? Change and Continuity in East-Central Europe*, ed. Christopher G. A. Bryant and Edmund Mokrzycki (London: Routledge, 1994), 191–217.
[6] The best sources on the regionalization of the late Soviet economy are Sapir, "Marchés régionaux," and Philip Hanson, "Local Power and Market Reform in Russia," *Communist Economies & Economic Transformation* 5, no. 1 (1993): 45–60.

over the contours of the monetary order mobilized and redefined power-ful social forces, the Russian state found itself faced with the need to choose allies and come to an accommodation with them. These choices and ac-commodations would institutionalize the power and priorities of particular groups. In 1998, when this book was completed, it was too soon to say how monetary consolidation would be accomplished in Russia (and for that mat-ter, whether it indeed would be at all). Vivid contrasts between the coali-tions backing different solutions to the problem of monetary order made it obvious, however, that this was a political struggle of enormous stakes and enduring consequence. Thus, as I seek to demonstrate in the concluding chapter, Russia's experience underscores how the deep imbrication of the national state in the structures that sustain a market economy—and in money above all—means that building a market involves conflict over the terms on which the economic and political sovereignty of the national state can be constructed. No resolution of such conflicts can occur without last-ing implications not just for the administrative and territorial structure of the state (especially for the division of power among levels of government) but also for its political character.

From "Market Reform" to "Monetary Consolidation"

In this book, I tell the political history of Russia's stalemated effort at monetary consolidation. There was another choice—I could have used the emergence of barter to illustrate the difficulties, or even the failure, of mar-ket reform in Russia. My preference for "monetary consolidation" over "market reform" is not just a way of specifying my topic more precisely: it is a choice of narrative frame. Narrative frames make a difference both for research and for explanation. Their significance is analytic, not just stylis-tic. They direct attention to some facts and not to others and suggest in-terpretations of those facts. To choose a narrative frame is to make an assertion about where to hearken to what Schumpeter once termed "the thunder of world history."[7]

For some social scientists and for very many journalists, market reform has been the master narrative of the post-Soviet experience. They focus on policies adopted, measuring them against recommended market reforms. What market reform means is somewhat hard to pin down, since the term has been hostage to the changing agendas of international financial bod-ies. Usually, however, market reform is defined through checklists of mea-sures designed on the one hand to eliminate the differences between the state socialist economy and the textbook market economy, and on the other

[7] Joseph Schumpeter, "The Crisis of the Tax State," in *The Economics and Sociology of Capital-ism,* ed. Richard Swedberg (Princeton: Princeton University Press, 1991), 99–140 at 101.

to achieve the "structural adjustment" of the resultant market economy in line with policies developed to deal with third world etatism. Thus (in roughly chronological order), fixed prices must be liberalized, state enterprises must be privatized, inflation controlled, budget constraints hardened, subsidies withdrawn, hopelessly inefficient industries dismantled, resources allowed to flow to their most profitable uses, monopolies broken up, property rights secured, contracts enforced, and taxes rationalized (the last four being somewhat more recent additions to the list).[8]

Whatever its virtues, or vices, as policy advice, the progress of market reform is a dangerous narrative frame for anyone trying to make sense of the course of Russian politics and economics after the collapse of the Soviet Union. It is dangerous because it winds up obscuring the most vital questions facing Russian politicians and the Russian state. To present, and advocate, a checklist of policies that the national government should adopt is to assume that this government has already gathered to itself the sovereign powers, dominance over money among them, that underpin a market economy of national scope. So if there are deviations from the desired policies, they must be explained by the politics of the cash register—conflicts over who gets how much from a general till, contested at the national level.

These assumptions are a fundamental mistake. The politics of the cash register in Russia, to the extent that they are significant, are driven by another, deeper politics: the politics of sovereignty, that is, of rule and control.[9] At stake in this politics of rule and control are issues that don't translate quickly or directly into monetary terms. They involve contests over matters such as in which political arenas are the critical decisions made, who has the capacity to enforce them, and to what extent legal regulations structure interactions in the economy. I hope to demonstrate that as a narrative frame, monetary consolidation does a much better job of capturing these issues. First, though, I want to argue that the focus on market reform has led to a systematic misunderstanding of the nature of politics, the character and political significance of the state's role in a market economy, and the structure of state-society interactions.

The category of market reform impairs understanding of politics by being at once too broad and too narrow. It is too broad because it lumps policies involving distribution of resources already in the hands of the state (such as the revenue from inflationary currency issue) together with the creation of new institutions (such as a unified monetary system) that allow

---

[8] A convenient summary of the conventional wisdom is World Bank, *From Plan to Market: World Development Report 1996* (London: Oxford University Press, 1996).

[9] The contrast between "rule and control" and "cash register" or "allocation" images of politics is drawn from Stephen Krasner, "Approaches to the State: Alternative Conceptions and Historical Dynamics," *Comparative Politics* 16 (January 1984): 223–246.

successful businesses to benefit from market opportunities. In both cases, wealth or income is allocated, but the administrative capacities on which this allocation rests and the political arenas in which its contours are contested are radically different. These differences cannot be systematically examined once the question is posed as one of how far a country has advanced down the reform agenda. What is left is a narrow, least-common-denominator vision of politics, in which the state is an allocator of resources implicitly (and illegitimately) conceived in monetary terms. (Money only becomes the measure of all things as the result of a process of institutional formation!) On this view, any state that does not implement policies leading to a perfectly competitive market is allocating rents. Since the fundamental political significance of state action is allocation, the politics of market reform either revolve around technocratic efforts to placate losers without placing too great a drag on the entrepreneurial energies of winners, or around the effort to carry out a more complete market reform over the objections of wealthy rent-seeking interests who benefit from less than consistently liberal policies.[10] In either case, the substantive content of government policy is denuded of administrative meaning, reduced to its implications for the transfer of wealth or income.

Throughout this book, I argue that the reasonable materialist focus on the distributive implications of policy should not distract us from looking at the mechanisms through which such distribution takes place. An analysis of the creation of such mechanisms is at the heart of any adequate investigation into the politics of institutional origins. In this regard, the assumption that "what is basically at stake in regulatory processes is a transfer of wealth" (widely used in what has been termed the "positive political economy") is fatal to a study of the creation of the institutional underpinnings of capitalism.[11] Of course it should be no surprise that an approach that compares the results of regulation to what would be produced by an unregulated free market eviscerates investigation into the complex institutional bases of any market that approximates this ideal.

[10] The latter position has been especially popular in the analysis of Russia. See Joel Hellman, "Winners Take All: The Politics of Partial Reform in Postcommunist Transitions," *World Politics* 50 (January 1998): 203–234; Daniel Treisman, "Fighting Inflation in a Transitional Regime: Russia's Anomalous Stabilization," *World Politics* 50 (January 1998): 235–265; and Anders Åslund, *How Russia Became a Market Economy* (Washington: The Brookings Institution, 1995). Though all three exemplify the surrender of the terrain of politics to an externally defined reform agenda, the first two are vastly more sophisticated.

[11] The quotation is from Sam Peltzman, "Toward a More General Theory of Regulation," in *Chicago Studies in Political Economy*, ed. George Stigler (Chicago: University of Chicago Press, 1988), 234–266, at 237 but is representative of a large literature. The programmatic statement of positive political economy in political science is James E. Alt and Kenneth A. Shepsle, eds., *Perspectives on Positive Political Economy* (Cambridge: Cambridge University Press, 1990).

The least-common-denominator vision of politics as allocation resonates with a second concomitant of the focus on market reform. The economic argument for market reform has as a side effect the implication that market reform is a public good. Thus one should expect that no collective action will be produced on its behalf.[12] The benefits of market-oriented reform, it is argued, will be lower prices and a more efficient allocation of resources, benefits that will be experienced by consumers as individuals in the context of their daily transactions. Given the complexity of the economic processes that precede the consumptive transaction, consumers are unlikely to draw the connections between the prices they pay and, say, liberalization of capital markets or the breakup of monopolies. This is all the more true to the extent that these policies take time to bear fruit; they are, after all, predicated on a view of how market processes operate *over time* to consumer advantage. However, even the consumer sophisticated enough to share a liberal economist's view of the benefits of marketization is unlikely to get politically involved in its defense. Prices and the other benefits of market reform are nonexclusionary public goods, so there will always be a temptation to watch the battle for free markets from the sidelines. The cheaper fruits of consumer-oriented markets will only taste sweeter to those who expended no effort to make them possible. But from the ranks of those contemplating such a pleasant "free ride" into the consumer paradise no movement is likely to spring, leaving *für sich* an endlessly unreachable distance from *an sich*. Where the political organization of those who stand to gain from markets is hindered by the nontransparency and universal availability of the eventual benefits involved, the political organization of market opponents is held to be a matter of inevitability. Market-oriented measures such as the withdrawal of subsidies, privatization, demonopolization, and so on are likely to cause immediate pain to a compact group that has no trouble in identifying itself and is likely already to possess organizational form. The political logic suggests that only strong and insulated executive officials deaf to the well-orchestrated howls of anguish of these rent-seeking forces will be able to improve the lot of the multitudinous victims of monopoly, who are apparently no less worthy of such care for all that their selfishness chains them to political passivity.

Thus the view of market reform as a public good gives rise to what might be called a voluntarist vision of the state: If key state apparatuses are staffed by market reformers with the vision and political will to ignore the iron political logic (or the skill to soften it through strategic partial manipulations), economic reform will go forward. But without the presence of such dedicated individuals, the state degenerates into a tool of rent-seeking forces in

---

[12] Mancur Olson Jr., *The Logic of Collective Action: Public Goods and the Theory of Groups* (New York: Schocken, 1965). Cf. Hellman, "Winners," 206–207.

a bacchanalia of corruption.[13] Voluntarist approaches accordingly analyze policy as stemming from the political views and incorruptibility (neither subject to further analysis) of those who control key institutions.[14]

Both the interpretation of politics as allocation and the voluntarist image of the state conceive society as an assemblage of individuals who can be united only in demanding unwarranted subsidies that reduce social wealth.[15] This is why using market reform as a narrative frame has also proven to promote an exceptionally narrow vision of state-society relations, which are seen as structured above all by the "credibility" of government policy. The roots of this approach grow on the one hand from János Kornai's classic writings on soft-budget constraints, and on the other from the rational expectations research program in economics, which focuses on the effects of economic actors' predictions about government policy on their economic behavior.[16] Analysts writing in this latter school believe that if governments could make a credible commitment to a restrictive monetary policy, economic actors would adapt more quickly, reducing the recessionary costs associated with ending inflation. Developing together with expanded social-scientific interest in game theory, the credibility approach sought to view the relationship between a central policy-making authority and economic actors as a strategic interaction, in which each side sought to predict the other's future actions and act appropriately. In other words, as an authoritative survey put it, credibility school analysts "have been motivated by an effort to understand how a leader-follower game of two players—a dominant centralized policy-making body and a private sector consisting of many spatially separated atomistic agents, each of whom, being aware of no perceptible influence on the actions of others, takes as given the behavior of other participants in the game (including that of policy makers)."[17] This image of economic actors abstracts from their institutional

---

[13] Åslund, *How Russia Became a Market Economy,* is especially symptomatic.

[14] Hellman, "Winners," cleverly moves beyond the good bureaucrats–bad bureaucrats implications of trying to explain "market reform" by arguing that the voting public can become the defenders of the public good against rent seeking, and he thereby suggests democracy as the key institutional feature likely to promote market reform. This analysis (the validity of which depends on the substantive character of the policies democratic electorates were voting for, an issue not adequately investigated), though politically more interesting, in all other respects shares the anemic vision of the state criticized here.

[15] For an exceptionally direct formulation of this viewpoint, which is more often left implicit, see Maxim Boycko, Andrei Shleifer, and Robert Vishny, *Privatizing Russia* (Cambridge: Massachusetts Institute of Technology Press, 1995), 27.

[16] János Kornai, "The Soft Budget Constraint," *Kyklos* 39, no. 1 (1986): 3–30. For a survey of "credibility" in economics, see Keith Blackburn and Michael Christensen, "Monetary Policy and Policy Credibility: Theories and Evidence," *Journal of Economic Literature* 27 (March 1989): 1–45, on which this paragraph draws.

[17] Ibid., 8.

context.[18] It also assumes that any horizontal interactions between actors have no systematic consequences for their macroeconomically relevant behavior. Those analysts who embrace the policy credibility approach have no real way of investigating whether these assumptions are true and are naturally led away from studying the concrete institutional structures within which an economy functions.[19] What will shape behavior in society and economy are predictions by each individual agent about the state's behavior in allocating rents, or, equivalently, judgments on the political will of those presently in government.

In short, all too often, a focus on market reform has led to the assumption that politics is the allocation of rents, unless such is forestalled by political will credibly broadcasted. Reinhard Bendix once argued that in the course of nation building, a key historical passage occurs when "politics ceases to be a struggle over the distribution of sovereign powers [in which he included 'control of the currency'] ... and becomes a struggle over the distribution of the national product and over the policies and the administrative implementation which affect that distribution."[20] The distorting lens of market reform has made it appear that this transition has already taken place, that the heart of Russian politics lies in an endless siege of the cash register, not the acquisition of the power to rule and control.

These assumptions have been especially pronounced in the discussion of monetary matters, where they were given a surface plausibility by the notion that it would be relatively easy to get a state-socialist economy to adopt money as its guiding principle. Before the Russian government launched its radical market reforms, the general and largely implicit assumption was that monetary consolidation was a trivial matter of removing the restrictions on the use and role of money that characterized the Soviet economy. This simple model of how monetary consolidation would come about might be dubbed the "Bender's revenge" approach. In a famous novel published in 1931, *The Golden Calf,* Soviet satirists Ilf and Petrov chart the adventures of their con-man protagonist Ostap Bender as he pursues his dream of becoming a millionaire. Bender finally achieves his goal, just as the first five-year plan is opening, only to discover he has been pursuing a chimera. Bender had sought money in the sense described by Mary Douglas, "general purchasing power over all marketed goods."[21] Yet the luxuries that Bender had imagined money would buy him proved all but inaccessible.

---

[18] Ibid.

[19] Kornai's work is, in this regard, quite different from what followed it.

[20] Reinhard Bendix, *Nation Building and Citizenship: Studies of Our Changing Social Order,* new enlarged ed. (Berkeley: University of California Press, 1977), 129.

[21] Mary Douglas, "Primitive Rationing: A Study in Controlled Exchange," in *Themes in Economic Anthropology,* ed. Raymond Firth (London: Tavistock, 1967), 119–145, at 120.

Spaces in hotels were reserved for agricultural specialists or others doing useful work, and not simply any paying customers. Meals in dining halls were sold only to members of trade unions. Although money was still a necessary part of these regulated transactions, it was not sufficient to complete them.[22] Despite the monetary riches that he had worked so long and so deviously to obtain, Bender found himself confronted by what Douglas would have described as a system of "primitive rationing," designed to "restrict and channel the purchasing power of money."[23] Ilf and Petrov's use of the curbing of money's power to illustrate the achievements of the Soviet order was typical of an environment in which money was always something of a guilty afterthought, never comfortably integrated into the Soviet ideological self-image.[24]

Bender's frustration in seeking to spend his money in the consumer economy was nothing compared with that felt by the leadership of the Soviet enterprise. The Soviet productive organization existed not to make money, but to make the plan, a plan conceived and drawn up fundamentally *in natura*. Its dealings with money were conditioned primarily by the notion of "control with the ruble," the use of the motions of money in enterprise bank accounts to track mandated transactions, rather than to motivate voluntary ones. When goods had moved, money was supposed to follow (though when for some reason it did not, punishment was usually not ferocious). "Control with the ruble" was accompanied by substantial control *of* the ruble to ensure that enterprises could not make use of their so-called cashless (*beznalichnyi*) account money in ways that would contribute to macroeconomic destabilization. Enterprise money was allocated to accounts dedicated to particular purposes to prevent its use to feed the notorious "investment hunger" of the Soviet enterprise or its conversion into cash money for salaries that could sweep even more goods off barren shop shelves. The strict control over the use of money meant that it did not represent a "bearer of options" for enterprises that held it nor a major goal of productive activity.[25] It is true that under the classical command economy, efforts to use money to stimulate economizing behavior meant that having more money was better than having less, and this did lead enterprises to pursue it. But such pursuit was as likely to involve surreptitious price rises as savings through productive efficiency, and in any event did not

[22] Cf. Richard Ericson, "The Russian Economy since Independence," in *The New Russia: Troubled Transformation*, ed. Gail Lapidus (Boulder: Westview, 1995), 37–78, at 60.

[23] Douglas, "Primitive Rationing," 120. Cf. Caroline Humphrey, "'Icebergs', Barter and the Mafia in Provincial Russia," *Anthropology Today* 7, no. 2 (1991): 8–13.

[24] Gregory Grossman, "Gold and the Sword: Money in the Soviet Command Economy," in *Industrialization in Two Systems*, ed. Henry Rosovsky (New York: Wiley, 1966), 204–236.

[25] The phrase is from Gregory Grossman, "Introduction," in *Money and Plan*, ed. Gregory Grossman (Berkeley: University of California Press, 1968), 1–16.

take the form of tailoring production to the needs of consumers with money.[26] Money remained an adjunct to a system of production and circulation of goods that moved according to entirely different principles.[27] When macroeconomic imbalances grew sharply in the waning years of the Soviet Union, even money's adjunct role began to wither, as enterprises turned to demanding in-kind payment for goods whose sale at fixed prices gave increasingly inadequate returns.[28]

That Soviet authorities erected formidable barriers against the unsanctioned use of money, that nonetheless these barriers often proved porous, and that barter formed so clearly a way around official price restrictions all contributed to the view that monetary consolidation was merely a matter of lifting the limitations on prices and uses that kept money from playing its "natural" role. Indeed, little more than half a year after price liberalization was implemented, its architect, the acting prime minister Yegor Gaidar, was able to hail (quite accurately) the universal acceptance of the ruble in payment and proclaim (quite prematurely) the end of the barter economy.[29] With Bender's revenge complete, it was easy to assume that at issue in Russia was no longer monetary consolidation, but monetary policy.

Monetarist theories of inflation could thus set the agenda for political analysis.[30] Accepting that the causes and cures of inflation can be sought in fiscal and monetary policy set at the discretion of central state authorities, this literature focuses on institutions at the apex of the political system, seeking the circumstances in which iron-willed reformers can insulate the budget and the central bank against what is held to be nearly universal political opposition to stabilization.[31] At stake in the politics of stabilization are

[26] Thus, even Soviet money's tendency to "activization" (cf. Grossman, "Gold," 233–234) as enterprises tried to acquire more of it had little in common with the pursuit of a choosing consumer's money under a market system.

[27] A partial exception to this was the cash in which households received wages. For a fuller discussion of the institutional details of the Soviet monetary system, see chapter 1.

[28] Michael Burawoy and Pavel Krotov, "The Soviet Transition from Socialism to Capitalism: Worker Control and Economic Bargaining in the Wood Industry," *American Sociological Review* 57 (February 1992): 16–38.

[29] Reported in *Svoi Golos*, no. 33 (August 27–September 3, 1992), 5.

[30] On Russia, David Lipton and Jeffrey Sachs, "Prospects for Russia's Economic Reforms," *Brookings Papers on Economic Activity*, no. 2 (1992): 213–283, at 253–260; for a similar analysis of Latin American inflation by political scientists, see Stephan Haggard and Robert R. Kaufman, eds., *The Politics of Economic Adjustment: International Constraints, Distributive Conflicts, and the State* (Princeton: Princeton University Press, 1992). Cf. also Åslund, *How Russia Became a Market Economy.*

[31]Jeffrey Sachs has argued that the relevant actors are even narrower, especially in the first phase of stabilization: "[K]ey progress on stabilization can be achieved at the outset by a very small group of reform leaders centered at the Ministry of Finance and the Central Bank. It is usually possible to achieve a 'temporary stabilization' on the basis of a credit squeeze, and (usually) some foreign exchange reserves, even before fiscal policy is firmly consolidated." Jeffrey Sachs, "Russia's struggle with stabilization: Conceptual issues and evidence," *World Bank Research Observer, Annual Conference Supplement* (1994): 57–80.

whose hand will be on the money valve and how wide it will be opened, as well as how steady this hand will be, since only a credible commitment to monetary restriction can promote restructuring.

The problem with this approach is that it assimilates the Russian experience to a vision of politics drawn from countries with a consolidated monetary order, in which virtually all goods are sold exclusively for state-authorized money. In a consolidated monetary order, a focus on the apex of the political system of the sort just described is analytically appropriate only because of a *prior* political process of the accumulation of power at the center. And, as already suggested, it was just such a centralization of power that was the major challenge facing Russia's government in the uncertain fall of 1991.

The explicit intent of the Russian government would not be a good reason to choose monetary consolidation as a narrative frame over market reform. After all, the government aimed at both, and at the latter far more explicitly than the former. Yet there are compelling analytic reasons for a focus on monetary consolidation. The widespread attainment of monetary consolidation in contemporary nation-states is presumably no accident. There are grounds to suspect that it is driven by powerful confluences of state imperatives and private interests. Because most students of market reform believe it has an extremely tenuous political base, they fear that the market reform agenda is in constant danger of being rendered irrelevant. But no contemporary economy, however far from the market ideal, can avoid pursuing some regulation of the issue of money.

More important, a focus on monetary consolidation takes money seriously as a complicated institution for facilitating voluntary exchanges that is accepted by individuals and administered by the state. It therefore offers the possibility for a richer vision of politics, the state, and state-society relations than that imposed by an analysis of market reform. In the study of monetary consolidation, politics appears as a politics of sovereignty fought out in multiple fora by political actors whose identities are not just revealed but even constituted by the process. The state is not reduced to a collection of actors displaying a greater or lesser degree of devotion to the eternal verities of liberal economics. Instead, it is an actual or potential organization-for-itself.[32] It engages in projects to ensure its fiscal capacity and effective sovereignty against a variety of contenders and attracts allies to the extent these projects appear capable of realization.[33] Society is not a collection of atomized individuals (or at best firms) coming to isolated predictions re-

[32] Theda Skocpol, *States and Social Revolutions* (Cambridge: Cambridge University Press, 1979).
[33] Kiren Aziz Chaudhry, *The Price of Wealth: Economies and Institutions in the Middle East* (Ithaca: Cornell University Press, 1997).

garding the likelihood of state largess, but rather a "sphere . . . of lively interaction," replete with efforts to put this interaction on a relatively predictable footing, efforts that may contribute to, collide with, or even be shaped by the projects of the state.[34]

The project of the rest of this book is to demonstrate that focusing on monetary consolidation allows proper attention to these issues, and that they are central to the evolution of post-Soviet Russia. The two concluding sections of this introduction are intended to provide provisional security for some the assertions of the preceding paragraph. First I make a brief excursus into the general nature of money as an institution, and then I suggest how money is implicated in center-regional relations in Russia's specific context.

A Sociological-Institutional Approach to Money

Economists reflecting on the reasons money is preferred to barter have generally focused on how money reduces the cost of transacting for individuals. In a version associated with Austrian-school economists such as Menger,[35] stress is placed on the inconvenience of the double coincidence of wants that barter requires. Searching for an exchange partner who not only desires what one has to offer but also offers what one is seeking can be time-consuming. Exchanging first for a widely desired good and using it to acquire the directly desired good speeds up the process. In time, some widely desired good will attain to the status of money as a universal medium of exchange. More recent accounts of why individuals will come to embrace money stress that the quality of goods and therefore their economic value is hard to measure precisely. By making the investments required to become expert in judging the worth of a single good—money—and insisting on conducting exchanges through its medium, individuals can minimize the costs involved with overvaluing poorly known goods.[36]

Economic approaches to money, then, emphasize money's role in conceptually separable transactions between pairs of individuals entered into one at a time. Money arises from individuals' predictions about the form these transactions will tend to take. Money is a medium of exchange, an item acquired with an eye to a future exchange. Economic approaches also assume that humans are endowed with a capacity to calculate economic advantage that simply finds its expression in money exchange, since money arises as a result of individuals' efforts to reduce preexisting transaction

---

[34] Simmel, *Philosophy of Money*, 101.
[35] Carl Menger, "On the Origin of Money," *Economic Journal* 2 (June 1893): 239–255.
[36] For a summary of such views, see Thrainn Eggertsson, *Economic Behavior and Institutions* (Cambridge: Cambridge University Press, 1990), 231–246.

costs. Competing sociological views of money, by contrast, stress that money is an institution connecting the transactions of many individuals and standardizing their behavior in these transactions, in part by creation of a new capacity for rational economic calculation that is not part of humans' natural mental equipment. The originator of the sociological approach to money was Georg Simmel. Much of his wide-ranging masterpiece *The Philosophy of Money* is devoted to arguing that the use of money does not express numerical calculation but rather allows it. Accepting a broadly Austrian vision of the origin of shared media of exchange, he nevertheless notes that the process can be driven by a relatively diffuse capacity to compare alternatives and a desire to achieve a rough-and-ready sort of equality in exchange. This equality only begins to acquire a numerical interpretation with the spread of precisely divisible monetary units. Thus where one function commonly ascribed to money is "standard of value," Simmel would argue that the gesture at a preexisting value that money merely measures is fundamentally illegitimate.[37] Just as the abstraction of "length" can be defined only after a measure of it is agreed upon, so the abstraction of "value" comes into being only with its measure, money. In a language that would have been anachronistic for him, Simmel's argument can be rephrased as follows: humans are endowed only with an ordinal sense of utility; they attain something like a cardinal sense of utility ("value") only through the habit of making calculations in money.[38]

As a side effect of its creation of a standard of value, money creates a network of obligations between people denominated in *the same units*. The most significant formulation of the implications of this point was attained by Georg Knapp in *The State Theory of Money*. Money, Knapp argues at the conclusion of a discussion in which he develops a number of graceless but exceedingly precise neologisms, is a "chartal means of payment."[39] In conventional usage, a "means of payment" is what settles a legal obligation, as opposed to a medium of exchange, which is acquired with an eye to a later trade. Knapp uses "chartal" to characterize a means of payment that bears a sign indicating its value in nominal units. He distinguishes a chartal from a "pensatory" means of payment, which fulfills an obligation to pay through delivery of a given weight of a given material. This distinction may appear

[37] Simmel's reasoning has great kinship with the viewpoint argued in Philip Mirowski, "Learning the Meaning of a Dollar: Conservation Principles and the Social Theory of Value in Economic Theory," *Social Research* 57 (Fall 1990): 689–717, an essay that decisively influenced the readings presented here of both Simmel and Knapp.

[38] I thank Peter Woodruff for suggesting this formulation.

[39] Georg Friedrich Knapp, *The State Theory of Money*, trans. H. M. Lucas and J. Bonar, Abridged ed. (London: Macmillan, 1924), 38.

just a tedious scholasticism, but in fact it expresses rather precisely the critical idea that makes a sociological approach to money sociological. The unit of value finds its source not in the individual, who wants material things susceptible to material operations such as weighing, for example, but rather in social conventions.

With a pensatory means of payment, Knapp writes, "the unit of value was defined 'really,' i.e. in terms of material." Then a great transition occurs. The law mandates that the old pensatory means of payment be replaced by some new chartal one. Material operations can no longer define the unit of value, which is set by "the declaration by the State how many of the present units (say marks) go to discharge the debt expressed in the former unit (say thaler). To know the means of payment we need, not a mere historical definition, but a special description of the pieces, and a statement of how many units of value each piece is worth. The resulting validity is purely authoritative; a definite content for the pieces is neither demanded nor excluded."[40]

With a materially defined means of payment, transactions can be truly bilateral—one party weighs out the amount of material the other has agreed to accept. Once the means of payment is chartal, however, no transaction is truly bilateral, because all transactions inevitably involve implicit reference to the human institutions defining the means of payment. This is the basis for Knapp's provocative opening claim that "money is a creature of law."[41] Once there is no purely material way to determine whether something proffered in payment is acceptable, then it is only shared, instituted social standards that can allow the determination. To the sociological insight that the "value" money measures is an effect of money itself, Knapp adds the institutional insight that the definition of the unit of value rests on the rules specifying what counts as a means of payment in settlement of a legal obligation.[42]

Monetary Consolidation and Center-Regional Conflict

The sociological-institutional argument that money is a means of payment, finding its definition in legal institutions, rather than a medium

[40] Ibid., 54.
[41] Ibid., 1.
[42] Polanyi, *Great Transformation*, 196, adopts a position identical to Knapp's. See chapter 4. One implication of thinking of money as a means of payment is that there is an important difference between contending variants of the legal means of payment and alternate currencies held as a medium of exchange or store of value, rather than for the purpose of paying legally incurred debts. This is why Russia's fight against dollarization is not formally part of monetary consolidation as I have defined it here, and also why its politics have been so different. Dollarization is not considered in this book.

of exchange whose use is explained by individuals' predictions about their future transactions, reveals the connection between money and state building. Monetary consolidation depends on winning political battles over sovereignty because it involves control over what counts as making a payment of a legally recognized obligation. It further depends on the administrative capacity to enforce these rules. Thus the sociological-institutional view of money suggests an alternate path by which an existing monetary system can lapse into barter. Traditionally, economists have argued that in the course of hyperinflation there can be a "flight from money," because individuals are unwilling to hold a depreciating money long enough to use it as a medium of exchange. This argument resonates with the atomized vision of society criticized earlier, in which individuals qua individuals judge the credibility of a distant and a priori centralized state, gauging how much money the state is likely to issue.

But Russian barter and other varieties of nonmonetary exchange emerged as inflation was falling. The sociological-institutional view of money suggests that the root of this phenomenon was a loss of control over what counts as making a payment. Above all, it was Russian provincial governments that challenged the central state's exclusive claim to monetary sovereignty. Local authorities asserted the power to define nonmonetary means of payment for legal obligations denominated in rubles, both through taxing in kind and encouraging local enterprises to arrange payments among themselves in similar manner.

Provincial governments' willingness to undermine the coherence of the monetary system arose largely from the character of their interactions with the local economy. Simmel argued that the arrival of a money economy simultaneously increased the number of people on whom one is critically dependent while making one independent of any particular person. Independence should thus be characterized as abstract rather than concrete dependence, a dependence on categories rather than the unique. The residents of modern cities with a developed division of labor, "even though they require innumerable suppliers, workers and cooperators and would be lost without them . . . [are] not dependent upon any of them as particular individuals but only upon their objective services which have a money value and may therefore be carried out by any interchangeable person."[43] A person independent in this sense need be concerned only with the earning of money, for money can buy whatever is necessary.

In developed countries, not just individuals but government bodies are largely independent in Simmel's sense. They can adequately provision themselves by purchasing with money taxes what is produced consistent

[43] Simmel, *Philosophy of Money*, 300.

with the demands of money profit. They are abstractly, not concretely, dependent on the economy. The roots of center-regional conflict over the definition of the means of payment lay in the fact that the plausibility of conceiving of dependence on the economy in purely abstract terms was distinctly less for Russia's local governments than it was for central authorities. The cash register image of politics implies that the stakes of politics, like money, have an inherent commensurability. Winnings and losses can be accurately and adequately described by a number; they are dimensional in nature; losses here can be made up in gains there. What this view of politics obscures is the distinction between the formal and substantive senses of "economic" delineated by Karl Polanyi:

> The first meaning, the formal, springs from the logical character of the means-ends relationship, as in *economizing or economical;* from this meaning springs the scarcity definition of *economic.* The second, the substantive meaning, points to the elemental fact that human beings, like all other living things, cannot exist for any length of time without a physical environment that sustains them; this is the origin of the substantive definition of *economic.*[44]

Russian local authorities were unable to take the attitude that the substantive economy will continue to operate as a by-product of the formal one. Like any developed industrial society, the Soviet Union had an incredibly complex substantive economy. It possessed the ever more ramified technological and organizational infrastructures of the sort that have passed rapidly over the last century from the realm of high-tech exotica to that of bedrock necessities, creating patterns of settlement and occupation that simply could not be sustained without the reliable operation of an endless proliferation of railroads, electric power networks, water mains, and the like. Even in capitalist systems, the uniqueness and indispensability of such structures represent a limit to the Simmelian independence of consumers or government bodies. But they are partitioned into independent organizations, which have grown up in the context of a monetized economy.

The parallel structures in the Soviet economy were much more weakly delineated from the rest of the economy. The Soviet economy had no reason to draw distinctions between "public" and "private" infrastructure. Technical systems from sewage plants to heating networks were predicated on the continued existence of *particular* enterprises whose primary activities may have been entirely different. If such enterprises exited the money economy, local authorities were in no position to demand that they return to it. This was even more true of technical systems that were relatively well

[44] Karl Polanyi, *The Livelihood of Man* (Boston: Beacon, 1977), 19.

organizationally partitioned (such as electric power supply in large, but not small, towns), which tended to be even more thoroughly indispensable. Weber once suggested that in-kind taxation retarded the development of capitalism, constraining production to service concrete demands of the state rather than freeing it to pursue money profit.[45] The situation in Russia's regions had the opposite form—a rigid structure of production bound the local state to in-kind taxation. The origins of the uneasy relationship of the Soviet Union's substantive economy to the formal abstractions of money form the topic of the next chapter.

[45] Weber, *Economy and Society*, 1:199.

CHAPTER ONE

Making Money Multiple, 1924–1933

Money is an instrument of the bourgeois economy which Soviet power has taken into its own hands and adapted to the interests of socialism.

—Iosif Stalin

For more than a decade after the introduction of the concilia-
tory, market-oriented New Economic Policy (NEP) in 1921,
monetary policy was a critical axis of political contention
among the leaders of the Bolshevik Party. It is of course unsurprising that
the arguments familiar from the rich historiography of the extraordinarily rich economic policy debates of this period—over whether to
make industry or agriculture the basis of growth, over the speed of industrialization, over the degree of coercion that could reasonably be directed against the peasantry—had implications for monetary policy. But
historians have perhaps underemphasized that arguments about how to
organize the monetary system and how much money and credit the state
should create had extraordinary political significance in their own right.[1]
Bolsheviks of all stripes were intensely aware that the practical issues raised
by the ongoing difficulties of managing of the financial system were of
deep political significance. The debate over monetary policy became a central arena in which adherents of the various economic *Weltanschauungen*
did combat.

---

[1] Welcome exceptions are Iurii Goland, "Currency Regulation in the NEP Period," *Europe-
Asia Studies* 46, no. 8 (1994): 1251–1296 and Simon Johnson and Peter Temin, "The Macroeconomics of NEP," *Economic History Review* 46 (November 1993): 750–767.

Although this debate had concluded more than fifty years before Mikhail Gorbachev came to power, understanding it is essential to understanding both the fate of his economic reforms and the difficulties of monetary consolidation facing the post-Soviet leadership. An inquiry into the genesis of the Soviet monetary system helps to specify the nature of the "institutional legacy" facing both sets of reformers. The term *institution* is notoriously difficult to define. Ronald Jepperson's effort to identify the core of sociological usages of the term locates it in a vision of institutions as "standardized activity sequences that have taken-for-granted rationales, that is, in sociological parlance, some common social 'account' of their existence and purpose."[2] Jepperson argues that these accounts may not be known to those engaged in the behavior that maintains the institution, but that they do have a sense that such an explanation is available. The notion of "account" is worth specifying more closely, for an account of an institution's existence and purposes only makes sense as part of a view of the world. The most important intellectual component of an institution is the ontology with which it operates. Mary Douglas is a thousand times right when she argues: "It is naive to treat the quality of sameness, which characterizes members of a class, as if it were a quality inherent in things or as a power of recognition inherent in the mind. . . . Institutions bestow sameness."[3] To put it differently, institutions embed an ontology. But institutions do more than this. They not only define classes of possible events and give rules for relating particular events to the appropriate class, they also specify algorithms for reacting to these events. In fact, it is these algorithms and the resources available for carrying them out that—in short, institutional capacities—that are usually understood when institutional legacies (or endowments) are discussed. Yet as will be argued in subsequent chapters, an institution's implied *Weltanschauung* is an equally important legacy.

Acceptance of this argument implies a privileged position for inquiries into an institution's origins for determining the nature of its "legacy," that is, its likely effects in a radically changed environment. It is in the nature of the "taken-for-granted" to be hard to specify. James Murphy has provided a fascinating discussion of the relations between customary and stipulated varieties of social order. He argues that "legal stipulation presupposes custom," both because customary categories serve as a point of

---

[2] Ronald L. Jepperson, "Institutions, Institutional Effects, and Institutionalism," in *The New Institutionalism in Organizational Analysis*, ed. Paul J. DiMaggio and Walter W. Powell (Chicago: University of Chicago Press, 1991), 143–163, at 147.

[3] Mary Douglas, *How Institutions Think*, (Syracuse: Syracuse University Press, 1986), 58, 63.

departure for stipulated ones and because those designing them hope they will become customary, or "prereflective."[4] One can suggest that negotiations over new stipulated behavior patterns and existing customary ones offer an opportunity to understand the kind of worldview being deposited in a new institution, to catch it, as it were, before it descends into the prereflective. At moments of institutional creation, ontologies, worldviews, and arguments to justify them tend to be on explicit view—and the object of political struggle.

This chapter identifies and analyzes the intellectual legacies embedded in Soviet monetary institutions through an examination of their genesis.[5] These legacies, I argue, were two. The first took the form of an unresolved tension between facilitating production and monetary stability. The architects of the Soviet monetary system operated with a vision of the meaning of money for the productive unit that contradicted their vision of money on the systemic level. As a systemic factor, money was seen as a meaningful aggregate, with consequences for macroeconomic balance. Thus the monetary system was designed to control this aggregate. Sums of money in the hands of various production units were commensurable: from the systemic point of view the numeric total mattered. (I use the term *commensurable*, here and elsewhere in this chapter, to mean measurable in the same units, such that the arithmetic operations produce meaningful results.) But with respect to the individual production unit, money was seen as just a lubricant for its productive processes. The need for this lubricant derived from the technical specifications of production, which naturally bore no relation to the technical specifications of production elsewhere in the economy. The technical needs of production are not commensurable across production units: it would be absurd to say that one factory had to use fewer boards because another factory had begun to use more bolts. To the extent that money was conceived as a technical requisite of production, its commensurability across enterprises was equally absurd—yet this commensurability was precisely what macroeconomic control demanded. As the Soviet economy developed, the contradiction between a microeconomy that denied the commensurability of production in money and a macroeconomy whose stability depended on this commensurability manifested itself in the endless efforts of Soviet enterprises to slip their financial controls, and in constant inflationary pressures. Analysts of Soviet-type

[4] James Bernard Murphy, "The Kinds of Order in Society," in *Natural Images in Economic Thought*, ed. Philip Mirowski (London: Cambridge University Press, 1994), 536–582, at 548.
[5] I borrowed this language of ideas being "embedded" in institutions from Peter Blitstein. Cf. Robert Keohane and Judith Goldstein, eds., *Ideas and Foreign Policy: Beliefs, Institutions, and Political Change* (Ithaca: Cornell University Press, 1993).

economies have properly stressed that they tend to give primacy to production concerns—meeting the plan for gross output, calculated in physical terms—even at the expense of monetary stability.[6] Yet the historical evidence presented here suggests that the conflict between production and monetary stability, and its frequent resolution in favor of the former, did not stem just from the general preferences of planners.[7] One must also look to the weakness of the intellectual resources for legitimating financial controls over enterprises available in the implicit account (in Jepperson's sense) embedded in the Soviet monetary institutions.

The proximate origins of Soviet monetary institutions lie in the sweeping "Credit Reform" of 1930 and various modifications and improvements to it made over the following decade in an effort to restrain the tendency to mint new money automatically to pay for all production. Cumulatively, these modifications produced what might be called a "partitioned money."[8] To prevent the flood of money issue brought about by the Credit Reform from undermining the priorities of the first Five-Year Plan, Soviet central officials created an elaborate set of controls over when and by whom goods could be bought and sold. Such controls, used to "restrict and channel the purchasing power of money,"[9] in some spheres were so extensive that authorities were in effect allocating physical goods. In such cases, especially common in enterprise supply, the movement of money between economic actors only registered a transfer of goods that had happened for other reasons. The possession of money by the recipient of the goods was not a sufficient, and at times not even a necessary, condition for the transfer to go forward. However, the mechanisms for partitioning money also allowed for the creation of realms *within* which money did represent

---

[6] As Gregory Grossman, "Note," in *Stagnation or Change in Communist Economies?*, ed. Karl C. Thalheim (London: Centre for Research into Communist Economies, 1986), 49–54, at 51, puts it, "the basic tenet of the soft budget constraint, that is, an enterprise must not falter in its production tasks, and its employees must not be laid off for want of means of payment, has been honoured, *de facto* if not *de jure*." Cf. Joseph Berliner, *Factory and Manager in the USSR* (Cambridge: Harvard University Press, 1957), 282–287.

[7] That more than a general bias for more production rather than less must be at stake is illustrated by the familiar efforts of Soviet planners to *rein in* excessive construction.

[8] Much of what I discuss under this heading is described as the "partial demonetization of the Soviet economy after 1929" in Gregory Grossman, "The Structure and Organization of the Soviet Economy," *The Development of the USSR: An Exchange of Views* (Seattle: University of Washington Press, 1964): 41–60, at 51. I am also much indebted to: Gregory Grossman, "Gold and the Sword: Money in the Soviet Command Economy," in *Industrialization in Two Systems*, ed. Henry Rosovsky (New York: Wiley, 1966), 204–236 and Gregory Grossman, "Introduction," in *Money and Plan*, ed. Gregory Grossman (Berkeley: University of California Press, 1968), 1–16.

[9] This phrase is drawn from Mary Douglas, "Primitive Rationing: A Study in Controlled Exchange," in *Themes in Economic Anthropology*, ed. Raymond Firth (London: Tavistock, 1967), 119–145, at 120.

real, general purchasing power. To achieve this in an environment of fixed prices required not just removing requirements other than money for making a purchase, but also bringing the amount of money available to all potential purchasers roughly in line with the amount of goods available for sale.

The politics surrounding partitioned money contested, essentially, where to draw the partitions, and it is this politics of inclusion and exclusion that I consider to be the second major idea embedded in the monetary institutions established in the 1930s. As I will argue, the politics involved in deciding how to restrict and channel money's purchasing power represented a sharp break from the politics of monetary policy characteristic of the 1920s. In this earlier period, the value of the ruble was regarded as universal for all in society, and political contention focused on how, and how jealously, to guard this value, in light of the class implications of various policies. Society as a meaningful collectivity was conceptually prior to monetary policy, though the various classes of society would react to different policies differently. From the 1930s, however, the partition of money, by making the meaning and value of money very different in different realms, *created* meaningful collectivities, rather than merely influencing them.

In line with Murphy's observation that new stipulations are shaped by prior customs, the analysis that follows begins in the 1920s, examining the class politics of monetary policy in this period and the institutions and models governing money management. Then I turn to the debate over the Credit Reform, using the arguments advanced in this debate to help specify its critical intellectual assumptions. Next I treat the initial implementation of the Credit Reform in 1930, and the partition of money that ensued as modifications were introduced over the following decade. A concluding section returns to the two legacies of the monetary transformations of the 1930s already mentioned. In particular, I elaborate on the role of Soviet partitioned money in creating meaningful collectivities through some contrasts to Simmel's arguments on the role of money in capitalist societies.

Theoretical Basis of the Worker-Peasant Alliance: The Bolshevik Class Analysis of Inflation

From the October revolution into the early 1920s, the Bolshevik regime made extensive and rather gleeful use of seigniorage as a taxation mechanism. In fact, during these years of "War Communism" the state collected no money taxes whatsoever, and all money spent by the government came directly from the printing presses. Party doctrine during this period—as the Bolsheviks themselves were later to note, seconded by innumerable Western analysts—made a virtue of this necessity. Hyperinflationary evaporation of the currency's value was heralded as the first step toward money's disappearance under Communism.[10] The use of seigniorage was also seen as part and parcel of the class struggle manifested in the Civil War. As the economist Preobrazhensky put it in 1920, the state's money-printing operation constituted "the machine gun of the Commissariat of Finance that poured fire into the rear of the bourgeois system and that made use of the laws of currency circulation for the purpose of destroying it and of financing the revolution."[11]

The end of War Communism and the move to the somewhat market-oriented NEP in 1921 was to bring a new and more subtle class analysis of inflation, but the process took some time. Although NEP's course toward voluntary market relations was a course toward monetization, with the fiscal apparatus in ruins it was not immediately possible to attain full monetization. Indeed, the cornerstone of early NEP policies was the *prodnalog*, or tax in kind, assessed on peasant production. Hyperinflation continued apace, with seigniorage still the central means of government finance. Hyperinflation raised difficulties for promoting rational behavior in state industry, but far more important were its political implications. The political basis of NEP was the *smychka*, an alliance between worker and peasant, entailing an end to forced requisitions of grain and the establishment of terms of trade between city and countryside that would be promote voluntary peasant participation in the market.[12] The most immediate threat to the *smychka* was the so-called scissors crisis of 1921 to 1923, when industry (which NEP had left largely in state hands) used its monopoly position to raise prices on its goods far faster than agricultural producers could. Eventually this problem was dealt with through the imposition of price controls.

Aside from the scissors crisis, however, the *smychka* was threatened by the circumstances of inflation themselves. Bolshevik leaders understood inflation much as most present-day economists do: as a tax on the holders of money balances.[13] They usually described this tax as the "emission tax." In circumstances of inflation, who pays the emission tax depends on who can turn money over faster, since the longer money is held, the more value it loses. The winners from the emission tax are those into whose hands newly printed money is delivered. Naturally, as Marxists, the Bolsheviks were in-

---

[10] This view was expressed, e.g., by Bukharin and Preobrazhenskii in Alec Nove and D. M. Nuti, *Socialist Economics* (Harmondsworth, England: Penguin Education, 1972), 39.

[11] Quoted in Arthur Z. Arnold, *Banks, Credit, and Money in Soviet Russia* (New York: Columbia University Press, 1937), 95–96.

[12] On the *smychka* see Stephen Cohen, *Bukharin and the Bolshevik Revolution: A Political Biography, 1888–1938* (Oxford: Oxford University Press, 1980), 133, 135.

[13] Although Sokolnikov was exceptional, in general it appears that Johnson and Temin, "Macroeconomics," somewhat underestimated the Bolsheviks' sophistication in monetary policy.

clined to view the distributional issues raised by the inflation tax in class terms. Grigorii Sokolnikov, Soviet minister of finance until late 1925 and the architect of the currency reform that ended hyperinflation in early 1924, developed the class analysis of the inflation tax on the basis of analogies between Russia's inflation and the postwar inflations in France and Germany. In both European countries, he suggested, the bourgeoisie had used inflation to support heavy industry at the expense of the workers and peasants. This intensification of the class struggle, however, brought on a political crisis that forced the bourgeoisie to turn away from inflation to avoid popular uprisings.[14]

Sokolnikov felt that the European experience held important lessons for Soviet Russia. The demands of socialized industry for inflationary monetary emission on its behalf did not, naturally, constitute a form of class struggle. Yet the interests of state industry could come in conflict with those of "the state as a political organization,"[15] in particular, with the state's responsibility to maintain the class alliance between workers and peasants. Direct emission-created revenues to state industry forced the peasantry to pay the inflation tax. Peasants, given their lack of rapid communication with towns, could not turn over their money as quickly, nor adjust prices as quickly, and therefore tended to suffer much more from inflation. For this reason, Sokolnikov argued, "an economic split between town and countryside is the inevitable consequence of an inflationary policy. In contrast, the *smychka* between city and countryside, that *smychka* about which so much is being said, is possible only on the basis of a stable [*tverdaia*] currency."[16] Without a stable currency, the Soviet state ran the risk of the same sort of political crisis as had brought down Poincare in France and forced the bourgeoisie's retreat from inflationary support of industry in Germany. Later, in a more ominous analogy, Sokolnikov located the causes of the revolt against the Jacobins in the inflationary issue of *assignats,* implying that a retreat from hard-money policies threatened the Bolsheviks as well with Thermidor.[17]

One could accept Sokolnikov's point about the distributional implications of money emission without sharing his political preference for preservation of the *smychka*. By the late 1920s, on the eve of the first Five Year

[14] This argument is advanced in a speech of July 1924; Grigorii Iakovlevich Sokol'nikov, *Novaia Finansovaia Politika: Na Puti k Tverdoi Valiute* (A new financial policy: On the way to a hard currency) (Moscow: Nauka, 1995), 200–201.

[15] Ibid., 201.

[16] Ibid., 202–203. On the extra burden of inflation on the peasantry due to their inability to turn money over as quickly as city dwellers, cf. Alec Nove, *An Economic History of the Soviet Union* (Harmondsworth, England: Penguin, 1982), 95.

[17] From a 1925 speech; Sokol'nikov, *Novaia Finansovaia,* 274. Cf. Sokol'nikov in 1924; *Novaia Finansovaia,* 196.

Plan, political debate among the Bolshevik leadership had polarized between a left wing, led by Stalin, which advocated rapid industrialization at the expense of the peasantry and a right wing, led by Bukharin, which wanted a slower industrialization and more balance between agricultural and industrial investment.[18] Much of this debate centered on monetary policy. Rightists, as Sokolnikov had, defended hard money as the key to voluntary exchange between town and country and thus preservation of the *smychka*. Leftists argued that hard money played into the hands of the class enemy, the rich peasant or *kulak*, who tended to hoard money. If inflation could expropriate these money hoards in favor of industrial development led by the working class, so much the better.[19] Despite their disagreements, both sides employed the framework of the class analysis of inflation, a framework that presumed that money had a value universal across society. This framework was to be destroyed in the course of the Left's eventual victory. But to understand how this came to pass, we must first turn to how the problem of monetary management was conceived in the 1920s.

Monetary Management in the Era of the *Smychka*

Bolshevik theorists in the middle and late 1920s tended to perceive the problem of monetary management as divided into three spheres, and they assigned each sphere its own regulatory principle, not necessarily compatible with the others.[20] The first task was to maintain the gold value of the ten-ruble note, or *chervonets*. This was done not by a legal guarantee of convertibility on demand, but by selling gold for rubles on legal and semilegal domestic markets to prop up the *chervonets* as necessary. Similar interventions were made in foreign markets on which the currency traded. Gold-price regulation also involved maintaining a stipulated ratio between currency outstanding and gold reserves, to make credible the prospect of gold sales in support of the ruble. The second area of monetary management was credit policy, regulated by the Real Bills doctrine. Essentially this doctrine stated that *chervontsy* could be issued to finance short-term commercial loans to state and private businesses without fear of inflationary effects. The final sphere of monetary management was price policy, in which the Bolsheviks tended to operate with a rough-and-ready quantity theory

---

[18] This debate had been going on at least since 1925; the best source is Alexander Erlich, *The Soviet Industrialization Debate, 1924–1928* (Cambridge: Harvard University Press, 1960).

[19] See, e.g., *Torgovo-promyshlennaia gazeta*, 22 October 1929, 3.

[20] For documentation of the assertions in this paragraph, see the more detailed discussions that follow.

of money. It was held that printing money to finance the budget deficit would drive prices up or, when prices were fixed, would intensify shortages (known in these years as the "goods famine"). Conflicts between the three principles were resolved variously. Thus while rough-and-ready monetarism was applied largely to dealing with prices and shortages, links were also sometimes drawn between an increased money supply and problems in maintaining the gold price of the ruble. Such arguments occasionally led to direct quantitative controls on the amount of money issued for commercial credit, in violation of the Real Bills doctrine. On even rarer occasions, the gold principle trumped monetarism as an instrument of price policy; here the argument ran, in "nominal anchor" style, that stabilizing the gold price of the ruble was necessary to stabilize all other prices. For much of the 1920s, however, the three spheres were monitored and manipulated separately, and it was considered perfectly consistent for one person to endorse all three regulating principles. It was only in the late 1920s that the contradictions became sharper as the inflationary impact of the Real Bills doctrine became increasingly manifest, exacerbating relations between city and countryside and hastening the breakdown of the *smychka*. The remainder of this section treats the three principles of monetary management in turn and concludes with a discussion of how they played into the political debates adumbrated at the close of the preceding section.

The *gold standard* was in substantial part an answer to the question of how to maintain confidence in the new currency both at home, where tsarist gold money was still considered the paradigm of what money should be, and abroad, where the Bolsheviks' repudiation of tsarist debts had naturally undermined the willingness of creditors to extend loans to representatives of the new state. Russia depended heavily on international markets for industrial and especially capital goods, and the Bolsheviks could not afford a thoroughgoing exit from them. Monetary policy was critical to the effort to restore access to commercial credit in international markets. Adopting "orthodox" monetary policies was a signal to international markets of Russia's reliability as a business partner. The Bolsheviks' situation was very much analogous to that of third world countries in the late twentieth century whose dependence on international financial markets compels them to adopt the austerity programs in favor among the players on these markets. Thus the Bolsheviks established gold reserves, many held in foreign banks, and regularly published information about the amount of money being printed and the amount of gold available to back it. Though backed by gold, the currency was not redeemable for gold on demand. However, up through early 1926, efforts were made to support the currency at its gold par on both domestic and foreign markets. Spending money for this purpose, to the extent that it benefited domestic speculators and foreign capitalists, naturally appeared to contradict Bolshevik class loyalties and was a matter of some tension.[21]

Competing with and complementing the gold standard as a guide for monetary policy was a second principle, the so-called Real Bills doctrine. A brief summary of this doctrine is in order, given its importance in Soviet debates of the late 1920s and the origins of the mature Soviet monetary system. Roy Green has defined it as follows: "The central proposition [of the doctrine] is that bank notes which are lent in exchange for 'Real Bills', i.e. titles to real value or value in the process of creation, cannot be issued in excess; and that, since the requirements of the non-bank public are given and finite, any superfluous notes would return automatically to the issuer, at least in the long run."[22]

To understand the significance of the Real Bills doctrine in Russian circumstances of the late 1920s, one needs to understand something of bank practice at the time, namely discount policy.[23] *Discounting* is the practice of making a loan to a party on the security of a loan that party has itself made to a third party. The discounting bank pays out the full amount eventually to be received from the creditor's debtor, less interest—the "discount" that gave rise to this term.[24] Usually discounting is a form of giving credit for so-called self-liquidating commercial transactions. For instance, a wholesaler might give goods to a retailer on credit, accepting the retailer's note that it expects will be repaid when the retailer sells the goods to the final consumer. This note then serves as the security for a loan from the bank— the note is "discounted." In the 1920s, the Soviet State Bank would discount bills of exchange presented to it by its customers. These bills of exchange, known in Russian by their German name of wechsel (*veksel'*), consisted of a promissory note with two signatures, that of the seller and buyer in a commercial transaction. After discounting the bill for the seller, the bank would collect the money from the buyer when it came due. If the buyer could not pay, the bank would "protest" the wechsel, forcing its other signatory, the seller in the original transaction, to make good the loan.

---

[21] Goland, "Currency Regulation."

[22] Roy Green, "Real Bills Doctrine," in *The New Palgrave: Money*, ed. John Eatwell, Murray Milgate, and Peter Newman (New York: W. W. Norton, 1989), 310–313, at 310.

[23] This summary is based especially on Arnold, *Banks*, 345–346; F. D. Livshits, "Problema sovetskogo vekselia" (The problem of the Soviet wechsel), *Vestnik Finansov*, no. 6 (1929): 47–64; A. I. Morin, G. L. Piatakov, and V. V. Sher, *Reforma kredita: doklady i rechi na soveshchanii upravliaiushchikh filialami Gosbanka 18–22 iunia 1929 g. i tezisy pravleniia Gosbanka* (Reform of credit: reports and speeches at the conference of managers of State Bank branches, June 18–22, 1929 and the theses of the Gosbank board) (Moscow: Gosfinizdat SSSR, 1929). For background on discounting, see David S. Landes, *Bankers and Pashas: International Finance and Economic Imperialism in Egypt* (New York: Harper Torchbook, 1969), 4–8.

[24] In Russian, discounting is known as *uchet*, and discount policy as *uchetnaia politika*.

In Russian circumstances, the Real Bills doctrine indicated that the State Bank (Gosbank) should discount wechsels that represented real, self-liquidating commercial debt and that this policy was a sufficient guarantee of both its commercial soundness and of a noninflationary monetary emission policy. Printing money to make such loans was consistent with "hard money" and was, according to Sokolnikov, an "entirely different affair than printing a sinking currency for tax purposes."[25] It is precisely this analytical leap from commercial soundness to macroeconomic adequacy that has drawn the fire of critics of the Real Bills doctrine. However, in the 1920s the theoretical argument was far from resolved. As late as 1913 the doctrine was enshrined as the basis for the actions of the U.S. Federal Reserve.[26] In fact, at least some Soviet economists viewed adoption of the Real Bills doctrine as a means of demonstrating the Soviet state's monetary conservatism. Thus F. D. Livshits noted that a reform eliminating the wechsel would be dangerous precisely for the USSR's image with foreign partners: "With the elimination of the wechsel, the present basis for emission of banknotes will be destroyed, and the activity of our State Bank—the main bank debtor in the USSR with foreign countries—will take on an unclear and mostly incomprehensible character for foreign countries. For to this day the majority of the main banks of issue of the world base the emission of bank notes precisely on the discount of first-class bills of exchange as the most realistic indicator of the credit money required by the turnover of goods."[27] (It is worth repeating that despite the impression given here, the Real Bills doctrine was not the sole basis for emissions policy.)

Despite its bad odor among present-day economists, the Real Bills doctrine was not a recipe for unlimited monetary expansion. In fact, the degree of its expansive effects depended very strongly on the capacity of the bank to detect various forms of "unreal" bills—wechsels presented for discount that did not reflect a commercial transaction. Such bills are a chronic problem for bills-of-exchange-based lending.[28] Unreal bills might take the form of "accommodation paper" in which a firm would ask another to cosign the wechsel as customer, even though no actual transaction was involved, promising to supply the money before the bill fell due. Or two firms might each cosign the other's wechsel, appearing in one transaction as customer and in the other as supplier. Each could then go to the bank on this basis. Another common practice was the "advance" wechsel, in which a customer signed the bill well before delivery of the goods involved, allowing the supplier to operate with increased working

[25] Sokol'nikov, *Novaia Finansovaia*, 168.
[26] Green, "Real Bills," 312.
[27] Livshits, "Problema," 52.
[28] See Landes, *Bankers*, 6.

capital. By all indications, Russian industrial firms in the late 1920s made regular and extensive use of all these forms of unbacked wechsels as a means of improving their access to credit.[29] Determining the provenance and backing of a particular wechsel was largely beyond the capacity the State Bank. The general virtues or failings of the Real Bills doctrine as a method of monetary regulation aside, it was a recipe for an expansive policy given the weak monitoring capacities of the State Bank.

The unenviable task of dealing with deleterious monetary effects of the proliferation of unreal bills was left intellectually to a kind of rough-and-ready *quantity theory of money*, and institutionally above all to the Ministry of Finance. The main argument of the quantity theory is straightforward.[30] The cornerstone of formal versions of the quantity theory is the "equation of exchange,"

$$MV = PQ.$$

This equation represents the simple notion that the amount of goods sold in any period must be equivalent to the amount purchased. M is money; V, velocity (the number of times it is spent over the period); P, the price level; Q, the amount of goods sold. If one ruble is spent one time (M = 1, V = 1), then the value of the goods sold must be equal to one ruble. It is important to realize that the equation of exchange is just a tautology, not a statement about causality. It can as easily be read as a claim that an increase in prices will increase the money supply as a claim that an increase in the money supply will increase the price level, though the latter reading is somewhat more popular among economists. And it was in this latter version, that monetary expansion drives prices upward, that quantity theory had some currency among Soviet economists in the 1920s.

Although I have not encountered an algebraic formulation of the equation of exchange in the Soviet debates of the 1920s, many examples can be found of the implementation of the quantity theory as a rule of thumb. Even Sokolnikov, who cited only the gold standard and the Real Bills doctrine as the guarantors of the stability of the *chervonets,* spoke of decisions imposing quantitative restrictions on the amount of emission-funded bank credit.[31] Quantitative restrictions on credit were also the Politburo's reaction to problems in maintaining the gold price of the

[29] See, e.g, A. Blium, "Novye problemy v oblasti kredita" (New problems in the area of credit), *Ekonomicheskoe obozrenie,* no. 6 (1929): 25–37, at 31; Sh. Terushkin, "O bezveksel'nykh rashc-etakh i o bezveksel'nom kreditovanii" (On non-wechsel settlements and non-wechsel credit), *Ekonomicheskoe obozrenie,* no. 5 (1929): 76–92, at 80; Morin, Piatakov, and Sher, *Reforma,* 25.
[30] For a very clear and concise presentation, see Gavin Peebles, *A Short History of Socialist Money* (Sydney: Allen and Unwin, 1991), 80–82.
[31] See Sokol'nikov, *Novaia Finansovaia,* 288.

chervonets in late 1925.[32] Quantity theory arguments were also important in the debate over the feasible rate of industrialization, in which it was often pointed out that large construction projects spend money without immediately creating new goods for sale, thereby creating inflationary pressures unless financed from savings.[33] And there is evidence that by 1929, the State Bank was applying quantitative limits on credit beyond which it refused to discount further wechsels.[34] In general, the responsibility for "defense of monetary circulation" on a quantity theory rationale was laid at the door of the Narkomfin (essentially the Ministry of Finance), which was supposed to take excess money out of circulation through taxation and the issue of state bonds.[35] The prominence of quantity theory reasoning in the absence of a specific formulation or ideological defense is not as puzzling as it might seem. Not only would Soviet economists likely have been familiar with the theory's original formulations (despite Marx's contempt for them),[36] but in any event the arguments stemmed naturally from the widespread metaphor of "monetary circulation" (*denezhnoe obrashchenie*) to describe the workings of the monetary system; inflation occurred when the "channels" of this circulation overflowed.[37]

By early 1929, the increased flow of credit to industry as a result of the discount of unreal bills and the general turn toward greater promotion of industry meant that the task of ensuring monetary balance was becoming increasingly difficult. At this point, the practical conflict between the Real Bills doctrine and the quantity theory approach reached a head, and debate over which should be given priority began to intersect with the more general conflict between Left and Right. The Left promoted the Real Bills doctrine, since the new money printed to finance loans on wechsel security went into the hands of state industry. In fact, some years earlier Preobrazhensky in the *New Economics* had been quite forthright about the role of discounting in transferring resources from the private sector to state industry as part of "primitive socialist accumulation":

[32] Goland, "Currency Regulation."

[33] Erlich, *Soviet Industrialization,* passim.

[34] Z. S. Katsenelenbaum, "K reforme kreditovaniia tovarooborota" (On reform of credit for goods turnover), *Vestnik Finansov,* no. 7 (1929): 28–42, at 35. It is not clear how "hard" these limits were; see *Torgovo-promyshlennaia gazeta,* 26 July 1929, 3.

[35] For the role of tax policy in dealing with inflation, see Franklyn D. Holzman, *Soviet Taxation; The Fiscal and Monetary Problems of a Planned Economy* (Cambridge: Harvard University Press, 1962). Also, Piatakov to Stalin, top secret letter of 20 July 1930, 2. I am very grateful to Andrea Graziosi and A. Kvashonkin for making this source available to me.

[36] Karl Marx, *Capital,* trans. Ben Fowkes, vol. 1 (New York: Vintage, 1977), 220–221.

[37] Some Bolsheviks might have known Fisher's formulation from Tugan'-Baranovskii, *Bumazhnyia Den'gi i Metall* (Paper money and metal), Posmertnoe izdanie, s" izmeneniiami i dopolneniiami avtora (Odessa: Russkaia Kul'tura, 1919).

[W]e must not for one moment forget the economic source which really makes possible the *chervonets* issue and the loan operations by the bank out of the sources of this issue. If the bank issues 60 million *chervontsi* . . . this means, economically, that by one means or another the country's commodity values to that amount have been placed at the disposal of the State Bank for different periods. If we consider that this 'loan from circulation' is drawn from the state economy and from private economy, proportionally, let us say, to the share of each in the monetary circulation of the country, while the resources of this loan go to financing almost exclusively state and cooperative industry and trade, then we see swiftly passing before our eyes a process of socialist accumulation.[38]

For Preobrazhensky, then, crediting with new banknotes under the Real Bills doctrine was just as much an inflationary tax in favor of state industry as was a monetized budget deficit. Defense of the doctrine was an important part of the program of those who supported faster rates of industrialization at the expense of the peasantry, although they rarely approached the matter with Preobrazhensky's sophistication.

By contrast, the Right and its allies in Narkomfin argued that in a context of fixed prices, the increased money supply was causing serious shortages of goods (the "goods famine"), which amounted to an inflation tax on the holders of money. Investment in industry was thus being funded not by "real resources" but by forced savings.[39] Pro-Stalin economists faced with this accusation—that they were relying on forced savings—naturally denied it and tried to distance themselves from the disgraced Preobrazhensky, but they produced the impression of men protesting too much.[40] In a secret letter to Stalin, Piatakov was very clear that "Nepmen, kulaks, and the top seredniaki" should be denied opportunities to spend their money.[41] In public, a common strategy was simply to ignore criticism about finances.[42] The goods famine brought on by the excess currency issue naturally made the peasants less willing to sell grain—since nothing could be bought with the receipts—and contributed to the crisis in grain

[38] Preobrazhenskii, in Nuti and Nove, *Socialist Economics*, 136–137.
[39] For this argument, see *Ekonomicheskaia zhizn'*, 1 January 1929, 2. This article by an assistant director of Narkomfin used the term "anticipation of the national income" rather than the "forced savings" of present-day economists, but used it quite equivalently.
[40] For this exchange, see *Ekonomicheskaia zhizn'*, 1 January 1929, 2 and 13 January 1929, 2. For a slightly Aesopian endorsement of inflation in the "struggle for the socialist direction . . . of development," see A. Spunde, "Piatiletie Denezhnoi Reformy" (The fifth anniversary of the monetary reform), *Ekonomicheskoe Obozrenie*, no. 4 (1929): 64–71, at 69–70.
[41] Letter of Piatakov to Stalin, 20 July 1930, 4.
[42] Thus even a symphathetic review of anti-right-deviation economic literature chides it for systematically ignoring financial issues: K. Pavlov, "Ekonomicheskaia politika i pravyi uklon" (Economic policy and the right deviation), *Ekonomicheskoe Obozrenie*, no. 3 (1929): 165–169.

procurements that produced the expropriationary policies culminating in forced collectivization. As Bukharin noted, these measures were leading to a dwindling importance of money in organizing relations between city and countryside. And this meant the end of the *smychka*.[43]

Given the ultimate and total victory of the Left, one might have expected that the quantity theory approach would be abandoned while the Real Bills principle would become the main basis for regulating money emission. However, the actual outcome was an uneasy hybrid between these two contradictory regulatory principles. The next section traces the origins of this hybrid.

The Debate Over the Credit Reform

Nineteen twenty-nine was not only the year of the final defeat of the Right and the launching in earnest of collectivization and high-speed industrialization. That year also witnessed a huge, fairly public, and quite angry argument over the appropriate organization of the monetary system.[44] The main parties to the debate were Gosbank and the government organ managing industry, the Higher Council for the People's Economy, known by its Russian acronym as Vesenkha. The agenda for the debate was set by Gosbank's proposal for a "Credit Reform" that would eliminate all wechsels and instead move to a system of direct crediting, under which the bank would loan money directly to purchasers of industrial and other goods. Two major arguments supported Gosbank's position. First, it was becoming increasingly clear that the Real Bills doctrine was not effectively regulating the money supply in practice, due to the proliferation of accommodation paper. If monetary circulation was to remain under adequate control, it was time to break with the Real Bills doctrine and work instead with direct quantitative limits on the money supply. Thus the contradictions between the different money regulation principles discussed in the preceding section were recognized and brought into the open. Second, Gosbank needed to find a new role in the planned economy, and its leadership suggested that this role should consist in serving as a signaling device for problems with the fulfillment of the plan. Since it was possible to derive from the plan the maximum amount of credit each enterprise would need to carry out its planned tasks, each enterprise could be assigned a credit limit. When an enterprise exceeded this limit, this would

---

[43] Nikolai Ivanovich Bukharin, *Problemy teorii i praktiki sotsializma* (Moscow: Politizdat, 1989), 279.

[44] A complementary discussion may be found in David Shearer, *Industry, State, and Society in Stalin's Russia* (Ithaca: Cornell University Press, 1996), 70–74.

be a signal that there was a problem in plan fulfillment. In stressing that credit limits would derive from the plan, the centerpiece of the coming economic order, backers of the Gosbank project tried to give quantity theory considerations additional legitimacy.

Opposing Gosbank, Vesenkha officials and sympathizers argued for retaining the wechsel, both because it was the only reliable basis on which to emit currency and because discounting allowed essential flexibility to deal with an economy still far less than fully planned. Their commitment to flexibility seems to have been far stronger than their commitment to stability, however. Indeed, Vesenkha backed a crucial modification to the practice of discounting, whereby banks would discount wechsels as soon as they were presented, rather than waiting for acceptance by the buyer.[45] In general, Vesenkha officials also suggested that implementation of Gosbank's version of credit reform would lead to an unacceptable degree of bank dominance over productive activity and endless practical complications and conflicts, all of which would interfere with the main task of fulfilling the plan. They also professed concern that elimination of wechsels would weaken industry's ties with wholesalers and retailers, and thereby weaken their knowledge of the market for their products.

The short-term resolution of the argument was to adopt the Gosbank system, with, however, some extremely consequential compromises. And in the longer term the banking system developed in the spirit of the Gosbank vision. Both of these developments are discussed in the next section and need not detain us here. Here it is important to look at those aspects of the Gosbank project that were to have the most enduring impact on the Soviet monetary system. The counterarguments advanced by Vesenkha and other opponents are useful in drawing attention to these critical aspects of the Gosbank project. These were three:

1. Reaction to a systematic institutional weaknesses with inflationary consequences—Gosbank's inability to monitor the "reality" of industry's bills—with an even more institutionally ambitious project that like the Real Bills doctrine made successes in macrocontrol of the money supply dependent on repeated and regular successes in microcontrol of the behavior of enterprises.[46]

---

[45] *Torgovo-promyshlennaia gazeta*, July 26, 1929, 3. The author was M. Birbraer, at that time probably still "an official of the financial subdepartment of the planning department of Vesenkha"; R.W. Davies, "The Socialist Market: A Debate in Soviet Industry, 1932–33," *Slavic Review* 42 (Summer 1984): 201–223, at 205.

[46] Cf. Grossman, "Introduction," 10, who notes that the system of financial controls on enterprises in command economies "amounts to a *macro*-economic (anti-inflation) control by a means of a *micro*-financial control closely linked to the traditional management of the economy by micro-economic directives." The evidence presented here shows that, curiously

2. Closely linked to the preceding, complete reliance for control of the money supply on vertical control of the bank over individual enterprises, and no use of horizontal monitoring by enterprises of one another as a tool of monetary management.

3. Abandonment of a consumer-driven vision of economic value without provision of coherent replacement theory linking money to economic value. This left Gosbank without ultimately convincing arguments to counter the view of value promoted by Vesenkha and many Stalinists: economic value is created by production, which ought to be above monetary concern. The productionist theory of value thus remained a persistent, legitimate threat to the effectiveness of monetary control. On a deeper level, the consequence of the absence of theory of value underpinning the Credit Reform left the Soviet economy without standards of commensurability that could ensure rational choice between options.

In the remainder of this section these are dealt with in turn.

The issue of a complete reform of the system was first placed on the agenda after a special investigative report of the Workers-Peasants' Inspectorate (Rabkrin) in early 1929.[47] Shortly thereafter the idea was enthusiastically embraced by the leadership of the State Bank under its new head Grigorii Piatakov. Throughout 1929, Gosbank representatives repeatedly spoke out in the specialist journals and major economic newspapers about the need for a credit reform. They concentrated their fire on the practice of discounting wechsels. Here special ire was reserved for all the various forms of accommodation paper, which Gosbank spokesmen scored at every opportunity. Gosbank admitted it was completely unable to give any sort of statistical analysis of wechsels according to whether or not they were accommodation paper.[48] "Gosbank often does not know where its money has gotten to, whom it credited and for what."[49] The inflationary results were significant, since "the basic factor in the emission of banknotes is the emission of wechsels."[50]

Aside from simply suggesting that the bank did not have the institutional capacity adequately to implement the Real Bills doctrine, some supporters of the Gosbank position attacked, with varying degrees of obliqueness, the principle itself. Piatakov made much of the fact that Gosbank would henceforth be standing up to industry in questions of short-term credit. "The

---

enough, the origins of the link between microfinancial and macroeconomic control lie in capitalist methods applied prior to the creation of the command economy.

[47] Z. S. Katsenelenbaum, "K reforme kreditovaniia tovarooborota" (On the reform of credit for goods circulation), *Vestnik Finansov*, no. 6 (1929): 3–13, at 3; Shearer, *Industry*, 70.

[48] Terushkin, "O bezveksel'nykh," 80.

[49] Ibid., 83.

[50] Ibid., 82.

amount of short-term credit that will be extended in a given period of time to a given production organization will be determined in a process of struggle, in a process of argument."[51] Each request for extra funds must be weighed for inflationary effects.[52] Another defender of the Gosbank's project suggested that the Real Bills doctrine would be enough if the bank were only worried about getting its loans returned. "But Gosbank also bears the task of guarding the currency. And who now does not know that to guard the currency—this means above all not to allow the excess issue of money?"[53] The quantity of money necessary for each enterprise could be determined from the plan, implying that the plan had replaced the wechsel as the ultimate regulator of the money supply; it was inconsistent and archaic to speak otherwise.[54]

Despite the professed aim of the architects of the Credit Reform to design a monetary system to the measure of a planned economy, their ambitions in working out the details of the reform also bear the indelible impression of their experiences with the wechsel discount system. If the main frustration of the preceding system had been that the bank had been unable to track the use of credit, as the Real Bills doctrine mandated, then the new system would be geared above all to solve this problem. Thus credit would now be organized according to a "conveyer system," whereby the enterprise holding a good located somewhere in the cycle of production and sale would also have an outstanding debt to the bank for the money it had spent on purchasing the good. This debt would be paid back as the good was sold to the next link in the chain. Unlike the wechsel system, when money was given ostensibly to allow sellers to ship goods to buyers on credit, Gosbank would now loan its funds directly to the organization responsible to making the next sale of the good.[55] As Piatakov put it in *Pravda*, "The bank should conduct its work in complete correspondence with the material process of circulation."[56]

In the new system the general monetary stability would be guaranteed by ensuring that all individual enterprises stayed within their credit limits (determined on the basis of the maximum amount of loans each economic unit would need if it performed all its tasks under the plan). Gosbank officials predicted a huge administrative simplification from implementation of their scheme, since bank employees would no longer have to waste

[51] Morin, Piatakov, and Sher, *Reforma*, 7; cf. ibid., 10.
[52] Ibid., 51.
[53] Katsenelenbaum, "K reforme," no. 7, 29.
[54] Katsenelenbaum, "K reforme," no. 6, 12. Katsenelenbaum notes that there is some controversy in capitalist countries as well over the macroeconomic adequacy of the Real Bills doctrine but says that in any event it was accepted by the architects of the Soviet wechsel system.
[55] Morin, Piatakov, and Sher, *Reforma*.
[56] *Pravda*, 14 February 1930, 3.

effort in trying to differentiate Real Bills from accommodation paper. Indeed, the wechsel system's complexity was hindering Gosbank's ability to follow the Party line for "*orabochivanie i vydvizhenie*," that is, for employing more working-class persons in its apparatus through promotion from the ranks.[57] But whether the new system would indeed be administratively simpler was open to serious question, and opponents of the project hammered away at this point. A vigorous demolition of the Gosbank project in the Vesenkha newspaper suggested that an enormous number of variables would necessarily have to go into determining the credit limit, and discovering and calculating them would be far more difficult than just deciding whether a given wechsel was "healthy."[58] A more moderate critic pointed out that under the old system, industry had an incentive to monitor the financial circumstances of its retailer customers, because when wechsels were not paid in time their issuers were forced to cover them. Under the new system, Gosbank itself would now attempt to monitor all such customers. This would require "an apparatus so qualified and so perfect that it can only be created over the course of a number of years."[59] Furthermore, after shipping goods, industrial sellers were going to demand payment and be little interested in the state of Gosbank's relations with the buyers. And Gosbank was likely often to lose these arguments, leading to additional money issue.[60] (Despite advancing such arguments on a priori grounds, by and large Vesenkha supporters apparently believed that Gosbank would *not* lose these arguments, given their complaints of an intolerable dominance of Gosbank over the needs of production.)[61] In short, the bank, having failed to cope with the administrative burdens of the wechsel discount system, was now committed to an even more administratively difficult line, in which industry shifted from at least an occasional ally in the work of financial monitoring and monetary control to an out-and-out enemy.

The creation of an awkward and administratively burdensome system of monetary control was not, however, the most consequential legacy of Gosbank's design of the Credit Reform. This reform also destroyed the institutional basis of a consumer-driven theory of value without offering any theory of value in return. One of the persistent Vesenkha criticisms of the

---

[57] Terushkin, "O bezveksel'nykh," 76, 84.

[58] *Torgovo-promyshlennaia gazeta*, 26 June 1929, 3

[59] Ia. Kuperman, "Vzaimootnosheniia sovetskogo banka s ego klienturoi" (Relations of the Soviet Bank with its clients), *Ekonomicheskoe Obozrenie*, no. 9 (1929): 60–75, at 71.

[60] Ibid. Cf. *Torgovo-promyshlennaia gazeta*, 26 June 1929, 3. True, sellers had demanded immediate discount of wechsels under the old system—but they had to pay if the customer did not eventually pay off the bill.

[61] As Shearer notes (*Industry*, 70 n. 41), the critics "assumed that the reforms would be administered as planned."

Gosbank project, one that Gosbank officials never fully understood, was that with the elimination of wechsels, industry would lose touch with the state of the market for its products.[62] And indeed this was entirely accurate. Under the wechsel system, a factory that passed on a good to a wholesaler or retailer in return for a wechsel retained a strong interest in the good's eventual sale further down the line—for if this sale did not happen, the wechsel was likely to remain unpaid, and the bank would then extract repayment from the factory. Indeed, the whole point of the bill-of-exchange system was to allow for the workings of this *commercial* cycle. Industrial success depended ultimately on success with consumers. As Sokolnikov put it, "Production has no worth [*tsena*] if no sale follows it."[63] Further, the money in which customers made their purchases was also the unit of account in which industry should seek to economize, and without it, Sokolnikov claimed, there would be no basis for economic calculation.

This, of course, was a classic theme in the debate over the calculability of socialist production, a debate into which Gosbank did not enter. The Credit Reform as proposed by Gosbank made a definitive break with the institutions of a consumer-driven theory of value without *offering any alternative account of the nature of economic value.* Payment was now to be simultaneous with completed delivery of the product, unless the purchasing organization had exceeded its credit limit *at the moment of delivery*—a circumstance with no relationship to the salability of the producer's output. Producing a good that the customer could not pay for was an indication of problems with the *customer's* fulfillment of the plan, not the producer's. In eliminating the wechsel, designed for the world of the commercial cycle, Gosbank also eliminated industry's connection to the consumer while tying its receipt of money directly to the completion of production.

But then would it not be correct to say that Gosbank was merely institutionalizing a production-driven theory of value, one appropriate for a socialist economy? Only in the most sledgehammer of senses. "Value . . . analyzes fundamental beliefs concerning why seemingly diverse objects and human endeavors are comparable; and even more outlandishly, how such comparisons can be reduced to a single common denominator of *number.*"[64] Gosbank was implicitly taking the position that there was a meaningful commensurability of production in terms of money, in propos-

---

[62] Morin, Piatakov, and Sher, *Reforma,* 60.

[63] Sokolnikov speaking in 1922, in Grigorii Iakovlevich Sokol'nikov, *Finansovaia politika revoliutsii* (Finance policy of the revolution), 3 vols., vol. 1 (Moscow: Finansovoe izdatel'stov, 1925–1928), 251.

[64] Philip Mirowski, "Learning the Meaning of a Dollar: Conservation Principles and the Social Theory of Value in Economic Theory," *Social Research* 57 (Fall 1990): 689–717, at 695.

ing to reward and punish enterprises on the basis of their monetary performance. Gosbank's position, however, did not root the commensurability of production in money in the depositing of value in the process of production. In fact, the continued role of money at all was at best very weakly legitimated, though Gosbank did present two arguments in its favor. The first of these was that deviant monetary behavior—exceeding the credit limit—would signal that an enterprise was failing to fulfill the plan. Yet it was completely possible to be out of compliance with the plan without exceeding the credit limit.[65] Thus it was impossible to derive a logically valid justification for the commensurability of goods in money from the notion of the economic plan as determining enterprise behavior.

Aside from the signaling function of money flows, the only other justification for the commensurability of goods in money contained in the Gosbank project is the requirements of the "monetary circulation" as a whole. As already noted, this concern stemmed from the effort to overcome the inflationary problems created by accommodation paper. Piatakov argued: "Of course, under no system can there be a situation in which the State Bank extends credit in the amount that is demanded by industry, or consumer cooperatives, or any other organization. If affairs were organized in this way, we would get very quickly a very real inflation."[66] Elsewhere he suggested that each individual request for additional working capital must be evaluated from the point of view of monetary circulation. As another Gosbank spokesman argued, Vesenkha's argument that industry needed maneuverability could be accepted only if the interests of monetary circulation were given higher priority—allowing Gosbank to coordinate the financial maneuvers of the individual enterprises so as to avoid systemic problems for monetary circulation.[67]

For Gosbank's critics, the problem with the subordination of each enterprise's finances to systemic monetary imperatives was that these imperatives might bear only an adventitious relationship to the productive capacities of the enterprise or the productive goals of the society as a whole. The money in the hands of enterprises was commensurable, in the

---

[65] On this see K. L. [historians generally assume this was the official K. Lupandin], "Bor'ba za Kreditnuiu Reformu [Fight for the Credit Reform]," *Finansovye Problemy Planovogo Khoziaistva* (no. 7–8 1930): 19–29, at 20. Beyond this, one might point out, if one is seeking a single numerical indicator that would point at an enterprise's deviation from the plan, there is absolutely no reason to believe that enterprise behavior with money is the best one. It would be equally logical to count, say, the number of box cars entering and leaving plant grounds—and this would probably give a quicker signal of deviation from the plan. Or one could just as well multiply the prices of an arbitrarily selected subset of the inputs by one-half and come up with another indicator that would do exactly the same thing.

[66] Morin, Piatakov, and Sher, *Reforma*, 10.

[67] Katsenelenbaum, "K reforme," no. 7, 32.

limited sense that its aggregate had consequences. But this commensurability provided no guide to choice between uses of money, or, to put the matter differently, no guide as to who should suffer for the interests of the monetary system. "The argument [about whether to credit or not] . . . is about not just the needs and resources of the recipient of the credit [as it should be], but about the possibilities of the credit system," wrote a critic in the pages of the Vesenkha newspaper.[68] The economist Lev Shanin made the point in a deeper way. Suggesting that "we are Marxists enough to put material production organization [*material'noe khoziastvo*] in the first place," he argued that the interests of the financial system could not be defended at the expense of material production. Gosbank should not make important decisions regarding enterprises in line with its own conception of the interests of the monetary system. "The means of exerting pressure— and financing and crediting are means of exerting pressure—should not be in the hands of those who are partial, but in the hands of those who are the bearers of the synthetic basis."[69] While Shanin was vague on who exactly should serve as the "bearer of the synthetic basis," he made it clear that agencies involved in organizing production are better candidates than Gosbank. Gosbank, Shanin feared, would slide into rewarding production aimed to precisely satisfy current consumer wants. Such a policy will often lead to the wasteful abandonment of existing productive resources, which may in fact be able to produce an adequate replacement for what consumers currently want. Only those concretely involved in organizing production are in a position to make reasoned decisions on how closely to tailor production to consumer wants.[70]

Shanin's "synthetic basis," which amounts to society's theory of value, may be said to foreshadow the new politics of Soviet monetary policy. Monetary considerations can be overridden on a case-by-case basis in the interests of production. Rather than attacking Gosbank's ambition to rein in inflation as a capitulation to the hard-money interests of the *kulak*,[71] Shanin attacks Gosbank for investing monetary circulation with an unjustified importance. Indeed, inside the intellectual framework of the Credit Reform, its importance was *unjustifiable*. Gosbank's design granted money a dignity and importance transcending production, insofar as the requirements of the monetary circulation as a whole could mandate a limitation of production in any particular case, whatever the virtues of the productive project in question. But without an account of what made

---

[68] *Torgovo-promyshlennaia gazeta*, 26 June 1929, 3.
[69] L. Shanin, "Znamenatel'naia Reforma" (A signal reform), *Vestnik Finansov*, no. 6 (1929): 13–46, at 32.
[70] Ibid., 22–24, 44.
[71] Such attacks also sounded; see, e.g., *Torogovo-promyshlennaia gazeta*, 22 October 1929, 3.

money commensurable, such an approach was endlessly vulnerable to charges of irrationality, arbitrariness, and a failure to implement consistent values. Shanin's exploitation of this vulnerability was an early sample of a line of thinking that in the end was to react to the failure to establish money's commensurability in theory with the destruction of such commensurability in fact—through partition.

The Credit Reform in Practice

A Flood of Money

The Credit Reform as initially implemented represented a compromise between the desires of Gosbank and those of Vesenkha.[72] Gosbank, it will be recalled, wanted to eliminate wechsels in favor of direct crediting of purchasers. Assuming they had not exceeded their credit limit as specified by the plan, purchasers would receive a loan for the amount of purchase at the moment they officially "accepted" goods shipped to them. The money so loaned would then immediately be transferred to those who had produced the goods. Vesenkha, by contrast, wanted to retain the wechsel system, with the crucial modification that producers would issue a wechsel and present it for discount as soon as goods had been shipped, before customers had signaled their willingness to accept the goods and the responsibility to pay the wechsel.[73] Money creation (recall that the discounting of wechsels was generally done with new money) would thus take place immediately on the completion of production. The contest between the two approaches had only a limited overlap with the simultaneous debate between Left and Right. Vesenkha supporters did try to paint Gosbank's concern with the interests of the monetary system as tantamount to a Rightist surrender to the *kulak*. But Gosbank itself did not link its argument in favor of monetary stability to the need to preserve the *smychka*, striving rather for a more technocratic tone.

This perhaps explains why the Credit Reform went into effect largely as Gosbank had designed it. Wechsels were indeed eliminated. However, rather than paying producers only after customers had accepted the goods in question, producers were paid as soon as goods were shipped, with the intent that the funds would subsequently be deducted from the account of the purchaser. The origins of the decision to dispense with acceptances are somewhat obscure. It may have been a political concession to Vesenkha,

---

[72] For the immediate background of the Credit Reform and the views of various agencies, see Mariam Atlas, *Kreditnaia Reforma v SSSR* (The Credit Reform in the USSR) (Moscow: Gosfinizdat, 1952), 129–132 and Shearer, *Industry*, 70–72.

[73] This probably was a reaction to Vesenkha's separate struggle with sales syndicates, which had better access to commercial credit than producers. See Shearer, *Industry*, 60–66.

though a high-level commission containing representatives of both agencies had suggested that acceptances be used.[74] Another possibility is that the automatic payment procedure represented a temporary reaction to organizational difficulties; for instance, though the new system required that credit limits be calculated for each bank client, for the first two months after the reform began these limits apparently did not exist.[75] This left Gosbank completely bereft of a basis on which to deny payment to producers for shipped goods.

Whatever the importance of high-level political pressure on Gosbank or of implementation difficulties in helping to foster automatic payment, it is also the case that automatic payment within the general intellectual framework of the Gosbank reform project probably made more sense than not having automatic payment.[76] The issue was not only that punishing suppliers for their customers' violation of their credit limits was not very logical. The Gosbank project was, after all, based on the assumption of substantial success in planning. Without this it would be impossible accurately to calculate the necessary credit limits. If there were problems in the plan, Gosbank's idea seems to have been that its vantage point on the monetary system would give it the necessary tools to coordinate short-term plan adjustments. This was, of course, politically untenable; here industry's complaints that the bank was exceeding its brief were likely to be very compelling. Gosbank was trying to push too far into others' jurisdictions. Given the presumption of substantial plan accuracy built into the monetary reform, along with the politically unviability of substantial Gosbank control over short-term adjustments to planning, it must have been very tempting for the bank's leadership to take the further step of assuming that the plan's accuracy and fulfillment would prove good enough that it would not matter if payment were automatic. As an author in a Gosbank publication pitched to foreign audiences put it in March 1930, "The Soviet bank has reasons for 'trusting' all its clients, i.e. the enterprises in the socialised sector of national economy . . . the plan does not allocate tasks to unsound organisations which are unable to cope with the tasks of reducing cost of production, rationalising production, improving the quality of their

[74] Atlas, *Kreditnaia*, 144. However, in view of continuing objections by various agencies, a subsequent commission, headed by Ordzhonikidze, was convened, which came up with the final resolution implementing the reform.

[75] Ibid., 145.

[76] This is a different argument than that presented in Arnold, *Banks*, 358–363, also 363 n. 60, which suggests that Soviet bankers had gotten caught up in "leftist ideology" that foresaw a rapid withering of money. I am proposing instead that the basic design of the Credit Reform biased it toward automatic payment. Arnold's distinction between the "sound practices" of the initial proposal and what was actually implemented is thus slightly overdrawn.

goods, etc."[77] If such arguments were believed, then automatic payment would not create the risk of monetary expansion, since the purchasing enterprise will also have the necessary money available when the bill is forwarded to it. Although it is clear that at the time of Gosbank's initial drafting of its proposal, the bank did not share such optimism (and even still was criticized for making an overambitious leap toward the fully planned economy when real conditions were not ripe), it is conceivable that in the atmosphere of late 1929 Gosbank might have been converted.[78] Writing Stalin in mid-1930, Piatakov suggested as much when he linked part of the overissue of credit to failure by enterprises to fulfill the plan.[79]

However the practice of automatic crediting came to pass, it created a massive monetary emission. The payment to the seller became money creation pure and simple, while the debt due from the buyer accumulated as interbranch payments float [*mezhkontornye raschety*], which grew over 700% in the month after the Credit Reform was implemented on April 1.[80] The massive growth in the money supply stemming from monetization of this float had dramatic effects, making goods shortages critical, increasing rationing, and leading to a small change crisis as consumers hoarded silver coins that had become worth far more than their face value. Worse, the situation disabled the key mechanism the government used to rein in inflation—taxation. For as taxes too were paid at the moment of shipment of goods, they were also being paid in newly minted money. In short, 1930 witnessed an outpouring of new money from a multitude of sources, with virtually no control from central authorities. As David Shearer put it, "what had begun as a reform to enhance the state's control of the country's economic finances had rapidly turned into a complete breakdown of that system."[81]

Partitioning Money

The reaction to this flood of new money set the pattern for the Soviet monetary system for the remainder of its existence. In the opening section of this chapter, it was argued that institutions somehow store, in the way that they organize behavior, a meaningful formulation of their raison d'être. Yet the actual processes of institutional development would seem

[77] State Bank of the USSR, *Economic Survey*, No. 4, 1 March 1930.
[78] By this time the "plan" bore very little resemblance to a precise rational calculation, of course. Moshe Lewin, *Russia—USSR—Russia: The Drive and Drift of a Superstate* (New York: New Press, 1993), 95–114.
[79] Letter of Piatakov to Stalin, 20 July 1930, 7.
[80] K. L., "Bor'ba," 26.
[81] Shearer, *Industry*, 74.

to contradict this possibility. Certainly to the extent that its growth proceeds in fits and starts, any institution will represent the accretion of partial solutions to temporary problems. Indeed, Moshe Lewin has argued that the institutions managing the Soviet economy grew out of the Stalinist leadership's desperate and largely improvisational responses to the immense social chaos created by the twin drives for collectivization and industrialization, and a case can be made that the origins of the monetary system should be viewed in the same way.[82] This vision of institutional development would imply that the social scientist will be able to read the meaning of institutions only in the same sense that the geologist "reads" a rockface, discerning the features of past environments in patterns of erosion and compaction.

However, to argue that Stalinist improvisations were driven by the imperatives of circumstance is not to denude them of a *Weltanschauunglich* character, for these improvisations were reactions to problems created primarily by the intellectual structure of the Credit Reform. Indeed, what is striking about these efforts is that while they created relatively effective institutional solutions to the monetary problems stemming from the Credit Reform, they did nothing to address the fundamental intellectual contradictions of the reform.

This is most evident in the case of automatic payment, which continued to haunt the Soviet monetary system despite the quick elimination of its most direct form by installing the system of acceptances Gosbank had originally proposed.[83] The problem of what to do when a purchasing organization did not have funds available was not adequately solved, however, nor would it ever be, for it would forever remain difficult to justify punishing a plan-meeting producing enterprise for the financial sins of its customers. The basic tensions involved are quite obvious in the early resolutions addressing the problem. If the purchasing organization could not pay, after a certain period of time the good was to revert to the supplier to sell as it saw fit. Full implementation of such a measure would leave nothing of the planned economy, however.[84] And so it is no surprise to read in the same resolution that "in exceptional cases, when the good can be used only by this particular buyer" it could be passed on to the buyer, with the bank in-

---

[82] See Lewin, *Russia—USSR—Russia*. A similar point is argued in Hiroaki Kuromiya, *Stalin's Industrial Revolution* (Cambridge: Cambridge University Press, 1988).

[83] The key resolutions date from early 1931 and are in M. K. Vetoshkin, ed., *Finansovo–biudzhetnaia sistema SSSR: Zakonodatel'stvo SSSR i RSFSR* (The budget and finance system of the USSR: legislation of the USSR and RSFSR) (Moscow: Vlast' Sovetov, 1935), 652–658.

[84] I have not been able to trace further legal development on this point, but circumstantial evidence indicates it could not have persisted long.

structed to pay the supplier as soon as money appeared.[85] Once again production's specificity triumphs over money's generality. This problem of "nonpayments" for production was to be endemic to the Soviet economy.[86] Enterprises without money to pay for deliveries due them under the plan would simply fail to pay, leaving their suppliers to pressure Gosbank for credits to keep production going and wages paid.[87] Nonpayments seem usually to have been made good through clearing operations (*zachety*), whereby debts that enterprises had incurred to one another were netted out and new credit was injected to cover the debts of enterprises that could not pay for what they had consumed.[88] In this procedure, automatic payment for production had, as it were, its life after death.

The pattern of putting institutional patches over fundamental intellectual problems was continued in other measures adopted through the 1930s. Rather than developing a rationale for money's commensurability in theory, these measures simply made it incommensurable in practice. The first and most consequential way this was done was through an elaborate rationing system, which through various procedures of licensing created categories of purchases that money alone was not sufficient to accomplish. Rationing was driven by a number of practical pressures, most importantly the need to direct goods in line with the priorities of industrialization (or at least the present inclinations of the leadership) despite the massive and quite random money demand deriving from automatic payment for production. For producers' goods, rationing was implemented by the system of *fondy*, which allowed ministries to determine which enterprises would receive key goods in short supply.[89] Depending on the priorities of the ministry, identical amounts of money in the hands of different enterprises could have vastly different purchasing power. Consumer rationing also served to restrict purchasing power in line with social and production priorities. As Alexander Baykov noted, "From the beginning of the introduction of rationing it was stressed that it was based on the principle of differentiation and not on that of unification. . . . [A]ll

---

[85] Vetoshkin, *Fianansovo-biudzhet naia*, 657.

[86] For a brief discussion, see Jacques Sapir, *L'Economie Mobilisee: Essai sur les Economies de Type Sovietique* (Paris: La Decouverte, 1990), 56–57. For the fight against nonpayments in the 1930s see Atlas, *Kreditnaia* and Mariam Atlas, *Razvitie Gosudarstvennogo Banka SSSR* (Moscow: Gosfinizdat, 1958).

[87] Berliner, *Factory*, 282–287.

[88] See V. P. D'iachenko, *Finansovo-kreditnyi slovar'* (Finance and credit dictionary) (Moscow: Gosfinizdat, 1961), s.v. "Vzaimnye (kliringovye) raschety" (Mutual [clearing] settlements) and Raymond Park Powell, "Soviet Monetary Policy" (Ph.D. diss., University of California, 1952), 110–128.

[89] On *fondy* see Berliner, *Factory*, 22.

towns were divided into . . . groups, and all the population in these towns was divided into different categories on the basis of 'class'—production—distinction."[90] The rations available to different categories were radically divergent. Later, enterprises were given authority to supply scarce goods directly to their employees using their own schemes of differentiation.[91] In short, the power to command resources represented by any given sum of money depended almost entirely on the town in which one lived, the category to which one was assigned, or the factory for which one worked.

Another form of the partition of money was the creation of a strict division between short-term bank credit for temporary needs, on the one hand, and enterprises' "own circulating capital" (*sobstvennye oborotnye sredstva*), intended to meet permanent or year-round needs, on the other.[92] The Credit Reform had initially given each enterprise a single account, known as the *conto corrento* (current account), which could have either a positive or negative balance. A positive balance resembled an ordinary bank deposit, whereas a negative balance was an overdraft-like line of credit. The institutional difficulties of enforcing limits on this line of credit have already been mentioned, as has the fact that coming in inside the limit was no guarantee of plan correspondence. Beyond this, the *conto corrento* system provided no incentive to the enterprise to economize on its use of funds, as long as it stayed inside the limit—and these limits themselves were often fictional as they needed to be met only at the end of a given quarter.[93] Since overdraft credit was funded directly with money creation, enterprise willingness to make use of it translated into major macroeconomic imbalances.

By making a strict division between bank credit and enterprises' own funds, Soviet authorities addressed the problem of the articulation between monetary microcontrol and macrocontrol on a practical level without solving it on an intellectual one. Money continued to be viewed at once as a lubricant of the productive process in the individual enterprise and as a consequential aggregate on the level of the economy as a whole. The dichotomy between bank credit and the enterprise's own circulating capital reproduced this contradiction, addressing the issue through institutional partition rather than intellectual synthesis. The size of an enterprise's own circulating capital was calculated on the basis of its individual production

[90] Alexander Baykov, *The Development of the Soviet Economic System* (Cambridge: Cambridge University Press, 1950), 230. Cf. Kuromiya, *Stalin's Industrial Revolution*, 308–309.

[91] Baykov, *Development*, 231.

[92] For official documents on this division see Vetoshkin, *Finansovo–biudzhetnaia sistema*, 665–672.

[93] K. L., "Bor'ba," 22.

needs, quite loosely estimated on the basis of recent practice.[94] This method of assigning circulating funds quite explicitly did not view them as a scarce resource or try to make any decisions whatsoever about the relative benefits of different possible allocations. In other words, no effort to aggregate the working capital of different enterprises was made, nor was any commensurability of the sums involved across enterprises presumed. After this one-off initial allocation of circulating funds it would be difficult to get more; in essence, the idea was that an enterprise could get an increase of circulating funds only through its own economizing efforts. Aside from its own circulating funds, an enterprise's operations would be financed with short-term bank credit, now limited to strictly specified purposes.

Essentially the ideological maneuver that had been performed was as follows. The idea of money as lubricant of production was legitimized and institutionalized in the form of own circulating funds. Any additional requests for funds were less legitimate, however, and could be made only for a specific category of operations. Making the granting of short-term credit more difficult meant that there could be no automatic aggregation of "the needs of production" into money creation on a scale with dangerous systemic consequences. However, it was no longer this danger that served as justification to the enterprise for Gosbank's refusal to extend credit, but rather the idea that credit should only be required in circumstances exceptional for the enterprise in question. In addition, by necessitating explicit decisions on the granting of credit in each case rather than following the automatic overdraft method involved in the *conto corrento*, the new system made it easier to apply global limits on credit if necessary.

A final form of the partitioning of money was intended to make it possible to create spheres in which rationing would not obtain—realms inside of which money's purchasing power was relatively general and uniform.[95] To achieve this, new controls were created on the issue of cash money (as opposed to deposits in bank accounts, known in Russian as "cashless money," or *beznalichnye den'gi*), and new tools were created to balance the amount of cash outstanding with the prices of the goods available in the shops.[96]

---

[94] For the details of the rationale and implementation of the circulating funds reform see Atlas, *Kreditnaia,* 159–175.

[95] A major motive for the ending of rationing was the desire to make differential money pay a more meaningful stimulus—thus, to make differences in the quantity of money significant, which meant making it more commensurable. On this see Baykov, *Development,* 228, 250.

[96] The creation of these mechanisms is discussed in Atlas, *Razvitie,* 169–176 and 197–204, on which this discussion is based.

The development of the institutional mechanisms for cash planning in-volved many aspects, including trying to displace cash transactions that happened outside Soviet institutions (whether in black or tolerated mar-kets) with cash transactions inside Soviet institutions (i.e., the state retail network) or with noncash transactions. The number of transactions for which state enterprises were allowed to use cash was sharply narrowed. The payment of wages in cash continued, however, and much of the institution-building effort of this period consisted of attempts to gain control over enterprise wage funds. Permissible wage funds were tied closely to plan fulfillment. If an enterprise had not fulfilled its plan, it would not be allowed to pay as much salary. An enterprise that had over-fulfilled the plan could, however, pay somewhat more salary.[97] Although the firewall between cash and noncash circulation was notoriously porous,[98] it did allow Gosbank to draw up an economy-wide plan for the amount of cash money in circulation at any time and to attain a rough balance between goods available for purchase and the amount of money outstanding.

The contrast between the system of cash controls and the wechsel dis-count system of the 1920s is instructive. The wechsel discount system is-sued cash on the basis of a vision of the *commercial* cycle. Money serviced a purchase in the process of completion; consumption was supposed to drive the process. The 1930s system of cash controls issued cash on the basis of a vision of the *production* cycle—that is, it tied cash issue directly to the pay-ment of wages. At the same time, the balance between cash creation and goods available appears to have been calculated on the basis of something like the equation of exchange. This constituted a reprise of the 1920s contra-diction between rough-and-ready monetarism and the Real Bills doctrine—the latter now mutated into the claim that money should be issued to service production, rather than commerce.

In 1934 Stalin announced that "money will still remain with us for a long time, until the completion of the first stage of development—the socialist stage of development."[99] Money had become socialist through adaptation, an adapation that consisted in money's partition, that is, in the creation of multiple monetary realms within which money was commensurable. The paradigm of such a partitioned realm could be the "closed distributors," special shops whose purchasers were limited to "those persons who, on the

[97] This possibility meant that the cash plan of a bank division "could not serve as firm lim-its." Atlas, *Razvitie*, 198.
[98] Berliner, *Factory*, 282–284.
[99] Cited in R. W. Davies, *The Soviet Economy in Turmoil, 1929–1930* (Cambridge: Harvard Uni-versity Press, 1989), 323.

decision of the governing body, were 'tied' to this distributor."[100] The construction of such realms was made possible on the one hand by the system of ration controls, and on the other by instruments to control the amount of money in the hands of purchasers admitted to the realm. The size of these realms and the scope of the choice they involved were the product of deliberate policies, which could vary over time, and which were the subject of political conflict. Occasional efforts were made to reduce the role of rationing in industry, for example, and in the latter part of the 1930s, consumer rationing was gradually relaxed.[101]

The macroeconomic instruments that made construction of partitioned monetary realms feasible were themselves based on partition. The determination of allowable wage payments, like the setting of the balance between bank credits and an enterprise's "own circulating funds," established standards of "appropriate" behavior with money that applied to the *individual enterprise*. It was with respect to this within-the-enterprise notion of appropriateness that an individual enterprise's money was meaningfully commensurable.[102] Restricting access of the enterprise to money was never legitimated on the basis of the systemic needs of the monetary system but only on the basis of whether it had adequately dealt with its production tasks. The meaningfulness of aggregate sums of money for macroeconomic balance did not correspond to any meaningful commensurability of money as the basis for choice between alternative uses of resources across production units. Each enterprise became a monetary realm unto itself.

It has not been my purpose in this chapter to offer an explanation of the decline of NEP and the switch to forced industrialization, though the material analyzed does allow a few considerations on this topic to be presented. The academic debate around the reasons for the end of NEP has pitted those who believe Stalin's policies were mandated by the economic situation against those who believe there were feasible alternatives; a parallel debate contests the issue of whether room for a long-term accommodation of NEP could have been made in the framework of fundamental Bolshevik beliefs. Both sides have ignored the issue of the actual institutional capacities the Soviet government had to manage the acceptable operation of the market; as Kiren Chaudhry has argued in an important

[100] Baykov, *Development*, 238.
[101] On the former, see Davies, "Socialist Market"; on the latter, Baykov, *Development*, 251–276.
[102] Compare the similar development with regard to standards for capital productivity, which generally examined alternate uses only in the framework of a particular project. Gregory Grossman, "Scarce Capital and Soviet Doctrine," *The Quarterly Journal of Economics* 67, no. 3 (1953): 311–343, at 321, 342.

paper, it was as much administrative difficulties as either doctrinal or economic necessity that forced a retreat from NEP.[103] On the basis of the material analyzed here, one may say that in the monetary sphere in particular, an inability effectively to implement the Real Bills doctrine, best capitalist practice at the time, ensured an inflation that did much to foster the macroeconomic imbalances that hastened the demise of NEP. Administrative weakness led to inflationary difficulties that heightened tensions between town and countryside, and these tensions turned sinister in the hands of the ideologists of the class struggle. The hard-money-based *smychka* was undermined in practice before it was defeated in theory. Ironically, as we have seen, the institutional burdens implied by the monetary institutions of forced industrialization were much greater, but this was not a fact apparent before their adoption.

The Long Shadow of 1930

"Society," wrote Georg Simmel, "is the universal which, at the same time, is concretely alive."[104] Simmel was reaching for a conception of society that would avoid a mystical invocation of a group spirit while allowing for the fact that any interactions between persons are conditioned by, and in turn condition, a broader social context.[105] In money, Simmel found one embodiment of his conception of society:

When barter is replaced by money transactions a third factor is introduced between the two parties: the community as a whole, which provides a real value corresponding to money. The pivotal point in the interaction of the two parties recedes from the direct line of contact between them, and moves to the relationship which each of them, through his interest in money, has with the economic community that accepts the money, and demonstrates this fact by having money minted by its highest representative.[106]

This community as a whole, present in the individual monetary transaction through its role in creating and sustaining the institution of money, is at once universal and concretely alive.

In this vein, one might say that the monetary system that emerged from Stalinist industrialization transformed *Soviet* society into "the particular

[103] Kiren Aziz Chaudhry, "The Myths of the Market and the Common History of Late Developers," *Politics & Society* 21 (September 1993): 245–274.
[104] Georg Simmel, *The Philosophy of Money*, trans. Tom Bottomore and David Frisby from a first draft by Kaethe Mengelberg, 2nd enlarged ed. (London: Routledge, 1990), 101.
[105] Nicholas J. Spykman, *The Social Theory of Georg Simmel* (Chicago: University of Chicago Press, 1925), 26–27.
[106] Simmel, *Philosophy*, 177.

which is concretely alive." Partitioning money partitioned the communities in which a real value corresponding to money would be provided, and tasked concrete organizations with providing this value. The enterprise ensuring that its workers would find food in the shops, the ministry allocating *fondy*, monetary authorities attempting to balance the population's cash wages and goods purchases—these were the managers of multiple, particularized monetary realms.[107]

The contention that the passage from NEP to Stalinist industrialization represents a shift from society as a universal to society as an assemblage of particulars may seem unnecessarily abstruse. But this shift had major and definable consequences for the nature of politics. Sokolnikov's class analysis of inflation presumed a universal value of the currency for all in society. The classes of which his analysis spoke were defined by their place in the structure of production, which position shaped reactions to monetary policy. With the partition of money, *this* sort of class ceased to exist. The category of class became an ascriptive characteristic, rather than an economic one.[108] Inclusion in or exclusion from a particular monetary realm determined the value of money; the society for which money's value had been a universal no longer existed. The creation of partitioned and concretely managed monetary communities, to which political contention around money tended to gravitate, was one of the major legacies of the origins of the Soviet monetary system. The concrete manifestation of this legacy is described in the next chapter, which charts the breakdown under Gorbachev of the mechanisms that had allowed for large monetary realms to be created and managed from Moscow and that led to a proliferation of smaller realms.

That the mechanisms for monetary management proved so fragile in the face of economic reform is a consequence of the second major legacy of the Soviet monetary system: the unresolved tension created by the need to treat money as commensurate for purposes of macroeconomic control despite the incommensurability of production in money. In the effort to fashion a socialist monetary system, the Real Bills doctrine, born from the obsession of "the 'compleat' and orthodox banker"[109] to know his customer's business well enough to loan only on the most reliable of securities, was detached from its moorings in the commercial cycle and fused to an underspecified production-driven theory of value. Making money serve

[107] It is not my intent to deny that the choices offered bearers of money within a particular realm were often so narrow as to make the concept of "purchasing power" seem inappropriate, and the idea of a provision of value for money misplaced. But such cases of pure allocation of goods even less resemble the mechanisms of a Simmelian universal "society."

[108] Cf. Grossman, "Structure," 46–48, on the "adscription" accompanying Soviet industrialization.

[109] Landes, *Bankers*, 4.

the purpose of tracking and lubricating a productive process whose needs were not meaningfully denominated in numeric units undermined the credibility of and rationale for money's commensurability. Achieving macroeconomic stability, however, could only be understood as a task of balancing meaningfully commensurate money-denominated sums against one another. The absence in the initial design of the Credit Reform of a compelling explanation of why production could be measured in money, and of a reason to deny monetary rewards to enterprises whose customers could not pay, were thus not just infelicities of intellectual design relevant only to the aesthetic sensibilities of the external observer.[110] They created serious long-term difficulties for the practical tasks of Soviet monetary management and economic management more broadly. As we have seen, it was this contradiction that led to the partition of money and made systemwide monetary control dependent on serial successes in ensuring appropriate behavior with money. Such a model of macroeconomic management was extremely vulnerable to any economic reform aimed at giving enterprises more autonomy.[111]

Money's partition was never more than a practical solution to a problem that had not been intellectually engaged. In 1929, an author defending Gosbank's call to weigh systemic needs for macroeconomic balance in making decisions about extending loans to industry complained that industrial leaders never took this issue seriously enough:

> Some people think that individual enterprises' "getting around" Gosbank's credit plans is completely inevitable, for without this they will not be able to fulfill their production plans. In getting around Gosbank controls, or to put it differently, in spending more funds than the resources of the credit system allow, certain enterprises of the socialized sector reassure themselves by saying: *well it's true that in this case the currency will get a bit spoiled, but on the other hand the plan is implemented, factories are being built, goods are being produced, etc.* Gosbank, the comrades reason, knows only one thing: to preserve the stability of the *chervonets*. If one doesn't get around it, then perhaps the *chervonets* will be strong, but we won't fulfill our plans. So therefore, let's sneak out from under the control of that stubborn Cerberus, *let's build our factories, make our goods: victors are not judged, after all.*[112]

---

[110] One can suggest it was precisely this contradiction that so hobbled Soviet monetary theory. The poverty of this theory is analyzed in somewhat different terms in Grossman, "Gold and the Sword."

[111] Grossman, "Introduction," 10.

[112] Katsenelenbaum, "K reforme," no. 7, 30. Emphases added.

It was a complaint and an analysis that any Soviet banker could have repeated at any time over the next sixty years. Production victories excused any monetary sins, not because production was valued at any cost, but because no convincing formulation of the sinfulness of exceeding financial limitations could be given. Setting up enterprise-specific standards of appropriate monetary behavior gave a local definition of "sin" that always seemed arbitrary and unfair to Soviet enterprise managers. That the managers were right did not make this imperfect method of macroeconomic control any less indispensable—a fact that Gorbachev's ill-starred economic reforms were to make painfully clear.

CHAPTER TWO

Things Come Apart, 1987–1991

Money provides an extremely efficient technique for despotism, as a means for incorporating into its rule the most remote places which, in a barter economy, always tend to separate and become autonomous.

—Georg Simmel

"The winter of 1984–85 was unusually frigid," writes Yegor Ligachev in his memoir. For the embittered and disillusioned former Politburo member who led conservative opposition to economic and political reform in the late 1980s, this cold winter recalled a warm memory: of how the Soviet people came together under the leadership of the Communist Party in an effective battle against crisis. Power plants' stocks of fuel were all but exhausted, and thousands of freight cars with loads of coal frozen too solid to be unloaded clogged the railways. The Politburo assigned Ligachev to run a special "operations headquarters" that would supervise and coordinate rail transport during the crisis. Much of the work of this operations headquarters was carried out at nationwide conference-call meetings. As Ligachev notes, these meetings had a meaning that was as much political as practical. "The size of the audience on the other end of the conference call was unlimited. . . . Without any special order, almost all the leading Party and other officials of the regions threatened with economic paralysis voluntarily gathered at their communications posts." As the heroic and successful battle against the elements went forward, this vast audience "constantly sensed the integrity of the national economic organism, and the calm, firm, organizing hand of the center, which enabled resources to be maneuvered and bottlenecks to be cleared." Ligachev also made sure that they heard the name of Mikhail

Gorbachev, at the time battling to become the General Secretary of the Communist Party to succeed the rapidly declining Chernenko. The aim was to ensure that local Party leaders would come away with an image of Gorbachev as "taking care of real business, stabilizing the economy even in a critical situation."

From this warm memory of a cold winter Ligachev turns to a bitter memory of a rainy fall, the fall of 1990, when the weather threatened to destroy a record crop. If only a state of emergency and moratorium on political struggle had been declared, "the battle for the harvest could have become a uniting factor. Success could have dissipated society's pessimistic mood and inspired people with new faith. . . . A remarkable opportunity was missed to achieve civic accord and, on that basis, to build a calm, smooth crisis-free transition to new economic relations." But the battle for political power got in the way. Democratically elected local leaders were more concerned with pressing their political agendas than with helping the peasantry. The national leadership was no less indifferent, leaving Ligachev to complain that he "really didn't recognize anymore the Gorbachev who had run things in the winter of 1984–85 and who was responsible for getting results."[1]

The two crises Ligachev describes were only superficially caused by the weather. Neither cold winters nor fall harvests are beyond prediction, after all. In the Soviet Union, "emergency headquarters" and "campaigns" were a routine reaction to routine problems with which the state-socialist economy dealt badly.[2] As Ligachev implies, however, while the manifest function of extraordinary Party actions was to deal with crises, these actions had latent functions as well. For Party members, fighting crises was a "combat task" that answered to the emotional traditions (however desiccated and ritualized) of Bolshevik heroism.[3] Effectiveness in solving economic problems was also a cornerstone of the Party's legitimacy, if we understand legitimacy in the Weberian sense as a principle on the basis of which the right to rule is claimed, not granted. Behind the trajectory from Ligachev's 1985 pride in defeating the elements (and his political opposition) to his 1990 grief at the victory of the elements (and his political opposition) is the breakdown of the Soviet model of political and economic integration. Gorbachev's economic reforms worsened the dysfunctions of central planning

---

[1] Yegor Ligachev, *Inside Gorbachev's Kremlin* (New York: Pantheon, 1993). Quotations are drawn from 58–65.
[2] Don Van Atta, "The USSR as a 'Weak State'," *World Politics* 42 (October 1989): 129–149; Thane Gustafson, *Crisis Amid Plenty* (Princeton: Princeton University Press, 1989).
[3] For an exceptionally insightful account of the defining importance of combat tasks to Leninist parties, see Ken Jowitt, *New World Disorder: The Leninist Extinction* (Berkeley: University of California Press, 1992).

just as his political reforms were eliminating the Party as the key agent responsible for dealing with these dysfunctions. Economic difficulties that had been an opportunity for the Party to affirm its right to lead were transformed into a political debacle that fragmented first the polity and eventually the state.

The changing political meaning of economic crisis was especially apparent on a regional level. From the 1930s, local Party leaders and their bureaucratic *apparat* had had important responsibilities both in production and consumption. In production, they were responsible for smoothing over difficulties created by the inevitable imbalances of the plan through facilitating informal exchanges.[4] In consumption, local Party officials were charged with maintaining the purchasing power of the ruble in local stores. Although in both spheres local Party actions were seconded by or, at times, in conflict with the efforts of enterprises themselves, the Party was nevertheless a national structure whose efforts to deal with local problems could not but affirm the importance of the national political arena. As the Party's economic role declined, the tendencies to regional autarky that had been pronounced throughout the state-socialist period and were only exacerbated by Gorbachev's reforms acquired a new political meaning and resonance.

The Credit Reform had bequeathed to the Soviet economy a system of macroeconomic control dependent on an enterprise-by-enterprise battle to enforce arbitrary standards of appropriate behavior with money. Gorbachev's efforts to achieve economic dynamism through allowing for greater enterprise autonomy and the creation of new private businesses had the side effect of weakening the mechanisms by which macroeconomic control had been achieved.[5] As a result, the Soviet government found itself printing money faster and faster. In the classic pattern of repressed inflation, too much money chased too few goods; with prices unable to move to equalize supply and demand, the holders of money found it harder and harder to locate goods to purchase. For consumers, the flood of new money meant more retail shortages, as the goods available in state shops at fixed prices were simply too few to soak up all the buying public's rubles. Producers of goods also experienced an increase in shortages. Plan authorities, far from all-powerful to begin with, were less and

[4] Jerry Hough, *The Soviet Prefects* (Cambridge: Harvard University Press, 1969); Aleksander Yanov, *Detente after Brezhnev* (Berkeley: Institute for International Studies, 1977); Peter Rutland, *The Politics of Economic Stagnation in the USSR* (Cambridge: Cambridge University Press, 1993).

[5] This dilemma for marketizing reforms was pointed out long ago in Gregory Grossman, "Introduction," in *Money and Plan*, ed. Gregory Grossman (Berkeley: University of California Press, 1968), 1–16, at 15.

less able to guarantee enterprises the inputs needed to meet mandated output targets.

These problems were not novel, though more severe than usual. Their political effect, however, was quite novel. Shortages in the Soviet economy had always tended to foster informal horizontal exchange relations at the expense of vertical relations organized in the plethora of economic bureaucracies rooted in Moscow. In particular, shortages tended to increase the economic role of the Party leaders at the level of the province or the smaller Union republics, who became the organizers of barter deals intended to help local enterprises get the inputs they needed to meet plan targets.[6] As Gregory Grossman put it, "passive money equals active Party."[7] But as interregional barter acquired unprecedented scale in the late perestroika years, it also began to be organized by provincial governments rather than the local Party branches, whose economic apparatus was scrapped in 1988.[8] Rather than networks of Party first secretaries, alliances of contiguous provinces, such the Siberian Agreement and the Big Volga Association, sprang up to help organize the barter trade.

The exigencies of this trade gave local leaderships particular political interests, for not all goods were equally scarce. Some of the scarcest goods, especially construction materials, served as effective "currencies" in the barter trade. To trade effectively, local governments needed to gain access to these especially scarce goods. As Vitalii Naishul', who has provided the most important analysis of interregional barter, puts it, "Regional economic autonomisation, with the related ban on taking goods outside regions, was a prerequisite of the efficient functioning of a regional barter market."[9] Before 1990, no formal mechanisms existed to put the output of local industry under the control of local governments. The informal scratch-my-back arrangements local Party leaders had used to solve the problem were no longer adequate in the face of vastly expanded barter. Nor were enterprises and the ministries that still exercised a dwindling but substantial control over them eager to part with scarce goods. To win the battle over who would control these goods, local government leaders needed either expanded powers or weakened competitors.

---

[6] Hough, *Soviet Prefects*, 214–255.

[7] Gregory Grossman, "Gold and the Sword: Money in the Soviet Command Economy," in *Industrialization in Two Systems*, ed. Henry Rosovsky (New York: Wiley, 1966), 204–236, at 236.

[8] Rutland, *Politics*, 215; on the dismantling of the regional party's economic apparatus, see Robert J. Osborn, "Phasing Out the Party Apparat as Economic Manager," in *Perestroika at the Crossroads*, ed. Alfred J. Rieber and Alvin Z. Rubenstein (Armonk, N.Y.: M. E. Sharpe, 1991), 157–177.

[9] Vitalii Naishul', "Liberalism, Customary Rights, and Economic Reform," *Communist Economies and Economic Transformation* 5, no. 1 (1993): 29–44, at 33.

Boris Yeltsin was in a position to offer them both, Mikhail Gorbachev could offer them neither, and this in substantial measure determined the outcome of the titanic struggle between the all-Union and Russian authorities that began in the fall of 1990 and culminated in total Russian victory after the abortive coup of August 1991. Weakened competition from the structures of the command economy was ensured by a vigorous assault on the all-Union economic institutions. Holding out the prospect of looser regulation and greater retained profits, the new leaders of the Russian Republic were able to convince enterprises and banks subordinate to all-Union structures to rebel against their bureaucratic superiors and register with Russian authorities. Meanwhile, responding to demands emanating from the interregional alliances, Yeltsin put his authority behind expanded powers for provincial governments to tax the production of local industry.

In short, this chapter argues that the partial decomposition of the command economy into interprovince barter in the face of rapid monetary expansion gave provincial leaders an interest in its further decomposition, because this would free them to engage in barter more effectively.[10] Yeltsin was able to turn this interest to his advantage in his battle against the all-Union government to win effective sovereignty. The arguments and evidence presented here are naturally far from an exhaustive account of the demise of the Soviet Union. But they do have important implications for the way the politics of this period must be studied, and the way that economic factors must be included in such a study. For many analysts who have focused on narrating political dynamics after Gorbachev's liberalizations, the economy figures as a factor in a general popular discontent that then serves as a resource for Gorbachev's opponents in the national political arena.[11] Philip Roeder's stimulating *Red Sunset* formulates the approach explicitly; from the outset he emphasizes that he is "limiting [his] analysis to that realm of behavior in which actors seek control over state policy."[12] However, this limitation leads to a misapprehension of the nature and the stakes of politics in these years. Prior to the battle over state policy is the battle over the instruments that can make policy decisions matter, by implementing them. The issue was whether Moscow would have the power to allocate goods centrally at all, not how they would be allocated.

The remainder of this chapter is divided into four sections. The first deals with the relationship between horizontal and vertical ties in inte-

---

[10] Of course, this was only true as long as prices were not liberalized.

[11] John B. Dunlop, *The Rise of Russia and the Fall of the Soviet Empire* (Princeton: Princeton University Press, 1993).

[12] Philip Roeder, *Red Sunset: The Failure of Soviet Politics* (Princeton: Princeton University Press, 1993), 10.

grating the Soviet economy. The second discusses how horizontal ties were strengthened at the expense of vertical ones as a result of the macroeconomic imbalance brought on by economic reforms. The imperative to expand horizontal ties led to a battle between ministries, enterprises, and provinces that sought to command the resources to engage in horizontal trade. This battle is detailed in the third section. The fourth section investigates how the leadership of Russia made political use of the processes of barter and fragmentation by backing interregional alliances that had emerged to handle the barter trade. In the concluding section, I offer some arguments about why the Russian leadership won out over that of the Soviet Union.

Horizontal and Vertical in the Soviet Economy

The organization of economic life under Soviet socialism had a vertical aspect and horizontal aspect, but it would be a mistake to facilely associate the former with a formal "command economy" and the latter with an informal "market." Vertically, the characteristic managerial structure in Soviet industry (agriculture had a somewhat different structure) was a three-link system involving branch ministries at the top, enterprises (as the Soviets came to term the basic organizational unit in industry, despite the word's inappropriate entrepreneurial connotations) at the bottom, and between them some sort of intermediate agglomeration of enterprises. These last had varying form due to frequent reorganization.[13] As authors in the vigorous school of Russian students of the "economy of getting approval" have emphasized, much of what took place inside the vertical structures of the command economy had in fact the form of an exchange.[14] Higher-up organizations bargained with lower units in negotiations in which producers sought to swap plan fulfillment for material and financial resources. (Burawoy and Krotov have noted the resemblance of such dealings to a "putting out" system.)[15] In Soviet discourse, these vertical

---

[13] Gertrude E. Schroeder, "Organizations and Hierarchies: The Perennial Search for Solutions," in *Reorganization and Reform in the Soviet Economy*, ed. Susan J. Linz and William Moskoff (Armonk, N.Y.: M. E. Sharpe, 1988), 3–22, gives a brief and insightful history of organizational change in Soviet industry; for a description of the various models of subordination circa 1975, see O. Kuschpeta, *The Banking and Credit System of the USSR* (Leiden: Martinus Nijhoff, 1978), 95–115.

[14] Petr O. Aven and Viacheslav M. Shironin, "Reforma khoziaistvennogo mekhanizma: real'nost' namechaemykh preobrazovanii," *Izvestiia sibirskogo otdeleniia adademii nauk SSSR: seriia ekonomika i prikladnaia sotsiologiia* 13 (1987): 32–40; and Naishul', "Liberalism," whose usage of vertical and horizontal I am adopting.

[15] Michael Burawoy and Pavel Krotov, "The Soviet Transition from Socialism to Capitalism: Worker Control and Economic Bargaining in the Wood Industry," *American Sociological Review* 57 (February 1992): 16–38.

relationships were often seen as imbued with a dangerous "agency patriotism" partaking of elements of clannishness and selfishness.[16] Agency patriotism referred to behavior placing the interests of an individual ministry above those of the plan or of local authorities. It was manifested most dramatically in ministries' efforts to attain autarky in production of critical inputs, even when these inputs were produced more cheaply by other agencies. Reliable control of within-ministry flows of goods was much to be preferred to relying on the plan and supply organs that coordinated transfers between branches.[17]

However enthusiastically pursued, ministerial autarky was never perfect, and supplies not adequately provided through official channels were often sought through illegitimate horizontal exchange. Although sometimes this took the form of purchase of goods for money (especially cash) on the black market, often it was in the form of barter. The coordination problem of finding a partner who had what one needed and could take what one had to offer was solved in three ways. One was for the enterprises involved to handle it directly, perhaps through employment of the *tolkachi* (fixers) made famous in Joseph Berliner's classic study.[18] Second, enterprises might make use of variously institutionalized "exchanges" at which partners could find one another, with greater or lesser degrees of official tolerance.[19] Third, and most interesting for present purposes, were efforts to enlist local Party authorities in organizing chains of barter transactions. As Alexander Yanov described the situation, enterprise directors in need of supplies would call the province Party committee first secretary, "the only person who has the authority and power to order an all-Union dragnet, so to speak, for scarce raw materials. He alone can call . . . the Masters of other provinces and offer them a deal. He always has in reserve some raw material that is in short supply in another province, and there is always an opportunity to exchange it for what 'his enterprises' need at any given time."[20] Boris Yeltsin's memoir gives the flavor of the situation from the point of view of a Party leader: "Gorbachev and I first met when we were both working as first secretaries, he at Stavropol and I at Sverdlovsk. . . . Quite often we needed to extend each other a helping hand, exchanging metal and timber from the Urals for food products from Stavropol."[21]

[16] I am using "agency patriotism" to translate the Russian term *vedomstvennost'*.

[17] Nikolai Shmelev and Vladimir Popov, *The Turning Point: Revitalizing the Soviet Economy* (New York: Doubleday, 1989), 114–128.

[18] Joseph Berliner, *Factory and Manager in the USSR* (Cambridge: Harvard University Press, 1957), 207–230.

[19] Gregory Grossman, "The 'Shadow Economy' in the Socialist Sector of the USSR," in *The CMEA Five-Year Plans (1981–1985) in a New Perspective* (Brussels: NATO, 1982), 99–115, at 106–107.

[20] Yanov, *Detente*, 24.

[21] Boris Yeltsin, *Against the Grain* (New York: Summit Books, 1990), 71.

Off-stage in these descriptions is the process whereby the Party secretary gained control over the scarce materials needed elsewhere. The basic pattern seems to have been the accumulation of sets of reciprocal obligations between the Party leader and local enterprises.[22] One can thus conceive of the Party leader as the organizer of something like a "barter clearinghouse," overcoming the difficulties of the double coincidence of wants when enterprises were unable to do this for themselves. To the extent that each time an enterprise made an "exchange" with the local Party leadership it involved a foregone "exchange" within the ministerial structures, the ability of local Party leaders to play this facilitating role might involve them in something of a bidding war for the scarcest resources.[23] The general impression is that when explicit struggle was involved, local Party officials lost more often than they won. As Shmelev and Popov suggest, "Local authorities, as a rule, are weaker than the [ministries] and often lose to them in economic arguments."[24]

The relation of monetary policy to the competition between the horizontal and vertical economies is somewhat ambiguous. It is certainly the case that the problems in controlling the amount of money issued made shortages more acute and forced firms to resort increasingly to what Grossman calls the "four b's" of the shadow economy: "barter, black market, *blat* [that is, pull or connections], and bribe."[25] However, resorting to these mechanisms need not be equal to decentralization or a diminished influence for national structures. The critical issue is whether what was involved was simply changing the terms of the stereotypical vertical exchanges of the "command economy" or whether they were horizontal ones. Decisive here was the effectiveness of the inflation-repressing mechanisms—fixed prices, rationing of goods, limitations on cash—in the hands of the agents of the vertical economy. Although the relevant data could never be gathered, it seems reasonable to hypothesize that up to some level of inflation/shortages, the influence of the command structures over subordinated enterprises increases, to the extent that this influence derives from the ability to distribute these scarce goods. But presumably at some level of inflation the repressive mechanisms cease to work as effectively. Higher organizations are not able to keep their side of the inputs-for-output bargain with their subordinate enterprises, prompting the latter to make alternate

[22] Hough, *Soviet Prefects.*
[23] The original discussion of this bidding war issue in the informal economy was Berliner, *Factory and Manager*, 219.
[24] Shmelev and Popov, *Turning Point*, 161.
[25] The "four b's" are discussed in Grossman, "Shadow Economy," 105–108; the link of inflation to resort to the shadow economy is discussed in Gregory Grossman, "Note," in *Stagnation or Change in Communist Economies?* ed. Karl C. Thalheim (London: Centre for Research into Communist Economies, 1986), 49–54.

arrangements.[26] (In the absence of such a threshold it would be hard to explain why the Soviet authorities made any effort at all to constrain the amount of money made available to enterprises.)

Tipping the Scales: Perestroika and the Disintegration of the Command Economy

Under Gorbachev, bad luck and worse policy combined to cripple the structures of monetary management that had, however imperfectly, served the command economy since the 1930s.[27] The magnitude of the monetary problems created in the Gorbachev period can be seen in the increase in the so-called ruble overhang. The ruble overhang accumulated as cash was paid out in wages but not recaptured by the state through taxes or the receipts of state retail stores. This money was thus available to consumers to buy any goods that appeared in the shops and thereby ensured the perpetuation of shortages.[28] The magnitude of the problem faced by Soviet monetary authorities can be gauged from table 1, which charts the percentage of consumer income left uncaptured by the official economy.[29] In interpreting these data it should be borne in mind that the monetary overhang accumulated over time, so that money left uncaptured one year remained to increase shortages in the next. While these data concern

[26] Joel Hellman, "Breaking the Bank: Bureaucrats and the Creation of Markets in a Transitional Economy" (Ph.D. diss., Columbia University, 1993), describes the point at which horizontal relationships become preferred to vertical ones as the "contracting threshold."

[27] This is the burden of Ellman's excellent survey (Michael Ellman, "The Monetary System: From Disequilibrium to Collapse," in *The Disintegration of the Soviet Economic System*, ed. Michael Ellman and Vladimir Kontorovich [London: Routledge, 1992], 106–136), on which the following draws. The story of how Gorbachev's policies managed to destroy the Soviet economic system is well known, and I claim little originality for what follows. A good general survey from the perspective adopted here is Petr O. Aven, "Economic Policy and the Reforms of Mikhail Gorbachev: A Short History," in *What Is to Be Done? Proposals for the Soviet Transition to the Market*, ed. Merton J. Peck and Thomas J. Richardson (New Haven: Yale University Press, 1991), 179–206.

[28] Some of this money, of course, represented authentic savings and no "threat" to goods in the shops, and it has even occasionally been claimed that forced savings was not a major phenomenon in the command economies before the 1980s; for a survey of this debate, see Gavin Peebles, *A Short History of Socialist Money* (Sydney: Allen & Unwin, 1991), chapter 5. Whatever the truth of the matter for earlier periods, the reality and significance of the monetary overhang in the perestroika years is indisputable. See International Monetary Fund [IMF], World Bank, and Organisation for Economic Co-operation and Development [OECD], *A Study of the Soviet Economy* (Paris: OECD, 1991), 396.

[29] This is the "propensity to save" as defined in Peebles, *Short History*, 12. Data from World Bank, *Russian Economic Reform: Crossing the Threshold of Structural Change* (Washington: World Bank, 1992), 320.

Table I. Percentage of consumer
income "uncaptured"

Year	Percent
1985	5.4
1986	6.3
1987	7.5
1988	8.9
1989	11.1
1990	12.7
1991	30.2

consumers, there is also substantial evidence that enterprises were accumulating money they were unable to spend in these years as well.[30]

In explaining how things came to such a pass, several factors must be cited. First are the dramatically increased budget deficits after 1986, financed in substantial part through the printing of money. These deficits had their origin in the twin fiscal disasters of the antialcohol drive and the sharp drop in world oil prices, as well as an ambitious investment policy associated with the policy of acceleration (*uskorenie*).[31] The budget deficit increased particularly sharply in 1991, when the struggle between the Union and the republics came to involve withholding of tax revenues by the latter.

A second stage, from 1988 onward, was the increasing monetary overhang stemming from the unintended effect of liberalizing reforms on the ability of monetary authorities to control the amount of cash issued to the economy. In particular, reforms allowed the creation of small, private cooperatives to handle lines of business and services poorly supplied by the state economy. Despite this intention, the bulk of cooperatives were created as adjuncts to existing state enterprises.[32] Although it is probably true that a major activity of the cooperatives was to transfer enterprise revenues to private pockets, this was not important for their effect on macroeconomic balance. What *was* important in this regard was that the cooperatives were not subject to the same strict limits on wage-fund cash that applied to state enterprises. Before the Law on Cooperatives, the Soviet enterprise had often had occasion to employ cash for purposes other than paying wages, and many ways of evading wage controls were developed.[33]

---

[30] IMF et al., *Study*, 390–391.
[31] Ellman, "Monetary System," 114.
[32] Michael Burawoy and Kathryn Hendley, "Between Perestroika and Privatisation: Divided Strategies and Political Crisis in a Soviet Enterprise," *Soviet Studies* 44, no. 3 (1992): 371–402.
[33] Grossman "Shadow Economy," 109–110.

But cooperatives' ability to set their own wage funds meant that the transfer of noncash to cash funds could happen on a much grander scale. Officials in Irkutsk Province reported that cooperatives in the first half of 1990 took more than twenty-three times as much cash out of bank coffers as they put back in, indicating a very substantial rate of conversion of noncash to cash rubles.[34] There is no reason to believe that this situation was not typical. If in 1988, less than 1 percent of all wages were paid out by cooperatives, by 1989 this figure was already over 6 percent.[35] At the same time, reforms in the bank system also weakened the State Bank's ability to monitor cash emissions by banks servicing enterprises.[36]

Other changes in the financial system also contributed to a decline in the ability of monetary authorities to contain the money supply and repress inflation.[37] The partitioning of enterprise money into separate accounts (an aspect of the partitioned money discussed in the preceding chapter) was weakened. Also, economic legislation created the possibility for the creation of new, cooperative banks. The Soviet system of bank transfers, known as the MFO (for *mezhfilialnyi oborot*, or interbranch transfers), was designed for a situation in which all banks were conceived as branches of a single bank. It was assumed that internal controls would prevent a branch of the bank from ordering the transfer of money not actually on account, which would be tantamount to printing its own money. With the arrival of the cooperative banks, this assumption became inaccurate. Indeed, banking officials later expressed relief that a worse monetary disaster was averted because the cooperative banks simply did not realize how much money they could have created.[38] In his otherwise rather unsatisfying memoir, the first head of the Russian Republic's Central Bank compared the MFO to mealtime in a "poor peasant family: one bowl is put on the table and whoever has the biggest spoon and is swiftest gets more porridge."[39] Whether or not new cooperative and commercial banks took full

[34] *Deng'gi i Kredit*, no. 4 (1991): 42. Cf. *Volzhskaia Kommuna*, 10 June 1990, 1. I have been unable to locate disaggregated monetary data that would allow a determination of whether the conversion of cashless to cash money was preceding at a higher rate. The argument linking the weakening of barriers to the conversion of noncash to cash money to cooperatives, and shortages to the excess money thereby produced was also made in a vigorous survey of the economic scene by the head of the Primorskii obkom economic apparatus, *Krasnoe Znamia*, 10 August 1990, 2.

[35] Calculated from IMF et al., *Study*, 97. I have been unable to locate figures for the last two years of the Soviet Union.

[36] Hellman, "Breaking the Bank," 111–112.

[37] These are drawn from Gur Ofer, "Budget Deficit, Market Disequilibrium, and Economic Reforms," in *Milestones in Glasnost and Perestroyka: The Economy*, ed. Ed A. Hewett and Victor H. Winston (Washington: Brookings Institution, 1991), 263–307, at 293.

[38] *Ekonomika i Zhizn'*, no. 30 (June 1992): 11.

[39] Georgii Gavrilovich Matiukhin, *Ia byl glavnym bankirom Rossii* (Moscow: Vysshaia shkola, 1993), 55. On the MFO see also Hellman, "Breaking the Bank," 105, 221.

advantage of the possibilities to issue money offered by the MFO, it seems clear that they did complicate the money management problem.[40]

At the same time as the increase of the money supply stemming from the weakening of the traditional management institutions was sharpening shortages, the vertical economy was increasingly losing its ability to control where goods in shortage were directed. Liberalized access for enterprises to both domestic and foreign markets created both new incentives and new opportunities to divert goods from the channels of the plan. Domestically, legalized *birzhi*, or commodity exchanges, where prices were not fixed by law, sprouted throughout the country—often on the basis of the structures of the state supply agency, which were thereby weakened.[41] As for international markets, a radical liberalization in April 1989 eliminated the state's monopoly on foreign trade. Direct access to foreign markets was open to any enterprise granted a license by the Ministry for Foreign Economic Ties (MVES), and fourteen thousand such licenses were issued in 1989.[42] Export deals were especially attractive, because many Soviet raw materials and metals could be sold easily on world markets at cheap prices, or bartered for consumer goods very much in shortage. Efforts to allow the state, rather than enterprises, to capture the difference between domestic and world prices through application of multiple exchange rates do not seem to have been very effective.[43]

The upshot of macroeconomic imbalance was that by 1990, enterprises were experiencing the relationship with their superior organizations as increasingly extortionate. The supplies and assistance that had previously accompanied higher-ups' demands to meet plan targets were gone, but output was demanded anyway. In response, to the extent they were able, enterprises exited these relations to use those of the horizontal economy. And this weakened the vertical economy still further. For the last several years of the Soviet economy, enterprises found themselves in a desperate and frustrating battle to conclude contracts for input supplies for the forthcoming year. Enterprises engaged in this activity often found that even when suppliers were obligated to sign such contracts (under the system of *goszakazy* or state purchase orders gradually replacing the plan), they would refuse to do so. Presidential and Council of Ministers orders to suppliers to "preserve existing economic ties" were ignored. In Primorskii Province, for instance, enterprises had only been able to contract for 9.2

[40] Ofer, "Budget Deficit," 293.
[41] On the *birzhi*, see Timothy Frye, "Caveat Emptor: Institutions, Contracts and Commodity Exchanges in Russia," in *Institutional Design*, ed. David Weimer (Amsterdam: Kluwer Academic, 1994), 37–62.
[42] Alan Smith, *Russia and the World Economy: Problems of Integration* (New York: Routledge, 1993), 132.
[43] Ibid., 133.

percent of required supplies for 1991 by October 1990.[44] A synthetic rubber plant in Samara Province had by December of the same year managed to conclude contracts for 30 percent of supplies for the forthcoming year. The problem, the plant's director explained, was the "extortion" of suppliers, who were demanding scarce goods (rather than just money) in return for those that they would ship. There was no choice but to agree with such proposals.[45] This was a conclusion to which ever more enterprises were coming.

Battling for Barter: Enterprise, Province, or Ministry?

The economic liberalizations of 1987 to 1990 weakened the partitioning mechanisms that were the heritage of the Credit Reform, but they did not change the characteristic boundary-drawing politics with which money's partition was associated. What emerged by 1990 was a decentralized redefinition of monetary realms and a struggle to acquire the resources to make money work within them. This struggle centered around efforts to capture goods that were in particularly sharp shortage and had the status of virtual currencies. These were such things as food, fuel, paper, tires,[46] construction materials (cement, bricks, etc.),[47] and consumer durables.[48] Producers of such goods had no need to arrange chains of barter, and no particular reason to share them with local authorities. And weakened but still important ministries (or their descendants in "concerns") were likely to fight particularly hard to control output in such cases.[49]

At stake in the battle for the barterable among ministries, enterprises, and local authorities was which consumers would be able to convert money into goods, or the size of the community embodied in money. The remnants of the planned economy were agents of a national community of consumers created in the attempt to balance the amount of goods available for purchase and the amount of money outstanding on the level of the country as a whole. The ideal at this level was the sale of consumer goods exclusively through the generally accessible retail network, with goods distributed regionally in proportion to the amount of salaries paid in each re-

[44] *Krasnoe Znamia*, 3 October 1990, 1.
[45] *Volzhskaia Kommuna*, 11 December 1990, 2. For similar stories about the weakness of central ministries in forcing suppliers to sign contracts and the eventual resort to barter, see *Krasnoiarskii Rabochii*, 20 October 1990, 3; *Volzhskaia Kommuna*, 4 December 1990, 2; *Volzhskaia Kommuna*, 16 February 1991, 2; *Krasnoe Znamie*, 23 January 1991, 1; also Burawoy and Krotov, "Soviet Transition"; and Burawoy and Hendley, "Between Perestroika."
[46] Naishul', "Liberalism," 33.
[47] *Krasnoiarskii Rabochii*, 24 August 1990, 1.
[48] Naishul', "Liberalism," 33; *Krasnoiarskii Rabochii*, 20 October 1990, 3.
[49] For a description of a tug-of-war between an enterprise and a postministerial structure over access to barter goods, see Burawoy and Krotov, "Soviet Transition," 29.

gion. Under such a system all currency would represent an equal chance to make a purchase. At the other pole was the balancing of salaries paid and goods sold on the level of the individual enterprise. Here retail institutions selling only to workers in a particular enterprise would increase the value of workers' wages by ensuring that goods could be bought for them.[50] Such in-enterprise distribution was a long-standing feature of the Soviet economy and was one of the way that enterprises sought to retain workers. The money paid out in wages to workers in such enterprises was no longer the same as money in the hands of consumers without access to such channels, and the community of consumers shrank to the employees of the particular enterprise.

Between the factory and the nation lay the province, a third potential community of consumers. The Party leader of a province was traditionally held to have some responsibility to ensure the balance between wages and goods available. The most famous example is Ligachev's contrast—at the 19th Party Conference in 1988—of his own successes as a provincial leader to Yeltsin's failures in the same post: "For more than 10 years the province in which I worked . . . has been supplied with food products entirely of its own production, and at a good level too, whereas you, Boris Nikolaevich, were province Party committee secretary for 9 years and got your province solidly stuck on ration cards."[51] In the late perestroika years this "currency community" became more important as residence restrictions on who could make retail purchases became increasingly prominent.[52]

The political meaning of the province as currency community had changed as well. For Ligachev, his success at avoiding rationing was an example of *Party* heroism. The solution of particular, local problems was still part of a mission to build socialism that found its inspiration and definition in Moscow. But with the dismantling of the Party's economic apparatus and the shifting of the weight of defending local interests onto the executive bodies, the efforts to put goods in the shops for local consumers rather than those in other provinces appeared as a political challenge to the center rather than a demonstration of fealty to it.[53]

The task facing provincial leaderships was to balance at the level of the province goods available for purchase and money available to buy them,

[50] Such practices are analyzed brilliantly and movingly in Caroline Humphrey, " 'Icebergs', Barter, and the Mafia in Provincial Russia," *Anthropology Today* 7, no. 2 (1991): 8–13.

[51] *XIX Konferentsiia Kommunisticheskoi Partii Sovetskogo Soiuza: Stenograficheskii otchet* (XIX Conference of the Communist Party of the Soviet Union: stenographic report) (Moscow: Politizdat 1988), 2:85.

[52] Gertrude E. Schroeder, "Perestroyka in the Aftermath of 1990," in *Milestones in Glasnost and Perestroyka: The Economy*, ed. Ed A. Hewett and Victor H. Winston (Washington: Brookings Institution, 1991), 459–469, at 467.

[53] For instance, the head of the economic planning office in Krasnoiarsk called for an end to "the right of central agencies to colonial control of our territory, enterprises, and natural resources." *Krasnoiarskii Rabochii*, 24 February 1990, 10–11.

in competition with similar efforts on the level of the country as a whole and within individual enterprises. There seem to have been two (overlapping) phases in the evolution of the interregional barter that served this goal. The first phase comprised the conversion of some of the implicit interregional "exchanges" mandated by the plan into explicit exchanges. Under conditions of perfect plan discipline, any two arbitrarily selected regions were likely to have a certain "balance of trade" expressed in flows of goods to one another. Since these flows were organized by the "command" economy, they were not exchanges between the regions and not perceived as such. Nor was information about the structure of these flows easily available. But as plan discipline declined, scheduled recipients of goods discovered that they were not receiving them. In those cases where the recipient organization had no direct way of affecting the supplier, it could turn to the regional leadership, which in turn would look for a delivery it could withhold from the region of the delinquent supplier. For instance, the former chairman of the executive committee of Krasnoiarsk Province related how the province had decided to retain some cement for local use rather than shipping it to Omsk as mandated under the plan. Shortly he was called by the governor of Omsk Province who explained that if the cement shipment was not made, Omsk would retaliate by blocking scheduled shipments of motor oil.[54] In February of 1990, Krasnoiarsk's key industrial supply and retail agencies were instructed to figure out which regions were failing to make deliveries and to develop ways of retaliating.[55]

There were limits to how far this transformation of the implicit interregional exchanges of the plan into explicit barter could go, however. Aside from the fact that planners had no reason to balance the bilateral flow of goods between any two arbitrary provinces, retaliation for failed plan deliveries was only possible if both sets of local authorities had decisive influence over how local enterprises disposed of their production, and this was often not the case. Either the enterprises themselves or superordinate ministries might object to being used as part of such a plan of retaliation. The second phase in the emergence of interregional barter involved efforts by local government to gain control over the output of local industry and use it to make new exchanges to provide for local needs, exchanges that were not mandated by the plan. In 1990 and 1991, all three of the provinces studied for this book sought to organize in-kind taxation of local industry for some form of "exchange fund" to barter for out-region food and industrial supplies.[56]

[54] Interview, July 1994.
[55] *Krasnoiarskii rabochii*, 22 February 1990, 2. For a similar story of retaliation for delinquent planned deliveries, see *Volzhskaia Kommuna*, 22 February 1991, 1.
[56] "In-kind taxation" is a slightly imprecise term. The ambition of local authorities was to be able to tell an enterprise to sell a scarce good at official prices to a particular buyer, without

Organizing such taxation did not prove simple in any of them. The problem was that the very resources that were most useful to the region for barter purposes were also those that were most useful to enterprises for keeping their production going and supplying their workers. One official in Primorye Province complained that enterprises were unwilling to start production of consumer goods the province could use for barter with other regions to put goods in its own shops. "It seems that they have forgotten that outside the factory gates the workers turn into purchasers."[57] But this official himself had forgotten, or was choosing not to remember, that workers were consumers *inside* the factory gates as well, and it was not easy to convince enterprise directors that their sense of responsibility to the province ought to exceed their responsibility to their own employees.[58] In the absence of effective "province patriotism," the problem of ensuring motivation reduced to the traditional choices of carrots and sticks, and provincial leaders found they had precious little of either.

The most elaborate effort to organize a local in-kind tax in the three provinces studied was encountered in Samara Province, where the Soviet sought to organize on a regional level the sort of "putting out" bargain that had operated in the vertical economy. Samara's "territorial purchase order" was explicitly modeled on the national "state order" system that had replaced, without fundamentally modifying, the plan. The ambition was to buy from 10 to 80 percent of the production of selected local enterprises, arranging for supplies of the necessary inputs. Incentives for joining included tax relief, scarce consumer goods, and land on which workers could start gardens.[59]

In practice it seems to have been sticks rather than carrots that played the main role in getting enterprises to make deliveries to the fund, though

---

insisting on some additional compensation. This compensation would then accrue to the region and constituted the "tax." Interregional barter would thus appear to have had no effect on enterprises' money receipts or money tax liabilities. Interview with the head of the Terzakaz office, Samara *oblast'*, April 1994; interview with the former Krasnoiarsk governor, July 1994. For the "exchange funds," see, e.g., *Krasnoe Znamia* 20 September 1990, 1; *Krasnoiarskii Rabochii* 24 August 1990, 1; *Volzhskaia Kommuna*, 15 April 1990, 2. For similar phenomena, see Philip Hanson, "Local Power and Market Reform in Russia," *Communist Economies & Economic Transformation* 5, no. 5 (1993): 45–60, at 49.

[57] *Krasnoe Znamia*, 14 August 1990, 2.

[58] On factory directors' sense of noblesse oblige as regards their workers, see Oleg Kharkhordin and Theodore P. Gerber, " Russian Directors' Business Ethic: A Study of Industrial Enterprises in St. Petersburg, 1993," *Europe-Asia Studies* 46 (November 1994): 1075–1102. A deputy of the Primorskii krai soviet suggested that enterprises participated in the exchange fund because of "nobility" (*blagorodstvo*).

[59] The draft regulation on the *terzakaz* was published in *Samarskie Izvestiia*, 21 November 1990, 5. The percentage of production subject to purchase depended on whether the enterprise in question was subordinate to local, republican, or Union authorities.

perhaps this impression is an artifact of journalists' news sense. One factory director warned that the use of threats like disconnecting electricity could provoke an "economic war with enterprises."[60] The territorial order system was scored as a "quit-rent in kind," the language being an unflattering allusion to the practices of prerevolutionary landlords.[61] The Soviet's chairman was unrepentant, however, threatening to block supplies of construction material and meat for worker cafeterias to those enterprises that refused to participate in the territorial order,[62] though he did confess to unhappiness with all the "knee-bruising" involved in ensuring deliveries.[63] Relevant officials in the Primorye and Krasnoiarskii Provinces indicated that similar knee-bruising went on there as well, along with efforts to give enterprises an interest in participating in province exchange funds, though it was not as public.[64]

It is virtually impossible to gauge the effectiveness or scope of these efforts to extract resources for barter purposes.[65] Speaking impressionistically, it appears that Primorye Province had the most difficulty in accumulating goods to barter, because it did not produce many of the goods in greatest demand.[66] As far as the national situation was concerned, a survey of approximately two hundred enterprise directors concluded: "Regional organs participated in the distribution and sale of production, but in insignificant measure (from 3 to 20% [of production])."[67] However, it should be remembered that this is a measure of the achievements of local governments, not of their ambitions, and it was their ambitions that were critical for their political interests.

Provincial governments' efforts to fight shortages by accumulating more goods for consumers to purchase were ineffective unless they could also set boundaries to the currency community they served by restricting pur-

[60] *Samaraskie Izvestiia,* 28 December 1990, 3.

[61] *Volzhskaia Kommuna,* 29 January 1991, 3.

[62] *Samarskie Izvestiia,* 9 February 1991, 2.

[63] *Samarskie Izvestiia,* 9 October 1990, 3.

[64] Interview with the former head of the Krasnoiarsk Head Planning and Economic Administration (GlavPEU), June 1994; interview with the former governor of Krasnoiarsk krai, July 1994; interview with the former deputy governor of Primorskii krai, November 1993.

[65] Repeated efforts to obtain access to records on barter in the pre-price-liberalization period in Samara were unsuccessful; in the other two provinces, it is not clear that these records even exist. On the difficulty of measuring the size of interregional barter, cf. Hanson, "Local Power."

[66] For references to the failure effectively to establish such a fund, see *Krasnoe Znamia,* 14 August 1990, 2; *Krasnoe Znamia,* 5 February 1991, 1; *Utro Rossii,* 14 February 1991, 1. In a November 1993 interview, the former deputy governor said his efforts to figure out how to trade the services of the krai's important ports and railroads in the interregional barter trade had met with complete failure.

[67] Irina Boeva, Tat'iana Dolgopiatova, and Viacheslav Shironin, *Rossiiskie Gospredpriiatie v 1991–1992: Ekonomicheskie Problemy i Povedenie* (Russian state enterprises in 1991–1992: economic problems and behavior) (Moscow: Institute of Economic Policy, 1992), 19.

chasing power. This was usually done by banning "exports" from the province and allowing stores to sell some or all goods to local residents only. These restrictions regularly provoked retaliations from nearby regions, often in the form of restricting deliveries due under the plan.[68] Local introduction of rationing systems shared the dynamic of plan-replacement barter. Breakdowns in plan discipline led to rationing systems, which in turn led to more breakdowns in plan discipline. The institutional foundations of the Soviet economy were spiraling to destruction.

Surfing Disintegration: Russia on the Rise

By 1990, Soviet instruments of macroeconomic management were decaying by the day. Price controls could be imperfectly maintained, but the institutions that prevented intolerable shortages by achieving a rough balance between purchasing power and goods available for sale in a national currency community were increasingly enfeebled. Both the vertical economy ensuring central allocation of goods and the monetary institutions that limited purchasing power functioned worse and worse. In these circumstances, in the summer of 1990, the newly elected Russian Congress of People's Deputies gathered for the first time. After heated debate, it chose Boris Yeltsin to head the smaller Supreme Soviet formed from its ranks, and passed, on June 12, a declaration of sovereignty for Russia claiming control over the Republic's resources. These events set off an unequal battle between the Soviet Union's leadership and Russia's, in which Russia had decisive political and administrative advantages.

For the Soviet authorities, the policy options were stark, and virtually none of them allowed cultivation of a political base, whether among mass publics, powerful economic actors, or regional elites. Mass publics were most affected by shortages. But to balance the amount of cash in circulation and goods in stores, the Soviet leadership had only had exceedingly blunt and unpopular instruments, such as restrictions on enterprise wage funds, the confiscatory exchange of high-denomination ruble notes in February 1991, or the sharp price rises enacted later that spring.[69] Worse, none of these measures was likely to have a permanent effect against the

---

[68] William Moskoff, *Hard Times: Impoverishment and Protest in the Perestroika Years* (Armonk, N.Y.: M. E. Sharpe, 1992), 46–55.

[69] For the dilemmas of economic policy from the point of view of key Soviet policymakers, see Valentin Pavlov, *Upushchen li Shans? Finansovyi Kliuch k Rynku* (Has the chance been lost? The financial key to the market) (Moscow: Terra, 1995); Nikolai Ivanovich Ryzhkov, *Perestroika : istoriia predatel'stv* (Perestroika: A history of betrayals) (Moscow: Novosti, 1992); and Leonid Ivanovich Abalkin, *Neispol'zovannyi shans : poltora goda v pravitel'stve* (A chance not used: A year and a half in the government) (Moscow: Izdatel'stvo politicheskoi literatury, 1991).

backdrop of the broader loss of monetary control. In the economic bureaucracy, ministries, responding to the same circumstances as provinces and enterprises, were increasingly focused on freeing themselves from their broader obligations to the vertical economy in an effort to maintain control over subordinate enterprises. Often this took the form of reorganization as a parastatal "concern."[70] On the local level, elections, shortage dynamics, and the withdrawal of the Party from the management of interregional barter, transformed center-regional economic relations into a zero-sum game. Perhaps the most successful political initiative of Soviet authorities (and this is very much damning with faint praise) was their effort to organize enterprise directors, especially those in the defense industry, to support a restoration of tighter vertical subordination.[71] But this new force had no institutions through which to act, and proved very ephemeral, as we shall see.

Russia's leadership, by contrast, won political support by accelerating the spiral of fragmentation gripping the command economy and by offering regional leaders and enterprises autonomy to act on the incentives this fragmentation gave them. In the summer and fall of 1990, for instance, Russian authorities launched a massively successful campaign to reregister subdivisions of the Soviet banking system as new commercial banks subordinate to Russian structures, in very short order destroying most of the remaining instruments of monetary control.[72] Meanwhile, in August 1990, shortly after his promise to "invert the pyramid of power," Yeltsin made a twenty-two-day tour of the Russian provinces.[73] The tenor of his remarks may be judged by what had to say in Primorye Province: "You yourselves will be the owners [*khoziaeva*] of your production and natural resources, you yourselves will decide how much wood to cut, how much to leave for yourselves, how much to sell. And it will be the same with fish and other raw material stocks."[74] Similar tactics were adopted with respect to coal miners, especially hard hit by shortages because their salaries, though unusually high, were virtually their only compensation. Mines where strikes occurred were brought under "Russian jurisdiction" and allowed to maintain greater shares of both their production and their monetary receipts.[75]

---

[70] Burawoy and Krotov, "Soviet Transition"; Simon Johnson, Heidi Kroll, and Santiago Eder, "Strategy, Structure, and Spontaneous Privatization in Russia and Ukraine," in *Changing Political Economies: Privatization in Post-Communist and Reforming Communist States*, ed. Vedat Milor (Boulder: Lynne Rienner, 1994), 147–174.
[71] On this effort, see Pavlov, *Upushchen,*144–146. The "directors corpus" so assembled was wildly hostile to Gorbachev.
[72] Hellman, "Breaking the Bank," 197–203.
[73] For a brief description, see Dunlop, *Rise of Russia*, 51.
[74] *Krasnoe Znamia*, 21 August 1990, 1.
[75] Stephen Crowley, *Hot Coal, Cold Steel: Russian and Ukrainian Workers from the End of the Soviet Union to the Post Comunist Transformations* (Ann Arbor: University of Michigan Press, 1996), 138. See also Pavlov, *Upushchen*, 128.

Since Soviet taxes served primarily as a means of removing excess liquidity from the economy, such measures only increased the imbalance between purchasing power and goods.[76]

The way the Russian government sought to reap political benefits from the dynamic of disintegration is especially clear in its relations with emerging alliances among provinces. These alliances were formed as provinces sought a means to coordinate and stabilize the plan-replacement barter described earlier.[77] Thus according to the first head of the Far East Association of Economic Cooperation, Far Eastern provinces first came together to deal with the breakdown of centralized distribution and later started to work for common interests such as investment in transport connections to the center of Russia and control over export licenses.[78] The origins of the Siberian Agreement go to a meeting at which provinces "tried to come to some agreement on fulfillment of contracted deliveries."[79] Finally, the "Big Volga" Association devoted much of its first meeting to determining "how we can coordinate to supply one another with material resources and in creation of the necessary industrial bases for their production."[80] These aspirations could not be attained, however, unless provincial leaderships could win their battle for the produce of local enterprises. Again, this fragmenting ambition provided a political opportunity for Russia's leadership. In 1990 and 1991, Yeltsin signed special decrees granting interregional alliances rights to some control over export and also rights to 10 percent of enterprise production for barter purposes.[81]

[76] Franklyn D. Holzman, *Soviet Taxation; The Fiscal and Monetary Problems of a Planned Economy* (Cambridge: Harvard University Press, 1962).

[77] In an extremely useful survey of the interregional associations (Andrew Bond, "Russia's Regional Associations in Decline," *Post-Soviet Geography* 34 [January 1993]: 59–66), it is argued that the associations had a "diversity of rationales for their inception—some had a purely economic raison d'être (strengthening the ties among members and coordinating external economic activity) . . . whereas the establishment of others primarily reflected political goals (greater regional autonomy, coordination of activity in national legislative bodies)"(59). However, this is not documented, and the argument for their primarily "political" nature in the text seems to apply to alliances of cities, rather than the interprovincial alliances.

[78] *Krasnoe Znamia*, 20–22 December 1991, 3.

[79] *Krasnoiarskii Rabochii*, 17 October 1990. One participant reported (interview, May 1994) that the participants showed up with lists of what they shipped to other territories—but not of what they received from them. Cf. also *Delovaia Sibir'*, no. 1 (January 1991): 2.

[80] *Volzhskaia Kommuna*, 22 February 1991, 1; the prominence of the barter issue for the Big Volga Association is also quite apparent in the first issue of its newspaper (*ABV: Ezhedel'naia Delovaia Gazeta*, "Nulevoi Nomer," October 1991, 2–6.)

[81] For the Siberian Agreement, see *Delovaia Sibir'*, no. 1 (January 1991), 2; for the Far East association, see *Krasnoe Znamia*, 20–22 December 1991, 3 (the description is slightly ambiguous and they may even have been granted more than a 10% share); for "Big Volga," *Volzhskaia Kommuna*, 24 June 1991, 1; *ABV: Ezhedel'naia Delovaia Gazeta*, "Nulevoi Nomer," October 1991, 1–2.

In 1990 and 1991, when in Moscow, Yeltsin was engaged in a furious argument for a radical and rapid transition to a market economy, a transition that Gorbachev and his close allies found unacceptable. Yet in dealings with the provinces, Yeltsin was engaged in cultivating a political base not for this market program, but for something entirely different: the decomposition of the command economy into its previously illegitimate horizontal ties. There was nothing automatic in the support of local leaders for a policy of maximal local control over resources; if this were so, no large country could sustain itself.[82] The appeal of Yeltsin's program of maximal local control depended on circumstances when fixed prices and an enormous monetary overhang made everything seem in shortage, so that control over resources seemed the road to local economic security. It mattered little whether goods went to export or domestic markets, whether they were competitive with international products or not. With everything worth more in the barter trade than it cost in the official economy, it was the rare politician who could look ahead to a time when it would be customers, rather than resources, that would be hard to come by.[83]

Conclusion

Soviet economic and political unification rested precariously on three pillars. The first was the monetary system, which ensured overall macroeconomic balance and minimized shortages by policing partitioned monetary realms. The second was a vertical bargaining economy, in which ministries and their subordinate enterprises contended over plan targets and the resources to fulfill them. And finally, there was a horizontal exchange economy, in which resources needed for plan fulfillment were procured, usually on a barter basis; in substantial measure, this informal exchange was not only tolerated, but indeed even coordinated by regional Party *apparatchiki*. Thus the horizontal economy, too, ended up affirming the political weight of the Party. Those local leaders who felt some indifference to the Party's universal mission nevertheless quite often found themselves, in their efforts to secure the resources to make horizontal exchange possible, in the waiting rooms of Moscow ministers. All three pillars of the Soviet economic system affirmed the political and economic centrality of the national capital.

[82] Taking the appeal of calls for decentralization for granted is an unfortunate feature of the useful studies by Dunlop (*Rise of Russia*, 54) and Roeder (*Red Sunset*, 240).

[83] An analysis of how late-perestroika conditions promoted disintegration of the organizations managing the logging industry for reasons that turned out to make little economic sense after price liberalization is in Michael Burawoy, "Industrial Involution: The Dynamics of the Transition to a Market Economy" (unpublished paper, 1994).

Gorbachev's perestroika first shook, and then toppled these pillars. Perestroika passed through a cycle familiar from earlier efforts to reform the Soviet economy: because macroeconomic balance depended on the effective partition of money, it was undermined by any effort to allow increased autonomy in the use of money. Thus reforms tended to end with the reasserting of central control needed to restore balance.[84] What was different about the spastic and unpopular measures to reassert economic control that the Union government took from late 1990 was that they happened in a political environment fundamentally changed by Gorbachev's own reforms. In a well-observed narrative of an afternoon in the early 1970s spent with a Soviet enterprise director who was appealing to the local Party leadership for supplies, Alexander Yanov describes how he and the director came to the conclusion that economic chaos was in fact an intentional mechanism for maintaining Party control: "The reason that [the Party first secretary] needs economic chaos, which dooms the country to stagnation, is that it is precisely this chaos that makes him a superarbiter, a general intermediary among the managers."[85] In this straightforward functionalist version—economic chaos benefits the Party, and therefore it exists because it benefits the Party—the argument is untenable. Too much of Soviet administrative history had revolved around efforts to tame the shortage economy, both through redrawing of organizational boundaries and through macroeconomic management, to allow serious consideration of the idea that the shortage economy was deliberately maintained as a prop of Party rule. But Yanov's functional argument does highlight what Ligachev understood very well—that addressing the perpetual crises thrown up by the command economy offered the Party an opportunity to make the resolution of local problems appear as the project and justification for a nationwide organization. In the monetary chaos unleashed by perestroika, it was local executives playing the role previously accorded to Party secretaries, and their activities were testimony to the center's weakness rather than its might.

Gorbachev never made a serious effort to bid against Yeltsin for the support of the regional organizers of the new barter trade, or the other structures seeking to kick the traces of the vertical economy, for what Yeltsin was offering them was in effect aid in destroying the all-Union state apparatus that Gorbachev headed. By embracing the localizing dynamic created by the decomposition of the state socialist economy, Russia's leaders were able to create a coalition to assert "Russian statehood" against the

[84] For an early expression of this view, see Gregory Grossman, "The Structure and Organization of the Soviet Economy," *The Development of the USSR: An Exchange of Views* (Seattle: University of Washington Press, 1964): 41–60; also see Naishul, "Liberalism," 33.
[85] Yanov, *Detente*, 27.

structures of the Soviet Union. The odd thing about this coalition was that it involved no economic rationale for why the provinces making up Russia ought to be united under a single sovereignty. The interprovincial alliances generated by the spread of barter helped to bring down the old order, but given their ambition to institutionalize autarky they could hardly be the building blocks of a new one. Yeltsin had forged a coalition not for a Russian national market, but against the remnants of the Soviet Union's national command economy. After the Soviet Union collapsed, Russia's leaders would discover that having exploded the Soviet monetary system and the forms of national integration it sustained, they now faced the challenge of building replacements that could unite a new, capitalist Russia.

CHAPTER THREE

Bender's Revenge, 1992–1993

And this is the path of the millionaire! Where is the respect, where is the
honor, where is the fame, where is the power?

—Ostap Bender

The tragedy of Ostap Bender, con-man hero of two famous novels by Soviet satirists Ilf and Petrov, was that success always reached him too late. In *The Twelve Chairs* (1927), Bender sought the one chair whose stuffing contained jewelry, hidden there in the midst of revolutionary chaos by a wealthy matron fearful of Bolshevik expropriations. After long and exhausting adventures, he and his partner Kisa Vorobyaninov finally did locate the right chair. By this time, however, Vorobyaninov had become so soured by the difficulties of the search and so eager to claim its prize that he slit Bender's throat and went off to secure the chair on his own—only to discover the jewelry had been sold, and the money spent to build a new workers' club. In *The Golden Calf* (1931), Bender reappears (with a scar on his neck), this time trying to become a millionaire by the direct route of finding an existing millionaire and extorting his presumably ill-gotten and nervously concealed wealth. Once again, exhausting efforts finally yield the desired result. Carrying his hard-won million rubles in a suitcase, Bender walks into a hotel and declares grandly that he needs a room and can pay as much as needed. But it is to no avail; the clerk informs him: "The entire Congress of Soil Experts has arrived to examine the Experiment Station. All the rooms are reserved for the representatives of science." It is this way everywhere; Bender's suitcase of money grows no lighter. To breach the partitions separating him from those bounded realms where money had purchasing power, Bender must present himself as socially useful, engaging in just the sort of chicanery money was supposed to obviate. To his sorrow, the great con-man had overlooked the momentous change in the meaning of money described in chapter 1 of this book and so precisely recorded by the two novels: In the 1920s, money meant the power to build a club; but by the 1930s, only the decision to build a club empowered money to purchase.

Bender's plaint on behalf of the disenfranchised cash-holder had particular resonance in the waning years of the Soviet Union. As chapter 2 showed, in these years the institutions allowing central authorities to harness money to their purposes decayed. Money was partitioned anew, now in a decentralized fashion. Factories tied money exchange to barter, demanding the right to make a purchase before agreeing to make a sale. Local leaders, now representatives of their territory rather than agents of an integral and integrating Party, built partitions of their own as they endeavored to shape how enterprises and consumers could spend money and for what purposes. Ilf and Petrov used Bender's frustrated desire to spend as an illustration of his irrelevance to a rising project for industrialization and national integration. Sixty years later, money's localized and fragmented purchasing power became a symbol of how that project had come undone. In these circumstances, Bender finally (once again too late) got his revenge. By introducing a sweeping price liberalization on January 2, 1992, Russia's leaders undertook to build a new economic system in which millionaires would indeed enjoy respect, honor, fame, and power—a system in which money, even Bender's money, would buy all.[1]

However, it was not the desire to appeal to a constituency of con-men (or even an embryonic bourgeoisie) that prompted the Russian government to pursue monetization. The project to invest money with universal purchasing power addressed the urgent task of state building. In the fall of 1991, the efforts of Yeltsin's Russia and of the other Union republics to break the power of the Soviet government by abetting the disintegration of the planned economy had reached a sudden and unexpected culmination. The failure of the August 1991 coup accelerated the demise of the executive structures of the Soviet Union, which in some cases collapsed of their own accord and in others were absorbed by the Russian government. All at once, Russian authorities found themselves in the position of governing a territory they had sought to render ungovernable.

New circumstances meant new priorities. The devolutionary processes that Yeltsin had aided now represented a barrier to the effectiveness of his own power. Local control of resources had progressed to the point where

[1] The final clause is adapted from the epigraph to Gregory Grossman, "Gold and the Sword: Money in the Soviet Command Economy," in *Industrialization in Two Systems*, ed. Henry Rosovsky (New York: Wiley, 1966), 204–236.

the Russian government was no longer in a position to supply even Moscow with goods and foodstuffs. Spastic efforts to recentralize on the old basis by retracting earlier concessions made to the provinces had little effect. "Life in the country today, given the paralysis of power, has become more disorganized," Yeltsin told the Russian Parliament in October of 1991. "Sharply increased centrifugal tendencies have exacerbated the already difficult position of the national economy and intensified the production decline. The weakness of Russian statehood and forced errors of tactics have made themselves felt particularly vividly in the new situation."[2] The price liberalization Yeltsin promised in this speech, and the monetization it was expected to bring, were ways to strengthen feeble Russian statehood.[3] Money would reverse the spiral of fragmentation brought on by barter, ensuring the economic power and political centrality of the national state.

This state-building project achieved important successes, but these successes were partial, and, to a substantial extent, temporary. In the aftermath of price liberalization, political contention shifted decisively to the national arena and acquired a new focus. Rather than debating control of physical resources, politicians began to argue about the allocation of money. As the first section of this chapter explains, Russian leaders, and many foreign analysts as well, assumed that these changes meant that monetary policy—decisions by national authorities on how much money the state should issue—had become the touchstone of politics. However, as the balance of the chapter demonstrates, the new importance of the national arena was deceptive, for it was as much a consequence of the persistence of Soviet monetary institutions as of the struggle to acquire rubles that now enjoyed nationwide acceptance.[4] In the new environment price liberalization created, Soviet monetary institutions began to shape a pattern of interactions between enterprises that amounted to decentralized generation

[2] Boris Yeltsin, "Statement to the RSFSR Parliament," in J. L. Black, ed., *Disintegration of the USSR* (Gulf Breeze, FL: Academic International Press, 1993), 278.

[3] Cf. Simon Clarke and Veronika Kabalina, "Privatisation and the Struggle for Control of the Enterprise," in *Russia in Transition*, ed. David Lane (Longman: London, 1995), 142–158, at 145.

[4] One important aspect of the persistence of Soviet monetary institutions was the "ruble zone" encompassing most of the post-Soviet republics, which at times amounted to a system of multiple central banks issuing the same money and competing to capture gains from seigniorage. The Russian monetary system only became fully and finally separate in the summer of 1993, though the unity of the ruble zone prior to that date can be overestimated. Unfortunately, the intricate institutional and political developments surrounding the ruble zone cannot be examined here. Although creation of a fully independent Russian monetary system with a single sovereign central bank was certainly germane to the project of monetary consolidation, it raised rather different issues than monetary consolidation on Russian territory itself. See Anders Åslund, *How Russia Became a Market Economy* (Washington: The Brookings Institution, 1995), 109–136.

of substitutes for money, raising huge fiscal and administrative difficulties for the national government, and also nourishing what appeared to be a powerful political opposition movement among industrial enterprise directors demanding changes in national policy. Yet once these Soviet monetary institutions were destroyed, the political and administrative challenges they created for the central government soon evaporated, a process substantially complete by the time of Yeltsin's violent dispersal of the Russian parliament in October 1993. Subsequent chapters will show, however, that this apparently rapid victory for monetary consolidation in the national arena was only a prelude to prolonged new struggles over monetary sovereignty, struggles that began on the local level.

Monetization as Centralization

The main architect of the effort to use price liberalization and monetization to address the "weakness of Russian statehood" was economist Yegor Gaidar, who became the country's de facto prime minister in late 1991.[5] Gaidar argued that the fragmenting dynamic that had contributed to the collapse of the Soviet Union stemmed from repressed inflation— the maintenance of price controls in the face of large-scale monetary emission. Since the price level could not rise to accommodate the increased supply of money, more and more goods quickly found buyers. Correspondingly, more and more would-be buyers could find no goods on which to spend their money. Repressed inflation led to the processes analyzed in the proceeding chapter—barter, the ignoring of state commands, and the increased unwillingness of regions to allow scarce goods to leave their borders—and had thereby stripped Moscow of its ability to ensure that even basic foodstuffs would flow to the consumers of large cities.[6] Defending his policies in August of the following year, Gaidar suggested that he had faced a very stark choice: "There are two groups of regulators that are capable of ensuring the vital activity of society: effective money and effective commands."[7] Effective commands were no longer possible; indeed, Gaidar claimed an attempt to impose them would end in violence.

[5] Gaidar was the main Russian architect of price liberalization. On the role of foreign advisers, see Åslund, *How Russia*, 16–21.

[6] The efforts of Gaidar and his supporters to demonstrate that his hand was forced by the situation continued to generate new revelations on the depth of the Fall 1991 crisis even as late as 1995. See *Izvestiia*, 4 November 1995.

[7] *Izvestiia*, 19 August 1992, 3. This important account of Gaidar's reasoning is also partially translated in *Current Digest of the Post-Soviet Press* [henceforth *CDPSP*] 44, no. 33 (1992): 4–7, from which some quotations are drawn. Although Gaidar did not produce such a comprehensive statement at the outset of the reforms, this seems to be an accurate summary of his thinking at the time. Cf. his television interviews as given in *Daily Report. Central Eurasia*, FBIS-SOV-92–004, 7 January 1992, 40–44 and FBIS-SOV-92–041, 2 March 1992, 29–33. Issues

Making money work through allowing prices to rise was thus, according to Gaidar, the only option. Monetizing the economy would ensure national integration and the effective sovereignty of national authorities over the Russian territory. As Gaidar put it in a March 1992 interview, "just as the road toward the collapse of the state begins with the collapse of the national currency, so the path to the rebirth of the state . . . begins with the stabilization of the national currency."[8] It is important to realize here how closely Gaidar was seeking to link asserting effective sovereignty of the national state, monetization, and fighting inflation. On the near side of price liberalization, what undermined money in its command-economy variant was repressed inflation. On the far side of price liberalization, the threat to money was open inflation, which if unchecked would end in hyperinflation and a general "flight from money." Open inflation needed to be fought just as repressed inflation could have been: by eliminating the budget deficit and restricting the issue of new money.

Gaidar expected that the main challenges facing the program to restore power to national authorities through price liberalization and restrictive fiscal and monetary policies would be political. He argued that fighting inflation would hurt the short-term interests of virtually all members of society, and maintained that therefore it was important for the government to take maximum advantage of the window of opportunity to run a radical policy before opposition coalesced.[9] He thus saw the political process not as a means of creating knowledge about how best to proceed, nor as an opportunity to build a coalition for reform, but only something that can interfere with or (less likely) facilitate a known, prior agenda.[10] Since giving in to demands to use an increased money supply to reduce the pain of price liberalization risked hyperinflation, Gaidar argued that in monetary policy, "it is necessary to concede only exactly as much as it is impossible not to concede, and not a grain more."[11]

With such remarks, Gaidar certainly invited a mode of analysis that seeks to rate the political strength of his government by measuring what monetary concessions he was in fact forced to make. A number of such accounts have been produced. Politics in Russia in this early period of economic reform, according to these accounts, centered around the efforts of the reformist government to restrict the money supply and prevent a retreat

---

of *Daily Report. Central Eurasia* will henceforth be cited only by their issue identifier (FBIS-SOV-YY–NNN).

[8] Russian TV, 1 March 1992; translated in FBIS-SOV-92–041, 2 March 1992, 29–33, at 31.

[9] *Izvestiia*, 19 August 1992, 3.

[10] In a TV interview translated in FBIS-SOV-92–041, 2 March 1992, 29–33, at 33, Gaidar accepted a comparison of his work to that of surgeon and added: "It is very dangerous to jog a surgeon's elbow, for example, when he is doing such an operation."

[11] *Izvestiia*, 19 August 1992, 3.

from price liberalization in the face of the hidebound, market-averse opposition of the "directors corpus," consisting of the leaders of large industrial enterprises. Together with their allies in the Supreme Soviet and, after July, in the Central Bank (in particular, its new leader, Viktor Gerashchenko, previously the Soviet Union's last Central Bank chief), the captains of industry demanded the printing of unlimited amounts of money to maintain their outmoded and uncompetitive enterprises. Conceptualizations of this industrial opposition to reform differ. It has been seen as a group constituted as part of a "corporate system of interest representation,"[12] or as the manifestation of a typical organic social rejection of an economic change imposed too rapidly from above.[13] Most often, factory directors seeking handouts are seen as rent seekers, rationally but nevertheless somehow atavistically interested in the particular benefit that newly minted money could bring to their individual enterprise, rather than in the nonexcludable public good of lower inflation.[14]

Whatever the disagreements about the origins of the industrialists' drive for loose money, however, the consensus viewpoint is that they were victorious.[15] Gaidar's government simply did not have enough political will to resist demands to issue new money. Moreover, Gaidar's pessimism about his government's political future served to encourage enterprise directors' predilection to delay adaptation to a market economy, making the consequences of continuing to pursue tight money policies more painful than they needed to be.[16] Political pressure from below and the insufficient political will at the top together caused a retreat from the policy of monetary restriction. The story of the central political struggle in the new Russia can thus be read in the figures for the money supply (figure 1).[17]

After some initial success in holding the money supply down, the usual story goes, the government's resolve was broken by June 1992. From late summer and into the fall, monetary discipline was further weakened by the willful actions of Viktor Gerashchenko at the Central Bank. Buoyed by support in the Supreme Soviet, and largely unapproved by the government, Gerashchenko indulged a willingness to create money endlessly in a hopeless effort to save the industrial dinosaurs created by the Soviet regime. Inflation rates that reached 26 percent a month by November finally terrified

[12] Michael McFaul, "State Power, Institutional Change, and the Politics of Privatization in Russia," *World Politics* 47 (January 1995): 210–243.
[13] Peter Murrell, "What Is Shock Therapy? What Did It Do in Poland and Russia?" *Post-Soviet Affairs* 9, no. 2 (1993): 111–140.
[14] Åslund, *How Russia*.
[15] Aside from sources already cited, see Michael Burawoy and Pavel Krotov, "The Economic Basis of Russia's Political Crisis," *New Left Review* 198 (March–April 1993): 49–69.
[16] Åslund, *How Russia*.
[17] M2 series from *Russian Economic Trends* 3, no. 2 (1994): 121.

Figure 1. Percentage growth in nominal money supply, January 1992–May 1993, by month

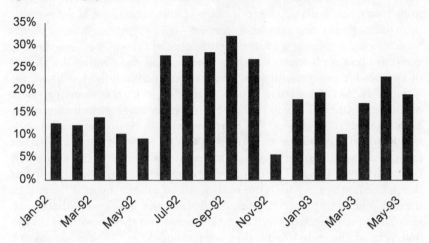

the government into bringing the Central Bank policy under its control, through the creation of a credit commission that had to pass approval on all new loans.[18] Nevertheless, some backsliding occurred in 1993, as new premier Viktor Chernomyrdin proudly proclaimed his affiliation with the "Red Directors" and allowed the money supply to increase. Only from May of 1993, when the Central Bank agreed (under pressure from the International Monetary Fund [IMF] and the government) to quarterly money supply targets and to peg its interest rates to market levels, was a real breakthrough on fighting inflation made (though backsliding would continue).

There are several shortcomings with analyzing Russian politics in the first year and a half of the reforms solely along the dimension of "more money-less money." Because price liberalization returned purchasing power to the ruble, it did set off new battles over centrally distributed money. Yet given the goals of the Russian government in launching the reform, to the extent that political struggle consisted in the efforts of regions and factories to win monetary subsidies, the fact that politics took this *form* demands far more attention than the specific outcomes of the battles. A major transformation in Russia's political physics had occurred. As Gaidar clearly realized, Moscow's printing of money in the Gorbachev years only worsened its difficulties in holding the country together, because increased money worsened shortages, promoting horizontal barter and local rebellion against the allocative efforts of the vertical economy. New

[18] On the commission, see Interfax, 12 October 1992; translated in FBIS-SOV-92–198, 13 October 1992, 24, and Boris Fedorov, "Monetary Policy and Central Banking in Russia," *East European Constitutional Review* 3, no. 3–4 (1994): 60–65.

money exercised a force of repulsion, pushing the subnational jurisdictions away from Moscow. After price liberalization, however, Moscow could print money with real purchasing power—and everybody wanted some. Moscow's money was now a force of attraction, not repulsion. Missed in the Western literature's frenzy to portray the supposed atavism of the chorus of appeals for government subsidies was how profoundly novel such requests were. As Gaidar put it, "The whole wide spectrum of demands made of the government is being replaced by a single, albeit most insistent, demand: give us some money!"[19] Efforts to maintain control of scarce goods in a fixed-price economy and efforts to win seigniorage-funded subsidies from the government in a monetizing economy are both, from a certain viewpoint, "rent-seeking" attempts to capture the gains from inflation, but the political arena in which the rents must be sought is very different. In the last year of the Soviet Union, enterprises and regions had battled to keep Moscow's ministries and agencies away from their resources; in the first year of the new Russia, they were trooping to Moscow to ask for money.[20] As one provincial governor complained, "Unfortunately it would be possible to list a great many examples in which a local territory is completely dependent on Moscow and has only one right—to appear in Moscow with hand outstretched."[21]

In the context of the Russian government's effort to make its sovereignty real, the fact of this pilgrimage was far more significant than its results. The Yeltsin leadership's concern over regions' efforts to restrict the flow of goods for the benefit of their own consumers had been manifest through the fall of 1991. As early as October Yeltsin tried to blunt the impact of his earlier efforts to put resources in the hands of local governments for the barter trade.[22] In early December, a strongly worded order on the Russian Republic's "single economic space" threatened local authorities with prosecution for blocking the movements of goods through Russian territory and pledged to cancel any local legislative acts restricting the free flow of commodities. The same order proclaimed the exclusive status of the ruble as the country's monetary unit.[23]

---

[19] *Izvestiia*, 19 August 1992, 3.

[20] Battles over resources, especially exportable commodities such as oil and metal, did continue. But central control over whether export would be allowed meant that the political effect of these was similar to the allocation of money.

[21] Supreme Soviet of the Russian Federation, *Vserossiiskoe Ekonomicheskoe Soveshchanie: Biulleten'* no. 1 [All-Russian Economic Conference: Bulletin no. 1] (Moscow: Respublika, 1993), 62.

[22] See Presidential Order No. 143, 15 October 1991, "On Economic Links and the Delivery of Goods and Products in 1992." From the Inforis on-line database (see Appendix), henceforth cited as Inforis.

[23] Presidential Order No. 269, 12 December 1991, "On the Unified Economic Space of the Russian Federation." Inforis.

Within months after prices had been freed, the dangers these orders had addressed appeared to have passed. Barriers to the movement of goods within Russia, according both to official remarks and available evidence, quickly eroded.[24] The organizations that managed the shortage-driven barter, and the local customs barriers that were intended to make it possible, either disappeared or strongly declined in importance.[25] By reducing barter and nationalizing the arena in which the politics of distribution occurred, price liberalization also reduced the potential threat from the interprovince alliances as alternate centers of political and economic coordination. In 1990 and early 1991, as Russia's leadership sought to improve its position by encouraging the localist attack on the crumbling command economy, key Yeltsin decrees had strengthened the interregional associations by granting special privileges to their members.[26] But from 1992, central authorities preferred increasingly to deal with provinces bilaterally, rather than with associations of provinces. A survey of 1992 issues of the official journal publishing resolutions of the government and presidential orders reveals that while dozens of documents offered benefits to specific provinces, only two orders were addressed to regional associations as a whole.[27] Although no deliberate policy of *divide et impera* was announced, this pattern of redistributive action was certainly easy to cast in such a light. Indeed, some members of the Siberian Agreement group felt compelled to call on fellow members not to seek such bilateral arrangements, but to insist on collective benefits.[28] The role of interregional alliances in coordinating barter trade also went into a decline in this period as this trade itself gave way to monetary exchange.[29] By 1993, the importance of nearly all the interregional associations was minimal.[30]

Against this background, it is no surprise that as early as August 1992, Gaidar displayed palpable confidence that the centralization he had

[24] *Svoi Golos*, no. 33 (August 27–September 3 1992): 5. *ABV: Ezhedel'naia Delovaia Gazeta*, 10 June 1992, 2. *Izvestiia*, 16 October 1992, 2, as translated in *CDPSP* 44, no. 14 (1992): 23.

[25] Interview with the director of the Samara oblast' *terzakaz* office, May 1994.

[26] See chapter 2.

[27] One of these two, actually signed by Vice President Rutskoi, allowed the Siberian Agreement group to found an agricultural products firm. The other granted special export rights to Far East provinces, though the resolution did not mention their interregional association. The survey was based on 1992 issues of *Sobranie Aktov Prezidenta i Pravitel'stva Rossiiskoi Federatsii* [Collected Acts of the President and Government of the Russian Federation]. The exceptional resolutions are in issues no. 7 and no. 13.

[28] *Svoi Golos*, no. 23 (15–22 July 1993), 5.

[29] *Segodnia*, 11 December 1993, 10.

[30] Andrew Bond, "Russia's Regional Associations in Decline," *Post-Soviet Geography* 34 (January 1993): 59–66. This survey identifies the Siberian Agreement and Far Eastern associations as somewhat more healthy, but with respect to the latter seems to be badly off the mark. See *Vladivostok*, 3 March 1992, 7.

hoped for had been achieved: "Stabilization of the ruble while control over monetary circulation remains in the hands of central agencies has strengthened the position of the Federation with respect to the regions. . . . The centrifugal forces that last autumn seemed to be on the point of tearing Russia to pieces have gradually been replaced. . . . The threat of the immediate secession of a region if a question of yet another privilege for it is not resolved is going out of style."[31] With the regional issue resolved, the main task was managing the politics of monetary policy so as to resist the dangerous demands of interest groups and Parliament to use seigniorage to cushion the impact of price liberalization. Or so it briefly seemed.

Soviet Monetary Institutions and Monetary Consolidation

Price liberalization naturally meant an enormous break from Soviet monetary practice, since fixed prices had been a central element of an economic system in which money was relegated to an adjunct role. By itself, however, price liberalization did not eliminate all aspects of the Soviet monetary order. Despite substantial and largely destructive changes in the banking system during the perestroika era, the basic payment institutions with which Russian enterprises operated in the period immediately following price liberalization still reflected the key ideas of the Soviet monetary system as analyzed in chapter 1: the origin of economic value is in production; the ability and willingness of consumers to pay for production is a secondary and technical matter.[32] At the moment price liberalization was introduced, most Russian enterprises settled their accounts with one another through the so-called payment order system. At the same time as goods were shipped the supplying enterprise sent a payment order to the bank of its customer, which would then pay it automatically from funds on the customer's account. When the customer had no available funds, unpaid bills accumulated on the so-called card file number two and were paid in the order of arrival. In short, customers were automatically extended short-term credit by producers (during the period that payments cleared) simultaneously with shipment of goods—that is, jointly with completion of production. When large amounts of such debt would accumulate in the card file, as occurred with some regularity, authorities would take steps to clear it in a *zachet,* or netting operation, a procedure that injected new money into the system to clear up the debts of those state enterprises that

[31] *Izvestiia,* 19 August 1992, 3. For a similar opinion from Yeltsin some time later, see *Izvestiia,* 21 July 1994, 4.
[32] Cf. Christian de Boissieu, Daniel Cohen, and Gaël de Pontbriand, "Gérer la dette inter-entreprises," *Économie Internationale* 54 (Second trimester 1993): 105–120.

had incurred more debts than they were due. It was not a system designed to encourage enterprises to care about whether their customers (largely mandated anyway) could pay. Although automatic crediting of customers by producers (and reliable ratification of the same by the monetary authorities) was a retreat from the direct and immediate monetization of production of the Credit Reform period (see chapter 1), the monetary system still very much bore the stamp of the ideas that gave rise to it—and made those ideas seem compelling, relevant, and practical to those who used it.

In the aftermath of price liberalization, enterprises began raising prices far beyond what could be sustained by demand backed with "official" rubles.[33] In January 1992, Russian consumer prices grew by 245 percent, and industrial prices by 383 percent. The money supply (M2), however, grew by only a little more than 12 percent. In short, the real volume of money in circulation was shrinking dramatically, and it would not begin to grow again until the fall. What made price rises possible despite this monetary restriction was the growth of debts in the card file. These debts not only made a major contribution to inflation,[34] they also created large social problems, since enterprises not being paid in official money had a hard time paying salaries. Furthermore, interenterprise debt—also known as "nonpayments" or "arrears"—posed serious tax collection difficulties.

Thus, both as a precondition for pursuit of the fight against inflation and for other reasons, after price liberalization the Russian government found itself confronted with the task of asserting and making good a monopoly on the issue of money.[35] This was a challenge that the government clearly understood; as a vice premier put it, the key cause of inflation was that "we are not controlling [monetary] emission within industry," in the form of nonpayments.[36] In the next few paragraphs, I construct an ideal-typical scheme of possible responses to this challenge, as a prelude to examining the actual course of the political battles and institutional

[33] By "official" rubles I mean M2: cash rubles and those created in a legal manner through the fractional reserve mechanism in the banking system.

[34] Jacques Sapir, "Formes et Nature de l'inflation," *Économie Internationale* (Second trimester 1993): 25–65, at 32–34.

[35] On interenterprise debt as a from of money, see Grigrory Yavlinsky and Serguey Braguinsky, "The Inefficiency of Laissez-Faire in Russia: Hysteresis Effects and the Need for Policy-Led Transformation," *Journal of Comparative Economics* 19 (August 1994): 88–116, at 100, who compare the situation to "free banking," and Jacek Rostowski, "The Inter-enterprise Debt Explosion in the Former Soviet Union: Causes, Consequences, Cures," *Communist Economies & Economic Transformation* 5, no. 2 (1993): 131–159, who argues that "every enterprise can . . ., for a short time, effectively create liquidity on a base of money as a reserve asset (which is needed to ensure wage payments, etc.)"; Gaidar ("Reforma: Finansovo-Denezhnyi Aspekt," [Reform: the financial-monetary aspect] *Finansy*, no. 10 [1992]: 3–11) referred to nonpayments as "low quality money."

[36] Interview with Grigorii Khizha on Russian television, 25 June 1992; translated in FBIS-SOV-92–128, 2 July 1992, 44–48.

transformations that pushed Russia's government toward particular solutions to it.

Tactics for Monetary Consolidation

The possible responses to a challenge to the state's monopoly on the definition and terms of creation of the means of payment may be divided into two categories: macro responses addressed to *confidence* and micro responses addressed to *costs* (see table 2).

Macro responses take as their point of departure the idea that alternatives to official money arise in credit, granted by economic actors confident that this credit will be repaid. This argument can inspire two possible responses from state authorities. On the one hand they can conceive such confidence itself as the problem and seek to eliminate it through pledging to carry out an economic policy that will make it irrational. Let us call this a strategy of *intimidation;* economists have usually analyzed it under the heading of making a "credible commitment" to a restrictive policy.

Rather than seeking to eliminate credit-creating confidence, a second possible response focuses on *ratifying and regulating* the creation of credit. The confidence of private actors becomes the basis for the emission of official money. The most familiar policy along these lines is government regulation of fractional-reserve banking. Here states allow bank deposits to serve as a perfect substitute for government-issued money, but they control how much money can be created in this way through mandating levels of reserves. A less familiar way of ratifying and regulating private credit decisions is implementation of the Real Bills doctrine, discussed in chapter 1. The Real Bills doctrine specifies that new official money will be created to fund credit issued in the course of verified commercial transactions.

Beyond such macro policies, which seek to bring the amount of private confidence in the economic future into balance with the amount of official money in circulation by modifying one or the other, there are also micro policies that seek to modify the costs to economic actors of choosing to use official money or some alternative. Authorities can either try to raise the costs of using nonofficial money through some form of coercion or punishment for those who create such money, or they can try to make it

Table 2. Strategies for monopolizing credit-money issue

Micro strategies (Addressed to costs)	Macro strategies (Addressed to confidence)
1. Complicate the use of alternate monies	3. Intimidate
2. Simplify the use of official monies	4. Ratify and regulate

less expensive to use official money than to use alternates. In short, they can try to *simplify* the use of official money or *complicate* the use of an alternate means of payment. Demanding that taxes be paid in official money is one way of accomplishing both goals.

If there is analytical purchase to be gained from this typological exercise, it will come in clarifying the way concrete historical situations constrain the options open to national executive organs seeking to uphold their monopoly on the definition and the terms of creation of the means of payment. The different policy measures discussed here have political and administrative preconditions that may not be present in all cases. Politically, both macro policies face a similar task: it must be possible to make a compelling case that they allocate in a rational, coherent manner either economic pain (if the policy is intimidation) or newly created money (if the policy is to ratify and regulate). If firms suffer under the restrictive policies implied by a strategy of intimidation, then it must be plausible to claim that their suffering stems from an inability to create economic value. Likewise, when bureaucrats issue new money to ratify private credit decisions, they must be in a position to argue that this issue is taking place according to defensible principles. (The language of compulsion here is too strong for real politics, of course, but is intended to illustrate the dilemmas that will face any policymaker who wishes to *justify* these policies.) Thus, in the case of a policy of intimidation, it is a matter of legitimating the workings of the market; a policy of regulation and ratification, by contrast, demands that the rationality of bureaucratic decisions appear sufficient. The administrative presuppositions of the two policies are therefore sharply different. The policy of intimidation requires nothing more than a bully pulpit from which authorities can broadcast their commitment to a restrictive policy, though the state must appear to dispose of powers that will indeed worsen the business climate. But a policy of regulated ratification implies both the articulation of a procedure for allowing private credit issue and the presence of an effective apparatus to influence it. The scale of the administrative burdens involved is exemplified by the difficulties plaguing Soviet application of the Real Bills doctrine in the 1920s (see chapter 1).

The political and administrative presuppositions of the cost-oriented, micro policies are somewhat harder to specify a priori. Politically, there is little to say beyond the obvious observation that the state must be prepared to claim sovereignty over such matters. Simplifying the use of official money might proceed under the heading of banking reform, anticounterfeiting operations, even investment in communications infrastructure. Complicating the use of unofficial money will most likely appear as a problem of combating tax evasion. Administratively, microlevel options naturally involve substantial amounts of regulation and coercion.

Contending Approaches to Monetary Consolidation in 1992–1993

These political and administrative concomitants of various policy options did much to shape Russia's changing approach to monetary consolidation in the aftermath of price liberalization. One may distinguish three phases. In the first, lasting until about mid-1992, the government under Gaidar focused on a policy of intimidation, while the Central Bank sought to complicate the creation of unregulated credit. In the second period, comprising the second half of 1992 and early 1993, the center of gravity on money policy shifted from the government to the Central Bank, which tried to apply a policy of regulated ratification, justified and organized on the basis of a production-centered theory of value. But by May 1993, it had become clear to the Central Bank that it did not have the administrative capacity or information to carry out such a policy in a coherent way, and it joined the government in a renewed effort at intimidation, beginning the third phase. In this chapter I deal with the first two phases, and the reasons for the more restrictive monetary policies that launched the third phase, whose effects are charted in the following chapter.

Phase 1: Intimidation and Complication, January–May 1992

After price liberalization, as already noted, the government conceived its main goal as using a restrictive monetary policy to prevent hyperinflation and forestalling the flight from money it might touch off. Yet prices in this period rose far faster than the Gaidar government had hoped, and the basis for this growth lay substantially in the expansion of interenterprise debt, which allowed transactions to go forward in the absence of official money. The reaction of the Gaidar team was an effort at intimidation, trying to convince enterprise directors that the issue of interenterprise credit was misguided given the government's policy of monetary restriction. The most notorious comments in this regard were those of economics minister Andrei Nechaev, who called for "instructive bankruptcies" and ridiculed enterprise pleas that money be given to their customers (to repay interenterprise debt): "No one wants to accept the fact that in a market economy the consumer, not the producer, dictates the price."[37] The idea behind such statements was that once directors came to realize that demand had indeed contracted, they would stop releasing goods without payment, and (as a by-product) it would be the state that determined the amount of money in the economy.

---

[37] *Komsomolskaia Pravda*, 9 April 1992, 2 as translated in *CDPSP* 44, no. 15 (1992): 13–14. For similar language from Gaidar, see his interview on Russian television, 5 January 1992; translated in FBIS-SOV-92-004, 7 January 1992, 40–44.

Pitted against this consciously uncompromising policy of intimidation was what rapidly came to be a powerful movement: the so-called directors' corpus. When arrayed along the more money-less money axis, this group appeared as supporters of inflationary subsidies that would subvert the monetarist project. For the directors corpus itself, however, the issue of how much money to print was not primary, but rather derived from an alternate institutional project for restoring the polictical and economic power of the national state. This project aimed at using the national monetary institutions to service an economy conceived *in natura*. In this conception, economic value reflected production costs and/or use-value, rather than consumer willingness to pay. The source of economic difficulties was organizational, not macroeconomic. The severing of production links between enterprises, for instance, stemmed not from decisions by upstream enterprises to seek more profitable outlets for their goods but from failures of political coordination. Marketization, while necessary, must be managed. Indeed, success in preserving the physical-technical economy against disorganization and short-term partial interests, followed by the coordinated transformation of this economy, could be the foundation of success in international markets. I will call this the "national productivist project" to emphasize the scope and rationale of its ambitions.[38]

The directors saw the cause of nonpayments in a failure to provide money to lubricate the production process, and it was this argument that justified their calls for transfers to enterprises funded by an increased money supply. The state should undertake an indexation of circulating capital, to compensate enterprises for funds lost to inflation. The backlog of mutual debt between enterprises should be netted out using the standard Soviet procedure (known as a mutual debt offset or *vzaimozachet*), which in effect implied that all production be paid for regardless of whether customers could themselves afford it.[39] These arguments reflected the productivist mind-set whose genesis was charted in chapter 1, and their popularity was certainly enhanced by the persistence of the monetary institutions that mind-set had helped to shape.

A nuanced understanding of the rationale for the directors' call to increase the money supply is important for understanding their political strength. It was ideas about the role of money that gave a collective character to opposition to the government's restrictive monetary policy. To organize a *coalition* around the idea that the government should in general be more generous in giving seigniorage-funded assistance to specific enterprises would be all but impossible—since, as Gaidar urged directors to remember,

---

[38] For a typical statement of the productivist project, see *Nezavisimaia Gazeta*, 11 July 1992, 4; translated in *CDPSP* 44, no. 29 (1992): 3–5.
[39] *Izvestiia*, 12 August 1992, 1; translated in *CDPSP* 44, no. 33 (1992): 7–8.

"to give money to each means to kill the money of all."[40] But calls to clear debts and restore lost circulating capital were phrased universalistically— the policies demanded applied to all state enterprises. These policies, for their supporters, held out the promise that the problems each enterprise faced individually could be resolved for enterprises in general. Indeed, the individual enterprises bombarding Moscow with telegrams demanding money on these bases were engaged in a form of collective action—even when this action was not specifically coordinated. The extraordinary apparent strength of the "industrial lobby" in the first half of 1992 must in substantial measure be traced to this fact. For the government, it was difficult to pursue a policy of divide and conquer with respect to a coalition organized around demands for an indexation of working capital and credit injections to clear interenterprise debt. Any concession to the latter demand was by definition a collective subsidy, and any individual concession to the former created a precedent.

Russia's leadership had been prepared to weather the vociferous political discontent of industrialists. Indeed, at several points the reformers expressed great satisfaction that the demands being made on them were couched in monetary terms—viewing this as emblematic of their victory in restoring money as a basis for the power of the national state.[41] Gaidar welcomed expressions of suffering on the part of defense industrialists as signs that the economy was indeed moving away from unnecessary production.[42] Gaidar's allies in government repeatedly rejected any debt-clearing operation that would pay for production that customers had not been able to afford.[43] Yet the prominence of nonpayments presented the government with other challenges not so easy to ignore. First, with no monetary income, enterprises had great difficulty in paying salaries. Although for some time banks were willing to advance cash against debts owed to enterprises, by late spring there simply was not enough cash to do this.[44] Even

---

[40] *Izvestiia*, 19 August 1992, 3; as translated in *CDPSP* 44, no. 33 (1992): 4–7.

[41] Ibid., e.g.

[42] *Segodnia*, 26 May 1994, 2.

[43] Interfax, 23 June 1992; translated in FBIS-SOV-92–122, 24 June 1992, 37–38.

[44] It has been argued that one reason for the growth of nonpayments was that enterprises who could show a positive balance of money owed to them against money they owed were able to get cash loans to pay their salaries; Barry W. Ickes and Randi Ryterman, "The Interenterprise Arrears Crisis in Russia," *Post-Soviet Affairs* 8 (October–December 1992): 331–361. There are very good reasons to doubt the importance of this factor even in 1992; certainly by 1993–1994, the extension of cash loans on the basis of receivables was extremely rare. Given the cash shortage of 1992, banks were able to sell cash rubles for several rubles in bank deposits (figures as high as 6:1 have been cited to me), which made the opportunity cost of giving cash rubles away against receivables of extremely dubious quality enormous. Whatever the circumstances of 1992, making this an important piece of the explanation of the ongoing arrears problem (Barry W. Ickes and Randi Ryterman, "Roadblock to Economic Reform: Inter-Enterprise Debt and the Transition to Markets," *Post-Soviet Affairs* 9 [July–September 1993]: 231–252, at 246) is incorrect.

those firms with money on account had trouble withdrawing it. With the bank payments system clogged, economic actors refused to deposit their cash, fearful that inflation would have eroded its value before the money could be transferred or withdrawn. Thus banks found themselves without cash. Nor could banks in their turn convert their deposits with the Russian Central Bank into cash, because for reasons that remain somewhat murky, the government failed to print enough cash to allow this. The dimensions of the problem may be shown by the fact that by the early summer, cash rubles could be purchased for bank rubles at a rate of about six to one.[45] Meanwhile, unpaid wages mounted to enormous levels.[46]

Local authorities reacted to the cash crisis by seeking to print ruble surrogates of their own.[47] The scope of this phenomenon should not be overestimated. However, its symbolic import was great in the context of the reformers' project to restore central power under the banner of monetization. Demands for a different approach to monetary policy from the directors could be written off as an inevitable political squall, which authorities would need to ride out. The appearance of local currencies, however, struck at the administrative bases of the centralizing project, and apparently caused great consternation among monetary authorities.[48]

Beyond the cash crisis, nonpayments raised a second administrative difficulty for the government simply because they could not be taxed. Interenterprise credit was allowing transactions to go forward, and taxes on the transactions were calculated. Yet without monetary receipts, there was no way to pay these taxes. In July, Gaidar said that at least 300 billion rubles of assessed taxes had not been collected for this reason, an amount equal to a third of government tax revenue for the first half of the year.[49] In essence, nonpayments broke the connection between fiscal policy and control of inflation. Nonpayment-driven price rises imposed new costs on the

[45] This is according to the Fall 1993 recollections of persons I spoke to in Vladivostok.

[46] For Krasnoiarsk, see *Svoi Golos*, no. 27 (13–20 July 1992): 2; for Samara, *Delo*, June 1992, 3.

[47] E.g., in Tatarstan: *ABV: Ezhedel'naia Regional'naia Delovaia Gazeta*, 5 August 1992, 2.

[48] Central Bank officials told Jacques Sapir that worries over local currencies had helped to prompt their decision to relax monetary policy in the second half of 1992; Jacques Sapir, "Inflation, stabilisation et dynamiques régionales en Russie: Analyse des trajectoires macroéconomiques et de leurs fondements micro et mésoéconomiques" (unpublished paper, Paris, Centre d'Études des Modes d'Industrialisation, 1993), 5. For Gerashchenko's concern over the need to maintain a single monetary system within Russia, see his remarks in *Vserosiiskoe ekonomicheskoe soveshchanie*, 28.

[49] See the interview with Gaidar on Russian TV, 13 July 1992, translated in FBIS-SOV-92–135, 14 July 1992, 12–17. Percentage of tax revenue calculated using William Easterly and Vieira da Cunha, *Financing the Storm: Macroeconomic Crisis in Russia, 1992–93* (Washington, DC : World Bank, Policy Research Dept, 1994), 36, and *Russian Economic Trends* 3, no. 2 (1994): 110.

government (for salaries and procurement) and yet were not amenable to taxation.

Summarizing, by June 1992, the nonpayments crisis was exerting substantial and mutually reinforcing political, administrative, and fiscal pressure on the government. The political pressure stemmed from the way that the directors' shared diagnosis of nonpayments' causes worked to make them seem a coherent and powerful political force. The administrative pressure resulted from local reactions to the shortage of money in the form of locally issued currencies. And the fiscal pressure resulted from the fact that nonpayments were not amenable to taxation. Together, these factors would promote major shifts in policy as the summer began.

Before turning to these shifts, however, one final policy measure aimed at stopping nonpayments must be discussed. In mid-May of 1992, the head of the Central Bank, Georgii Matiukhin, issued new regulations designed to make most enterprises responsible for collecting their own debts, in effect simply by dismantling the old card file debt-collecting system.[50] This measure, implemented from July 1, eliminated the mechanism whereby production had been converted into monetary receipts, and with it the major institutional symbol and implementation of the idea that value was created in the production of goods rather than their sale.[51] In terms of our typology of ways to assert a monopoly on the definition and terms of creation of the means of payment (table 2), abolishing the card file was an example of complicating the use of the alternatives to official money. Most enterprises' extension of credit to customers would no longer be automatically monitored by the bank, nor would banks assist in collecting such debts. All evidence indicates that this policy change was quite effective in reducing the willingness of enterprises to extend interenterprise debt, and demands for prepayment became standard.[52]

[50] Central Bank of Russia telegram no. 116–92, 15 May 1992, Inforis.

[51] The former head of the Russian Central Bank states: "We decided to abolish card file no 2 in order that the enterprises themselves, and not the bank, took care of their payments and calculated their expenses and income. . . . The system of payments should be such that if a purchasing enterprise has no money on its account, then no payment document can be created." His explicit aim was to break the old cycle of automatic payment for production. Georgii Gavrilovich Matiukhin, *Ia byl glavnym bankirom Rossii* (I was Russia's chief banker) (Moscow: Vysshaia shkola, 1993), 63.

[52] Ickes and Ryterman ("Roadblock to Reform," 238) assert that enterprises were instructed to shift to prepayment; I have seen no evidence that this is true and tend to credit what is reported in de Boissieu et al. ("Gerer," 111), that this shift was made at enterprise initiative. The original Central Bank documents on ending the earlier system (telegram no. 145–92, 30 June 1992 and letter no. 14 ["On the introduction of the regulation on cashless settlements in the Russian Federation"] 9 July 1992, Inforis) make reference only to refusing to transfer the shipping documents (the closest thing to a legal formulation of property rights available) when payment is not made on time and explicitly describe alternatives to prepayment, such as letters of credit. However, given the novelty of such alternatives, many enter-

Beyond its effects on enterprise willingness to ship goods on credit, elimination of the old payment mechanism destroyed the bases for the tacit collective action described previously. Without centralized records of payment orders in the banking system it became impossible for central authorities to carry out a mutual offset of any new debts. The plausibility of a general solution to the problems particular enterprises faced as a result of price liberalization and inflation waned. In essence, by destroying its capacity to implement a particular type of policy (a policy of issuing money passively to pay for production), the Russian state cut the ground from under the interest group constituted by the demand for that policy. One may conceive of the directors as what Claus Offe calls a "policy taker" interest group, that is, one that represents "collectivities that are specifically affected by state policies."[53] When the state's capacity to pursue the relevant policy disappeared, so to all intents and purposes did the interest group.

Phase 2: Search for a Coherent Ratification, June 1992–May 1993

The impact that the abolition of the card file was eventually to have on the directors' lobby was not immediately evident, since this abolition occurred in tandem with what appeared to be a major victory for this group. On May 25, 1992, in a joint resolution, the government and the leadership of the Supreme Soviet endorsed the money policies associated with the national productivist project, including a mutual offset of debts and extension of credits for working capital.[54] How exactly these measures were to be implemented was not specified, and a month would go by before any action was taken. Only in early July were the rules for distributing working-capital loans circulated.[55] Also in early July, the Central Bank attempted an unimplementable version of a mutual offset that involved transferring the debts of net-debtor enterprises to a special agency not yet in existence.[56] At the end of July, now under the leadership of Viktor

---

prises may have felt that only prepayment was left to them. See, e.g., the account of a sawmill in *Krasnoe Znamia*, 16 June 1992, 1.
[53] Claus Offe, "The Attribution of Public Status to Interest Groups: Observations on the West German Case," in *Organizing Interests in Western Europe*, ed. Suzanne Berger (Cambridge: Cambridge University Press, 1981), 123–158, at 139.
[54] Resolution No. 2837–1, "On Urgent Measures for Improving Payments in the Economy and Raising Enterprises' Responsibility for Their Financial Status." Inforis.
[55] "On Supplying Credit Resources to Normalize Payments in the Economy," Ministry of Finance letter no. 2–9, 3 July 1992. Inforis.
[56] Central Bank and Ministry of Finance of Russia Instruction of 3 July 1992, "On the Regulation of Mutual Non-payments of State Enterprises and Organizations in the Russian Federation." The outlines of this unworkable scheme were first drawn in a presidential order (No. 720) two days earlier. Inforis.

Gerashchenko, the bank launched a new version of the offset operation that amounted to a regulated ratification of enterprise issues of debt as a means of payment.[57] For each state enterprise, a special account was opened. The account was credited with an amount equal to the enterprise's receivables (debts owed to it by customers), and then used to pay for the enterprises' debts to suppliers. Since this procedure involved the assumption that all receivables would be paid, it had the effect of injecting credit to cover part of the payments due from enterprises whose net position was negative.[58]

Initially, the special accounts used for the offset operation were kept segregated from the rest of the monetary system, and enterprises with a positive balance were not allowed to convert this balance into regular money. After vociferous protests on this score and in the face of continuing fiscal difficulties, enterprises were allowed to use their positive balances to pay taxes, leading to a huge jump in government revenues.[59] In a sense, this revenue was seigniorage, but it would be a mistake to identify it with a straightforward decision to print money to cover the budget deficit. The amount of money printed was determined not by government spending needs, but rather by the amount of credit enterprises had issued to one another. Therefore, the conversion of decentralized debt issues into a means of payment was a form of regulated ratification of money issue by enterprises.[60]

Combined with an increased printing of cash, offsetting debts and giving loans for working capital did manage significantly to reduce the administrative, political, and fiscal pressure the nonpayments crisis had placed on the government. The cash crisis abated, and with it the impetus for regions to create their own currencies.[61] Meanwhile, the directors' movement began to unravel, as the directors discovered that beyond the mutual offset of debts (already behind them) and loans to restore enterprise working capital, they could agree on little.[62] The offset of debts rep-

[57] This point is forcefully made in Yavlinsky and Braguinsky, "Inefficiency of Laissez-Faire."
[58] Procedures for the clearing operation were described by bankers and a Central Bank official in Vladivostok in the fall of 1993. See also Ickes and Ryterman, "Roadblock."
[59] Interfax, 15 October 1992; translated in FBIS-SOV-92-203, 20 October 1992; Easterly and Vieira da Cunha, *Financing the Storm*, 6.
[60] Laurence Scialom and Yves Zlotowski, "Les fondements institutionnels de la crise monétaire russe: un éclairage théorique," *Revue d'Économie politique* 104 (September–October 1994): 701–718, at 710, characterize the mutual offset as the Central Bank's "attempt to restore its position at the heart of the monetary system."
[61] Thus in Nizhnii Novgorod, notes printed for use as a local currency were not issued, though later they were used to represent a local bond issue. Interviews in Nizhnii Novgorod, July 1993.
[62] See Elizabeth Teague, "Splits in the Ranks of Russia's 'Red Directors'," *RFE/RL Research Report* 1 (September 1992): 6–11.

resented not the victory of the "industrial lobby" but rather its last gasp. The efforts of rival claimants to the leadership of the lobby to produce more elaborate versions of a national productivist project for reconstituting the state's power to mandate the movement of goods and downgrading the criterion of profitability as the indicator of economic importance ultimately had little political influence. In the fall of 1992, however, the national productivist project found a last redoubt in the leadership of the Central Bank. In articles and interviews, Viktor Gerashchenko and his deputies made it clear that they continued to view the primary role of money as the lubrication of production, supporting both the offset of debts and an expanded indexation of working capital as means of implementing these viewpoints.[63] A second line of argument was that the Central Bank was forced to offer loans to enterprises whose production was socially necessary but which were unable to make a profit due to financial confusion and a distorted price structure.[64]

To carry out these policies in a coherent way, however, required substantial organizational capacities that the Central Bank found it simply did not possess. For instance, credits were given to commercial banks with the requirement that they be used for "priority tasks, connected with the production of agricultural and consumer goods, and fulfilling the life-sustaining needs of the economy." Yet as a bank official admitted, "We have not been successful in achieving a strict fulfillment of such requirements."[65] Officials' ability to monitor the use of loans was very weak, and many recipients appear to have made a practice of reselling them at a higher interest rate rather than directing them to the production-supporting uses for which they were intended.[66]

Those who interpret Russian politics in this period through the lens of the more money-less money struggle have not directed attention to these organizational concomitants of the Central Bank's expressed desire to use cheap, "earmarked" credits to support production, probably because this rationale was not taken very seriously. Yet there is evidence that the failure to achieve a coherent organization of productivist monetary policy was an

---

[63] *Ekonomika i Zhizn'*, no. 46 (November 1992): 1, 5; ibid., no. 30 (July 1992), 11.

[64] *Rossiiskie Vesti*, 13 January 1993, 3.

[65] *Ekonomika i Zhizn'*, no. 30 (June 1992), 11.

[66] In interviews, a number of bankers involved in distributing centralized loans cited their sense that Central Bank control over their use was minimal, though Central Bank officials tended to assert the opposite. For a discussion of the diverting of earmarked credits and a claim of extremely weak state control in this area by the country's then chief prosecutor, a political opponent of the government, see *Trud*, 4 August 1993, 2. For evidence of diversion of targeted credits in early 1992, see Joel Hellman, "Breaking the Bank: Bureaucrats and the Creation of Markets in a Transitional Economy" (Ph.D. diss., Columbia University, 1993), 227.

important factor in its abandonment. From the late spring of 1993, both the Central Bank and the government tried to tighten the monitoring of the use of earmarked credits. Unable to control effectively the behavior of enterprises, authorities chose instead to focus on the banks distributing earmarked loans. Representative is a May 1993 government resolution that vested responsibility for return of new government investment loans with a commercial bank that was supposed to distribute them.[67] The Central Bank implemented similar policies with respect to the earmarked credits it issued, and enforced repayment policies with vigor. Commercial banks quickly became reluctant to transfer these loans to enterprises unlikely to pay them back.[68] One Samara bank even took out full-page ads in all the local newspapers to ask to be spared from distributing centralized credits to farmers because of the fear that they would not be repaid.[69] This was not an isolated incident. By the spring of 1994, refusal by commercial banks to distribute centralized credits had reached epidemic proportions.[70] The scope of this phenomenon may be gathered from the fact that although the Central Bank authorized 1.3 trillion rubles in credits for the electric power industry in the first nine months of 1994, only 503 billion rubles in loans were actually made. Commercial banks, worried that their clients would default on the loans and leave the bankers with the liability for repayment, had refused to distribute a full 60 percent of the authorized loans.[71]

Closely related to the pressure on commercial banks to ensure repayment of government industrial loans was the May 1993 agreement between the Central Bank and the government that obliged the bank to keep its interest rates closely pegged to those set in the commercial interbank market.[72] Although the agreement was signed under IMF pressure,[73] this pressure is not sufficient to explain why the Central Bank consented to it and subsequently implemented it.[74] Indeed, the finance minister called

[67] *Rossiiskie Vesti,* 25 May 1993, 4

[68] Michael Burawoy, "Why Coupon Socialism Never Stood a Chance in Russia: The Political Conditions of Economic Transition," *Politics and Society* 22, no.4 (1994): 585–594, at 591.

[69] *Samaraskie Izvestiia,* 7 April 1994, 7. Bankers also assert that once taxes are taken into account even central credits that clients repay are a money-losing proposition (banks are allowed to charge only 3 percent more per annum on these loans than the rate at which they received the money from the central bank.) Burawoy, "Why Coupon," 591; interview with a Samara commercial bank vice president, 29 April 1994.

[70] Interview with the chiefs of the Central Bank Head Office for Samara Province (25 April 1994) and Krasnoiarsk Territory (June 1994). Also *Business-MN,* no. 18, 11 May 1994, 1; *Delo* (Samara), 18 March 1994, 8.

[71] *Finansovye Izvestiia,* 27 December 1994, 2.

[72] *Voprosy Ekonomiki,* no. 6 (1993): 4–6.

[73] *Rossiiskie Vesti,* 22 May 1993, 2.

[74] As a result the Central Bank raised what is misleadingly known as its refinancing rate rapidly throughout the balance of 1993. See, e.g., *Delovoi Mir,* 29 September 1993, 5.

Central Bank acquiescence on pegging the refinancing rate an "unexpected and major victory."[75]

However, if one sees the Central Bank as seeking to implement a coherent policy of using money to lubricate production, this agreement becomes much more comprehensible. Somewhat later, in April 1994, Gerashchenko revealed the structure of his reasoning. Discussing plans to auction credits to commercial banks rather than distributing them through the banks to enterprises, Gerashchenko noted: "Of course, credit resource auctions give no guarantee that the funds sold will be used to finance the smooth, uninterrupted work of industry and agriculture." This is very much the language of money as lubricant of production, it might be noted. He continued:

> Without a doubt, some banks, at the expense of the interests of their clients from the real sector of the economy, are going to look for the most profitable and least risky means to invest these funds. Therefore in order to avoid the resale of such credits on the inter-bank market and their conversion into hard currency the Central Bank is supporting at the auctions a fairly high level of interest rates as compared to the inter-bank rate.[76]

Starting from the argument that the role of Central Bank credits should be to finance production, Gerashchenko arrives at the conclusion that credit prices must be high—not because it is this that will ensure the money goes where needed, but because in the absence of a means of forcing banks to reloan cheap credits to chosen sectors, there is no reason for them to do so. Direct provision of loans to enterprises at subsidized rates is of course subject to the same reasoning. Thus the policy to peg interest rates on industrial loans to those set on the interbank market can be seen as admission of the Central Bank's inability to ensure that these loans would not be diverted to that market.[77]

The point at which the Russian government found itself by mid-1993 was pithily summarized by the economist Yevgeni Yasin, later minister of the economy: "The formation of a market is happening here in conditions of a weak state, and the only instrument, in effect, that the state can fight for

---

[75] FBIS-SOV-93–099, 25 May 1993, 32.

[76] *Den'gi i kredit*, no. 5 (1994): 21.

[77] The general caricature of Gerashchenko as the dark prince of inflationary finance (especially egregious in Åslund) thus misses the mark widely. As Yegor Gaidar put it, "After April 1993 when Yeltsin won his referendum on reform, Geraschenko started being very cooperative. From April 1993 he did exactly what the government wanted. After this point, any arguments about Geraschenko being the worst central-bank governor in the world are rubbish." My reading of what caused Gerashchenko's change in policy is different. Gaidar is quoted in Ben Edwards, "Can Yeltsin Keep His Nerve?" *Euromoney*, April 1995, 68–76.

is a strong ruble."[78] The destruction of Soviet monetary institutions, and the absence of substitute institutions that would have allowed monetary policy to be coordinated with a detailed industrial policy indeed meant that no *systematic* alternative to a hard money policy could be implemented.

Interenterprise Relations: The Declining Credibility of Central Subsidies

The demise of Soviet monetary institutions not only constrained the forms in which the state could intervene in the economy; it also prompted a major transformation in the way enterprises in that economy related to one another. So far, our narrative has viewed Russia's monetary consolidation largely from the point of view of the state—classifying the sorts of policies available to state leaders to pursue it, and demonstrating how the final dismantling of Soviet monetary institutions answered certain political and administrative challenges to the government's exclusive control over what would count as money. Yet money is only of interest to the state because it is also a means by which actors outside the state organize their relations with one another. I have argued that the growth of interenterprise arrears in the first half of 1992 stemmed from the persistence of Soviet monetary institutions capable of providing automatic payment for production, and which had regularly been used to provide such payment in the past. Enterprises were willing to ship goods to one another on credit because they believed the state could deliver money to settle the obligations of those firms unable to pay their own debts. Once the card file records of debts were eliminated in mid-1992, organizing such subsidies in a coherent manner was no longer possible. Interenterprise arrears did persist after this point, but in the new institutional context, they had different causes and significance, charted in the next chapter.

The literature on the nonpayments crisis has largely ignored the state organizational capacities underpinning enterprises' belief that nonpaying customers would eventually find sources of subsidies, and it has therefore provided an alternate explanation for the persistence of nonpayments. Given that the unpleasant political logic of a restrictive monetary policy implies that only the most committed governments will be able to resist the temptation to distribute inflationary subsidies, the state's main challenge is to make its commitment to hard money credible. Failures of political will, such as the decision in late summer 1992 to expand the money supply in the course of the debt-offset operation, undermine credibility and teach enterprises that the state eventually will pay off all debts. This lack of cred-

[78] *Moskovskie Novosti,* no. 33, 15 August 1993, 7.

ibility explains nonpayments.[79] If this argument were accurate, it would be difficult to justify a focus on monetary consolidation rather than monetary policy. The strategy of intimidation would not be one among a variety of policies designed to secure the state's monopoly on the definition of money, but simply the critical component of an anti-inflationary strategy pursued by national authorities with full control over all the relevant instruments of policy.

A closer examination of the development of the nonpayments crisis over time bears out the importance of organizational factors and demonstrates that a state's expressed willingness to subsidize is not sufficient to provoke profligate behavior by enterprises. The substantial expansion in the money supply in late summer and fall 1992, driven both by the debt offset operation and the effort to use cheap earmarked loans to support industry, was vigorously defended to all who would listen by the head of the Central Bank. In December, Gaidar was removed as head of government and replaced by Viktor Chernomyrdin, who proclaimed himself far more sympathetic to industrial interests. There seemed every reason to conclude that the monetarist project had suffered a political fiasco. Yet as figure 2 reveals, nonpayments declined in real (constant-ruble) terms in all but one of the months from November 1992 to October 1993. The effects a more credibly restrictive monetary policy was expected to have on nonpayments were also impossible to detect. Monetary policy began to harden from May of 1993. The violent dispersal of Parliament in early October seemed to portend increased government ability to implement its commitment to monetary restriction and elimination of cheap credits. The spirit of the moment was captured in the declaration of the minister of finance that "we have crushed the rebellion, [and] we will crush the inflation."[80] It would be difficult to construct a measure of government commitment to monetary restriction that would not mark October 1993 as its highest point. But

[79] On the lack of government credibility as an explanation for nonpayments, see John Odling-Smee and Henri Lorie, "The Economic Reform Process in Russia," International Monetary Fund working paper WP/93/55, 1993, 4; and David Bigman and Sergio Pereira Leite, "Enterprise Arrears in Russia: Causes and Policy Options," International Monetary Fund working paper WP/93/61, 1993. Both papers suffer from imprecision over whether the belief in coming government laxness exercises its effects on buyers or purchasers. See also Ickes and Ryterman, "Roadblock," 240. Ickes and Ryterman cite credibility alongside a number of institutional factors.

[80] Quoted in Jacques Sapir, "Conversion of Russian Defense Industries: A Macroeconomic and Regional Perspective," in *Privatization, Conversion, and Enterprise Reform in Russia*, ed. Michael McFaul and Tova Perlmutter (Stanford: Center for International Security and Arms Control, 1994), 164. Cf. Fedorov's press conference reported in *Delovoi Mir*, 13 October 1993, 1. In fact, monthly wholesale inflation fell from 19 percent in October 1993 to only 6 percent by August 1994 at the same time as nonpayments increased; *Russian Economic Trends* 3, no. 2 (1994): 149. This fact is particularly uncomfortable for those inclined to find the roots of both nonpayments and high inflation in the lack of reform "credibility."

Figure 2. Real overdue receivables in industry as a share of their December 1992 level

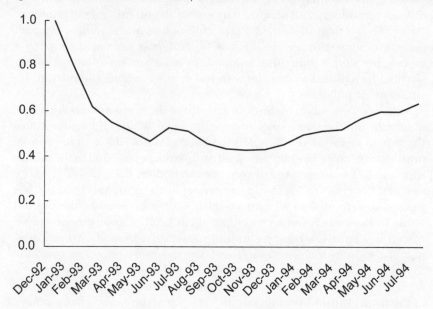

it was precisely at this moment that a new expansion in nonpayments began.[81]

Evidently, something other than perceptions of the government's ability to limit growth of the money supply was at work.[82] Far more important were the dismantling of Soviet monetary institutions and the consequent impossibility of implementing a coherent policy subordinating monetary issue to the needs of production. To students of János Kornai's theory of the soft budget constraint, it should not be surprising that this organizational transformation of the state prompted sharp changes in enterprise behavior. Kornai's theory is famous above all for its inquiry into the widespread willingness of socialist firms to run themselves into debt that their sales will not allow them to repay.[83] It is too little noticed, however, that three actors are involved. There is the softly constrained firm itself, its cred-

---

[81] The importance of October is shown by the fact that nonpayments (overdue receivables) jumped to 72 percent of the month's production from 54 percent in the previous month (*Kommersant*, 1 February 1994, 4–5), though some of this may have been due to a onetime adjustment in the method of calculating these nonpayments (*Voprosy Ekonomiki*, no. 1 [1994]: 53).

[82] One can make a case that the effects of credibility ought to show up with a lag, but efforts to choose a lag that could save the argument would be in vain.

[83] This discussion is based on János Kornai, "The Soft Budget Constraint," *Kyklos* 39, no. 1 (1986): 3–30.

itors, and the "paternalistic" state. The state steps in to rescue the firm after it has made the unsustainable expenditures, which were financed by the creditors (who may of course themselves have been parts of the state). Without this two-phase structure (first the loan-financed spending, then the rescue), the notion of the soft budget constraint is incoherent.[84] It is only the expectation of future political successes in extracting subsidy that can shape economic behavior, since a firm would have to regard any past subsidies unlikely to be repeated as an exhaustible resource.

The soft budget constraint, that is, enterprises' willingness to run into unsustainable debt, can therefore be undermined from one of two directions. Budget constraints can be tightened laterally, simply by the reluctance of creditors to extend the credit needed to run up debts. Or they can be tightened vertically, by a state that refuses financial help to ailing enterprises or that finds itself incapable of making the required expenditures. By mid-1993, Russian enterprises found budget constraints dramatically hardening both laterally and vertically. After July 1, 1992, payment regimes for almost all interenterprise trade were determined exclusively by the enterprises, and most enterprises sought to switch to payment in advance.[85] In part, the shift to prepayment reflected the well-known difficulties with recovering damages through the state arbitration system; earlier, banks would at least send payments for bills in the order received if and when any money arrived on the debtor's bank account. With the end of automatic bank bill collection, the general willingness of enterprises to extend credit to their customers shrank.

Reduced interenterprise loans were not the only component of the lateral hardening of the budget constraint. After bank reforms in 1988, many enterprises had been able to create "pocket" banks that would extend loans on easy terms. As the situation unfolded, however, these banks began to demand increasing independence to channel credit to profitable uses as they experienced heavy pressure from the Central Bank to keep their cash flow positive.[86] Inflation helped provide a means to realize this increased demand for independence. Because banks were forbidden to exceed fixed ratios between capital and assets (loans), inflation meant they

[84] As Kornai (ibid., 4) puts it with regard to the classical budget constraint, "the budget constraint is a constraint on ex ante variables . . . based on expectations concerning . . . *future* financial situation," emphasis added.

[85] This shift is discussed as an example of hardened budget constraints in de Boissieu et al., "Gérer la dette."

[86] On the "pocket banks" see Hellman, "Breaking the Bank," which predicts their increasing efforts to achieve autonomy. Such efforts are described by Burawoy, "Why Coupon," 585–594, which argues that in early 1993, pocket banks' impact was muted by a pattern of local government influence over local Central Bank branch operation. The cases I studied did not display this pattern.

constantly had to issue new stock. Since this process occurred in the context of shrinking enterprise financial power, it gave expanded influence to bank management as enterprise shares in the capital stock shrank and this stock became divided among larger numbers of smaller investors or fell into the hands of management itself.[87] The history of Samara Province's largest bank, which originally drew capital from large state enterprises, provides a good example of this trend. The bank's fifth issuance of stock in late 1993 saw the share of stock held by the four largest stockholders shrink from 47.6 to 32.8 percent, with only one stockholder owning as much as 10 percent. This was followed by a recapitalization of profit that was designed to increase the shares held by original bank founders, but by spring the bank's leadership was still able to announce that a much tighter approach to crediting bank founders would be followed.[88]

The tendency for lateral sources of credit to dry up was matched by a vertical hardening of budget constraints that stemmed more from the Russian state's weakness than from increased monetarist resolve. It was not only that the policy of distributing cheap, earmarked credits to support production proved impossible to sustain in face of the resistance of newly independent banks. Even subsidies directly funded by the budget were not reliable. Federal budget expenditures were made through an awkward system that passed expenditures through many agencies on the way to their intended recipient. Aside from the unintentional bureaucratic tangles the system created, inflationary conditions gave each link in this chain incentives to capture "float" on the money by delaying payment.[89] As a result, subsidies could be largely worthless by the time they arrived at their intended destination. Other promised subsidies simply never arrived. For instance, the government encouraged banks to make low-interest loans to ensure seasonal shipments to isolated Far North regions, promising to compensate the banks for the difference between the low-interest rate and the one at which they purchased funds from the Central Bank. Once the loans had been made, however, the promised compensation proved ex-

[87] This mechanism was described to me by the director of a Vladivostok commercial bank (interview, October 1992), the executive director of a holding company uniting many former state-owned factories (interview, November 1993) and the head of the central bank office for Krasnoiarsk Territory (interview, June 1994). For statistics reflecting banks' bumping up against asset limits defined by their capital stock see *Finansovye Izvestiia*, 15–21 May 1993, 3.

[88] *Delo*, 3 December 1993, 4 and 18 March 1994, 4; *Samarskie Izvestiia*, 16 March 1994, 1; interview with the bank's vice president, 29 April 1994; interview with chief economist for a founding enterprise, 29 April 1994.

[89] At least this is the picture drawn by officials of the *kaznacheistvo* or treasury office, which was still being set up in 1994, and which was supposed to improve the federal government's capacity to manage payments. Interviews in Vladivostok (November 1993), Samara (May 1994), and Krasnoiarsk (June 1994).

tremely difficult to extract.[90] Although their intended recipients could not tell whether such failures to deliver subsidies were due to a breakdown in disbursement institutions or to limitations imposed by revenue shortfalls, it mattered little from the point of view of the weight of the government's word.

By the end of 1993, the promises of generosity that many had feared would encourage profligate behavior by enterprises were manifestly hollow. Destruction of the card file payment mechanism meant that no new offset giving enterprises automatic payment for production not purchased was possible, however desired.[91] Moscow was essentially unable to make a credible commitment to subsidize.

Budget constraints on Russian firms grew ever harder. The impression grew that enterprises built to make the plan would now be able to survive only by making money. Creditors were less and less willing to loan money to enterprises in anticipation of an eventual government bailout. Banks grew more and more independent and jealous of their bottom line, and they began to refuse to bear responsibility for the return of government loans intended to help their customers. And the government itself, as much through incapacity as through political commitment, rescued failing firms less frequently and less reliably. By late 1993, even those firms that believed the government lacked a commitment to monetary rectitude found it difficult to find creditors who would advance the funds necessary to act on this opinion—at least with enthusiasm.

Conclusion

In the midst of the economic and institutional disarray confronting the leaders of the new Russian state, I have sought to show in this chapter, a focus on monetary policy could at once be attractive for politicians and crippling for students of politics. Karl Polanyi underscored the "integrating power of monetary policy," by illustrating how it drew together isolated members of society: "What the businessman, the organized worker, the

---

[90] On these loans, see *Kommersant*, no. 28 (1993): 27. The great difficulties in getting the federal government to pay the compensation were described by the head of the Central Bank office for Krasnoyarsk Province (interview, June 1994). For an early example of banks' refusal to distribute low-interest loans because federal budget compensation was not being paid on time, see the discussion from a provincial legislature reported in *Materialy dvenadtsatoi sessii Nizhegorodskogo oblastnogo Soveta narodnykh deputatov dvadtsat' pervogo sozyva, 22–23 sentiabria 1992* (Materials of the twelfth session of the Nizhnii Novgorod oblast' Soviet of People's Deputies in the twenty-first assembly, 22–23 September 1992) (Nizhnii Novgorod, 1992), 69–71.

[91] *Segodnia*, 18 February 1994, 1.

housewife pondered, what the farmer who was planning his crop, the parents who were weighing their children's chances, the lovers who were waiting to get married, resolved in their minds when considering the favor of the times, was more directly determined by the monetary policy of the central bank than by any other single factor."[92] The cast of characters in Polanyi's lovely vignette did not, naturally enough, include Ostap Bender, but it is not hard to see why Gaidar and the other authors of Russia's state-building project might want to write him in. Increasingly unable to spend the money the decaying Soviet state showered on them, Bender's descendants sought solutions in barter, localism, and subversion of central authority. Price liberalization, by restoring purchasing power to money, promised to reunite Russian society around a central institution. Even if monetary policy evoked not solidarity in anxious contemplation, but vigorous political protests, this would only demonstrate the decisive importance of national authorities.

After price liberalization, the fear that Russia would be subject to the same sorts of disintegrative processes that had brought down the Soviet Union passed quickly. Yet the political advantages a focus on monetary policy offered simultaneously created analytical dangers. It is profoundly misguided to reduce politics to a battle between proponents and opponents of monetary expansion when the very meaning of money and the character of the institutions that organize its circulation are in flux. The Russian government and its industrial opponents were arguing not so much about the appropriate amount of money in circulation as the appropriate role and meaning of money in economic life. To derive the motivations of the government's opponents from the vacuous principle that those who are hurt by monetary stringency will oppose it forecloses investigation into the actual arguments they advanced, the possibilities for political action created by these arguments, and especially the way a rapidly and massively changing institutional environment sustained some viewpoints about money and undermined others.

A premature focus on monetary policy also hinders an appreciation of the causes of the interenterprise debt explosion that challenged the government's control of the money supply. The credibility approach suggests, in effect, that enterprises extended credit to one another because of optimistic conclusions regarding "the favor of the times" in light of predictions about the *desire* of the government to subsidize noncompetitive firms. The institutional explanation advanced in this chapter focused instead on the instruments underpinning the government's *ability* to subsidize, and their

[92] Karl Polanyi, *The Great Transformation: The Political and Economic Origins of Our Time* (Boston: Beacon Press, 1957), 205.

effects on the behavior of creditors. Soviet monetary institutions made a policy of transforming interenterprise debts into official money both credible and feasible. Their destruction changed not only expectations, but also policy.

Gradually, discovering that they were bereft of the organizational structures needed to run a coherent policy of ratifying and regulating private credit issue, Russia's government and Central Bank converged on a policy of intimidation, trying to reinforce potential creditors' growing conviction that making loans was unwise. This strategy was effective in blocking the issue of unregulated credit, but only to the extent that it had been driven by the belief that the government's monetary policy would weaken. As it turned out, an unreflective faith in the largess of national government proved to be by far the least-enduring threat to the new Russian state's monopoly on the definition and terms of creation of the means of payment.

CHAPTER FOUR

Money Unmade, 1993–1994

> Mr. Edgewise, in whose purse already lie more of my Chits than he really
> likes to have out at any given time, has won from me a sum we both must
> view, less as any real Amount, than as a Complication to be resolv'd at
> some unnam'd date.
>
> —Thomas Pynchon, *Mason and Dixon*

Desperation is the mother of invention. As post-Soviet Russia
entered its third year in 1994 with a fall in production unprecedented in its short and depressing economic history,
the country's impoverished industrial enterprises were turning increasingly to barter. Unable to make ends meet at the prices prevailing in the
money economy, enterprises simply dropped out of it, continuing economic activity in kind. The new barter, which one might term the *barter
of the bankrupt,* was based on quite different motives than the shortage-
economy barter the Russian government had virtually eliminated through
price liberalization. For the roots of the barter of the bankrupt did not lie
in money's inability to command value. The spread of barter occurred despite falling inflation rates. In no way did it constitute a hyperinflationary
"flight from money."

The emergence of the barter of the bankrupt revealed fundamental flaws
in the Russian leadership's theory of the relationship between market transformation and the structure of political contention. In the chaotic fall of
1991, as the previous chapter detailed, Gaidar had thought that price liberalization would both remove the causes of the localized barter economy
and put pressure on firms that could not turn a profit in an environment
of market prices. Thus, dangerous challenges to sovereignty would be re-

placed by serious but ultimately less threatening challenges to a restrictive monetary policy. The politics of the cash register would replace the politics of rule and control.[1] National politics would supersede local politics.

However instructive about the relationship between money and the power of the national state, Gaidar's argument was mistaken. By creating new means of payment, the barter of bankrupt posed a new challenge to sovereignty. This challenge originated in political struggles fought out in local arenas, not in the national one.[2] To understand the character and significance of these struggles, and how they gave rise to a new wave of barter, it is best to relate them not to Gaidar's analysis but rather to a richer and more sweeping account of the relationship between capitalism and the nation-state, Karl Polanyi's *The Great Transformation*. Polanyi's developmental history, which focuses especially on England, deals with a far longer time period and treats sharply different circumstances. Yet it can nevertheless provide a template for constructing an explanatory narrative of Russia's own "great transformation," due to significant points of contact with the concerns of Russia's market reformers. Like Gaidar, Polanyi argued that unleashing market forces would produce an inevitable social reaction demanding the taming of their destructive effects. Furthermore, like Gaidar, Polanyi suggested that this reaction against markets contributed to the centrality of the national political arena.

Of course, what gives Polanyi's work its particular value for understanding Russian monetary consolidation are the points of difference. Polanyi's stress on the expansion of state capacities required for the creation of a full-blown market economy did not find an echo in the early thought of Russian reformers. More important, where Gaidar hoped his reforms would accomplish something like Schumpeter's "creative destruction," Polanyi argued that unfettered markets lead to destruction pure and simple. He accordingly located the source of the impulse to tame markets not in selfish efforts to pursue private gains at the expense of the public good but rather in a healthy societal impulse to self-protection.[3] As a result, Polanyi embarked on a detailed and important analysis of the institutional underpinnings of markets. Suitably modified, Polanyi's arguments on the administrative concomitants of market building and the

---

[1] The use of "cash register" and "rule and control" is adapted from their use to contrast statist and pluralist attitudes to politics in Stephen Krasner, "Approaches to the State: Alternative Conceptions and Historical Dynamics," *Comparative Politics* 16 (January 1984): 223–246.
[2] On the localizing effects of Gaidar's reform and the "articulation which exists between processes of regionalization and macroeconomic policy," see Jacques Sapir, "Différences économiques régionales, transition et politiques de stabilisation en Russie," *Revue d'études comparatives Est-Ouest* (March 1993): 5–55.
[3] Cf. Karl Polanyi, *The Great Transformation: The Political and Economic Origins of Our Time* (Boston: Beacon Press, 1965), 154.

institutional origins of demands to mitigate the baleful effects of unregulated markets can serve as an explanation for the emergence of the barter of the bankrupt in Russia.

Markets national in scope, Polanyi argues, did not arise through the accretion of spontaneous individual actions driven by a universal propensity to truck and barter. The destabilizing effects of markets—including the possibility that they might fail to provide for some most basic human needs—restricted them in the premodern world either to long-distance exchange or to segregated adjuncts of tightly managed and highly localized systems of provision maintained by towns. Steps toward a nationally integrated market became feasible only after monarchs of the mercantilist era with ambitions to a nationwide dominion stripped towns of their authority and forcibly uprooted localized systems of distribution and exchange.[4]

Concentration of economic powers with the national authorities was followed by Polanyi's famous "double movement," comprising a state-initiated impulse toward an all-encompassing system of self-regulating markets and then a spontaneous interventionist countermove aimed at averting the catastrophic social effects of such markets. The double movement represented the struggle "between two organizing principles in society . . . the principle of economic liberalism . . . [and] the principle of social protection aiming at the conservation of man and nature as well as productive organization." Self-regulating markets spawned social destruction because labor, land, and money were "fictitious commodities," treated as if they were "produced for sale on the market" despite the patent falsity of this conceit. Each of the fictitious commodities was associated with a particular kind of social destruction and evoked particular measures for societal self-protection.[5] The precious metals used as money at the dawn of the industrial revolution, for instance, were fictitious commodities because their production could not be increased rapidly in response to increased transactional demands or to compensate for flows of specie brought on by imbalances in trade. Drastic consequences could result as productive organizations succumbed to the effects of a deflation unrelated to their own activity. The protective impulse took the form of central banking, which was able to ensure orderly expansion of the money supply despite the limited quantities of precious metal by making use of the fractional reserve mechanism. Central banking produced a regulated nonmetallic means of payment of purely national scope—a sharp departure from a fully self-regulated market.

On Polanyi's account, because subnational authorities' ability to affect the operation of markets had been destroyed by the centralizing mercan-

---

[4] Ibid., 65–67.
[5] For quoted phrases, ibid., 132 and 72; in general, 68–76, 163–200.

tilist state, the double movement was from the outset both national in scope and a force for further national integration. The national state had the exclusive capacity both to unleash markets and to rein them in. When pressures to make the market system fully consistent mandated a huge expansion in the administrative functions of the state, these new functions devolved on central authority. When self-regulating markets began to demonstrate their incredible capacity to sow social havoc, only national authorities could implement protective measures. The double movement created a society that was not only territorially but also institutionally coextensive with the national state.[6]

Yet this argument for a clear separation between the centralization of economic powers and a subsequent double movement, which only reinforces national cohesion by fusing individuals into a "social unit," is difficult to sustain. Polanyi gives no explanation for why it was that only national authorities could provide protection against the deflationary perils of the application of the commodity fiction to money. The early establishment of the Bank of England was exceptional; in most countries, the mercantilist state did not achieve a full monopoly on the definition and terms of creation of the means of payment, which had to be pursued throughout the nineteenth century.[7] An exploration of the implications of this point for nineteenth-century Europe would take us too far afield, but its relevance to Russia is direct. Polanyi anticipates Gaidar in his overhasty assumption of a straightforward identity of society and state through the nexus of the monetary system. However, by eliminating this assumption, while retaining other elements of Polanyi's analysis, one can construct an account of how the attempt to effect a great transformation in Russia gave rise to the barter of the bankrupt.

Between 1992 and 1994, Russia passed through a "triple movement," in which the spread of the market principle through society ran into roadblocks first on the local and then on the national level. In the first phase of the triple movement, price liberalization had its intended effects of undermining barter-driven disintegration and threatening the existence of enterprises unable to cover their costs by sale of their products. The expected countermove began when, rather than simply going out of existence, enterprises were able to convince key suppliers to accept payment

[6] This point is beautifully expressed in a brilliant interpretation of Polanyi that has much influenced the one given here: Maurice Glasman, "The Great Deformation: Polanyi, Poland and the Terrors of Planned Spontaneity," in *The New Great Transformation? Change and Continuity in East-Central Europe*, ed. Christopher G. A. Bryant and Edmund Mokrzycki (London: Routledge, 1994), 191–217.

[7] Indeed, Schmoller, who initiated the interpretation of mercantilism on which Polanyi relies (*Great Transformation*, 278), sees the twin processes of centralization of state and market as extending well into the nineteenth century. Gustav von Schmoller, *The Mercantile System and Its Historical Significance* (New York: A. M. Kelley, 1967).

in kind at effectively lower prices. In many, though far from all, cases, these de facto price concessions were in effect coerced by local governments, which served as an institutional embodiment of the principle of social protection. (This usage is intended to highlight the relationship to Polanyi's theory, not to take an attitude on whether or not the destruction so avoided would have had a creative character.) In the final phase of the triple movement, central authorities found themselves not only unable to eliminate the barter economy emerging on the local level, but ultimately forced to enact policies that sustained it.

The origins of the triple movement lay in deep differences in the administrative and political circumstances of central and local authorities. The fiscal concerns that drove the initial federal reaction to the barter of the bankrupt were straightforward; as barter complicated tax collection, tax organs sought ways to force payment of taxes, in money. As it happened, they were not up to the task. Local authorities, by contrast, were much less likely to conceive their fiscal responsibilities in purely abstract, monetary terms. The builders of the Soviet economy had "hardwired" the ability to tax *particular* economic actors in kind into the very social infrastructure of Russia. For example, power and heating stations were often located on the premises of industrial plants even when they serviced residential consumers as well. These indispensable infrastructural services could not simply be purchased from other sources through the collection of money taxes. Furthermore, though local authorities certainly found it more convenient to tax in money, when circumstances began to require it, they were better situated to organize new forms of taxation in kind than were central authorities.

Political imperatives also made local authorities relatively more eager to protect enterprises whose inability to sustain themselves in the money economy prompted a turn to barter. As the literature on the "politics of stabilization" emphasizes, the burdens of market-oriented policies are more politically transparent than the benefits. Governments that sanction the liquidation of a factory that has run out of money must be able to allow themselves the luxury of abstraction, since the pain of the policy is felt by a concrete and compact group, whereas most of the benefits, should they eventually appear, will accrue to scattered individuals who are unlikely even to recognize their shared interests, much less act on them politically.[8] This dilemma affected both local and central authorities in Russia, but their thresholds of political tolerance were very different. The hypothetical beneficiaries of a more efficient economy will not necessarily live and

[8] E.g., Joan Nelson, "The Politics of Economic Transformation: Is Third World Experience Relevant in Eastern Europe?" *World Politics* 45 (April 1993): 433–463.

vote in the same region as the very palpable victims of policies intended to create it. Enterprises damaged by price liberalization had many opportunities to affect policy in the local arena, whether through formal consultative institutions such as the energy commissions that set local electricity rates, meetings of local authorities with industrialists' organizations of varying degrees of coherency, or simply through direct informal contacts between enterprise directors and local officials. Combined, these institutional and political factors meant that for a local government, the failure of a single factory employing several thousand people seemed an unacceptable disaster, whereas Moscow, however grudgingly, came to see it as an acceptable disaster in the light of broader economic goals.[9]

Despite its relatively greater political insulation from industrial distress, in the final stage of the triple movement, Moscow adopted policies that eased some of the destructive consequences of the widening exit from the monetary economy. These policies consisted in the distribution of money to affected regions and sectors of industry. The political origins of this concession lay in the organizational structure of the executive branch of government, which in effect transmitted and amplified demands for protection of industry from the local to the national arena. Under central planning, industry was grouped into sectors under the direction of particular ministries. Because of the importance of lobbying for scarce resources, the role of the ministries was as much representational as it was managerial.[10] Reforms under Gorbachev and Yeltsin eliminated many ministries (though some of these managed a tenuous resurrection as a loose quasi-private enterprise grouping or "concern"), consolidated others, and reduced still others to "committees" of nebulous authority and mandate. Nevertheless, key sectors of industry retained representation in the Russian Council of Ministers, also known simply as the government [*pravitel'stvo*]. (I use *government* through the rest of this book in this narrow sense, not in the broader sense of all state bodies as is common in America.) This representation was important, since the Russian government's power to make most critical decisions on economic policy rendered both of Russia's post-Soviet Parliaments virtual sideshows. The most prominent

---

[9] The point that central and local authorities are at loggerheads because the first are trying to promote economic reform while the latter must deal with the social consequences was made to me very forcefully by Iurii Moskvich, presidential representative for Krasnoyarsk krai. Cf. Philip Hanson, "The Center Versus the Periphery in Russian Economic Policy," *RFE-RL Research Report* 3, no. 17 (1994): 23–28; and the suggestive discussion in Christine Wallich, "Intergovernmental Finances: Stabilization, Privatization, and Growth," in *Russia and the Challenge of Fiscal Federalism*, ed. Christine Wallich (Washington: World Bank, 1994), 64–95, at 80–81, of "how [province] coping mechanisms may undermine stabilization."

[10] See, e.g., Thane Gustafson, *Crisis Amid Plenty* (Princeton: Princeton University Press, 1989).

sectoral ministries were the Ministry of the Railways (*Ministerstvo Putei Sob-shchenii,* or simply MPS) and the Ministry of Fuel and Energy (*Mintopen-ergo*). The latter had at least nominal supervisory functions for two vast parastatal enterprises descended from the former Soviet ministerial appa-ratus, the natural gas–producing monopoly Gazprom and the national electric power network United Energy Systems. The chiefs of these com-panies, though not formally members of the government, had regular ac-cess to the corridors of power.

The structure of industry's political representation thus tended to make central authorities more responsive to those issues that affected enter-prises qua sectors, as opposed to those affecting enterprises sharing other possible characteristics such as regional location or competitive position. Problems that could be presented as the problems of sectors—especially these sectors—got heard at the top. The problems of the individual en-terprise, by contrast, could increasingly get a hearing only on the local level. This asymmetry between local and national political arenas created the triple movement. Local governments sought to sustain a policy of con-doning the barter of the bankrupt either by directly appealing to the na-tional government for funds, or by pushing the costs of their policy onto the local branches of sectors with national political representation. The po-litical weight of these sectors at the national level allowed them to prevail on the government to deliver at least some monetary compensation for the effects of nonmonetary exchange. The triple movement was completed by the federal government's positive response to these regional and sectoral demands for monetary support.

In what follows, I focus in particular on the electric power and heat sec-tor, not as a case study but rather because of the crucial role of this sector in the emergence of barter.[11] As a critical supplier for all industries, power companies were immediately affected when many enterprises proved un-able to earn enough money by sale of their products to pay their suppli-ers.[12] Through examining how electricity suppliers and their customers reacted to this situation, we can trace the triple movement—drastic pres-sures on productive organization, followed by their mitigation through an exit from the money economy sustained first by local and then by national policy. Evidence on local policy was gathered in on-site case studies of three

[11] Electric power and heating (almost always provided through large stations serving entire neighborhoods rather than furnaces in individual buildings) are institutionally united in Rus-sia; cogeneration (use in the heating network of hot water heated for steam to turn electricity-generating turbines) often makes the unification physical as well.
[12] The other key industrial supplier that became an early center of the emerging barter econ-omy was the rail sector, which will receive only passing examination here. In the first seven months of 1994, less than half the payments made to the Russian rail system were in money (*Kommersant*, no. 31, 23 August 1994, 23).

Russian provinces: Samara, in European Russia; Krasnoyarsk in central Siberia; and Primorye, in the Russian Far East. Despite large differences in industrial profile, natural resources, and political history, all three were caught up in the sudden transformation of exchange practices throughout Russia in 1993 and 1994.

Enterprises Under Pressure

The prelude to the rise of the barter of the bankrupt was a transformation in the nature of the nonpayments crisis. What changed was who was not getting paid, and why. As noted in the preceding chapter, through much of 1993 nonpayments had fallen, as a consequence of the hardening of budget constraints and the absence of plausible grounds to think that the government would be capable of delivering payment to enterprises for production their customers had been unable to afford. From October of 1993, nonpayments started to rise again (see figure 3). This time, however, it was electric power companies throughout Russia that were discovering that fewer and fewer of their customers were paying their bills. Nonpayments to electric power companies, and by them to their suppliers in the fuel industry, were central to this new growth of nonpayments. Though the electric power sector made up only around 7 percent of the ruble value of industrial production in early 1993, it accounted for more than 30 percent of the real growth in nonpayments from October

Figure 3. Real overdue payments to sectors of industry, billions of rubles at January 1993 prices

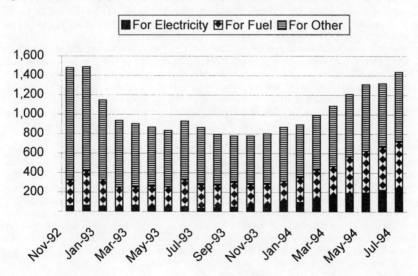

1993 to July 1994.[13] Overdue debt to electrical power companies swelled from about 5 percent to about 17 percent of all debt overdue to Russian industry.[14]

Power companies' sudden troubles in extracting payment were striking, since until the early fall of 1993 they had been exceptionally effective in receiving the money they were due. Up until August 1993, electricity producers had substantially fewer overdue payments from their consumers per unit of output than the average for industry as a whole. Electricity's success in collecting payments was particularly striking in comparison to the fuel sector, which performed almost twice as badly on this measure.[15] Both sectors were far from final demand, which according to some theories of the nonpayments crisis ought to have made them more likely to accumulate payments arrears from their customers.[16] Power companies, though, had the right to deduct their bills directly from their customers' bank accounts.[17] If customers had money they were holding in a legal manner, power companies could take it. While crude oil and natural gas suppliers also had the right to direct deduction, downstream refiners and distributors did not, nor did coal producers. As a result, it was much harder for the fuel industry to collect its bills. By the end of May 1994, however, the relative success of power companies in extracting payment from their customers was already a thing of the past; now

---

[13] Calculated from data in *Segodnia*, 1 September 1994, 11 and *Russian Economic Trends, Monthly Update* Excel file from *Russian Economic Trends* web site.

[14] *Segodnia*, 1 September 1994, 11.

[15] For a more detailed discussion of performance in payment collection, see David Woodruff, "Barter of the Bankrupt: The Politics of Demonetization in Russia's Federal State," in *Uncertain Transition: Ethnographies of Change in a Post-Socialist World*, ed. Michael Burawoy and Katherine Verdery (Boulder: Rowman and Littlefield, forthcoming).

[16] Barry W. Ickes and Randi Ryterman, "The Interenterprise Arrears Crisis in Russia," *Post-Soviet Affairs* 8 (October–December 1992): 331–361, at 354, suggest that final goods producers won't have late receivables, since their customers must pay cash, but they will be more likely to accumulate debts to their suppliers because those suppliers, responding to demand created by the availability of interenterprise credit, will have produced more than can be sold. See also Jacek Rostowski, "The Inter-enterprise Debt Explosion in the Former Soviet Union: Causes, Consequences, Cures," *Communist Economies & Economic Transformation* 5, no. 2 (1993): 131–159, at 136–137.

[17] For electric power, the railroads, and crude oil and natural gas suppliers the old payment order system was retained. Under this system the supplier notifies the payer's bank that a payment is due and the payment is automatically sent (this is known as *bezaktseptnoe sniatie*). See Christian de Boissieu, Daniel Cohen, and Gaël de Pontbriand, "Gérer la dette interentreprises," *Économie Internationale* 54 (Second trimester 1993): 105–120, at 111, and *Segodnia*, 22 February 1994, 11. Electrical energy's rights in this regard were confirmed in interviews with officials at power systems in Samara, Krasnoyarsk, and Vladivostok in 1994. Until May 1994, arrears for electrical energy were assessed very high fines of 2 percent a day; after this they were dropped to .5 percent a day. Interview with the chief engineer at Energonadzor (Samaraenergo), May 1994.

only fuel producers had more nonpayments from their customers relative to output.[18]

The explanation for the growing tendency for enterprises to shirk payment for electricity is short and simple. The power companies' direct access to bank accounts stopped bringing in funds because, by the early fall of 1993, much of Russian industry had run out of money. Many goods were going unsold. A study that examined tax documents for five enterprises in each of Russia's regions found that approximately a quarter of 1992 production went unsold, as did 14.5 percent of production made in the first half of 1993.[19] A detailed study of the textiles industry reported that millions of dollars of unsold goods had accumulated in warehouses by late 1993.[20] Other sources of funds besides sales were few. Working capital was no longer distributed by the state, as it had been in the Soviet era and in a haphazard fashion in 1992. Bank loans did not prove a lasting substitute. In a context where price liberalization had encouraged economic actors to count their money better, it had become much harder to find private loans for all but very certain and extremely lucrative ventures.[21] Few industrial enterprises fell in this category. It appeared that the ultimate principle of the market economy—that firms unable to sell customers goods they want at prices they can afford will not be able to sustain themselves—would soon claim its first victims. Enterprises could no longer pay for one of their most critical inputs, electricity. The potential for destruction of productive organizations was clear, and the first stage of the triple movement was complete.

Barter of the Bankrupt: No Money and No Markets

The epidemic of payment delinquency confronting power companies was accompanied by a second, no less significant development: those customers that did pay their bills increasingly did so not in money, but in goods of their own production. A Russian business weekly claimed that by February 1994, half of all payments for electricity in the country were in kind.[22] Two regional power companies in provinces visited for this study were able to furnish data reflecting a dramatic increase in payments in

---

[18] *Russian Economic Trends* 3, no. 2 (1994): 33.

[19] *Segodnia*, 6 November 1993, 12.

[20] *Russia's Textile Industry: Is There Any Chances* [sic] *for Surviving?* (Moscow: Russian Union of Industrialists and Entrepreneurs Expert Institute and the Higher School for Economics, 1994), 13.

[21] As we saw in the preceding chapter, even special subsidized state loans designed to support industry were regularly rejected by banks fearful of being forced to pay them back if their clients could not.

[22] *Kommersant*, no. 5, 15 February 1994, 31.

Table 3. Payments in Kind to Two Regional Power Systems[1]

Dal'energo (Primorye Province)

Date	Percentage of Payments in Kind
All 1993	25
January 1994	64
February	60
March	62
April	75
May	83
June	93
July	100

Krasnoiarskenergo

Date	Percentage of Payments in Kind
All 1992 (est.)	5
First quarter 1993	32
First semester 1993	30
Nine months 1993	37
All 1993	45
First quarter 1994	77
Second quarter 1994 (est.)	80

[1] Data from Dal'energo and Krasnoiarskenergo. Krasnoiarsk estimates were done by the commercial director, who supplied other numbers on the basis of accounting documents.

kind that moved in parallel with the general trend for growing nonpayments described above (see table 3).[23] In both regions, more than 75 percent of electric power payments were in kind by the summer of 1994.[24] Like nonpayment, in-kind payment could occur only with a complete absence of funds on enterprise bank accounts, since otherwise money payment would have been automatic.

The parallel growth of nonpayment and payment in kind for electricity had its origins in power companies' reaction to the poverty of their customers. Abstracting from institutional context, one might imagine that a firm faced with customers who cannot afford its goods or services has one

[23] The provinces were Krasnoyarsk krai in Siberia, and Primorskii krai in the Far East. On qualitative evidence, trends in a third province visited, Samara oblast' in European Russia, were similar, though exact data were not made available to me. Data from these cases is used in this section and the next to substantiate an argument about processes national in scope; some systematic comparisons are made below.

[24] It should be noted that, in an interview in July 1994, the deputy governor of Krasnoyarsk krai who headed the territory's energy committee disputed the accuracy of these figures, arguing that the power company would not be able to function at all in such a case; she conceded that occasionally the barter percentage had gotten as high as 50 percent.

of two options: refuse to sell to those customers, or lower prices for them. At this level of abstraction, one can say that power companies chose the second option of lowering prices. They did this by allowing their customers to pay fewer of their bills (leading to a growth in payment arrears) or by accepting payment in goods that for purposes of this exchange were assigned an "unrealistically" high price. It is analytically indispensable, however, to make only provisional use of the term "unrealistic" and to stress that conceiving nonmonetary payment as a form of price concession rests on an abstraction from institutional context. To speak of a "real" value for a good is to lapse into the mistaken assumption that economic calculation rests on some preexisting numeric metric, rather than on particular institutionalized practices.[25] As we shall see, a price concession that takes the form of allowing debts to accumulate or accepting alternate means of payment also has quite different institutional—and political—effects than one implemented simply by reducing money prices.

Power companies made forced concessions to reduced or nonmonetary payment because when the direct deduction rights that had held nonpayments for electricity to a minimum stopped working, companies suddenly found themselves in a weak strategic position vis-à-vis their debtors.[26] Among suppliers to industrial enterprises, electrical power companies are in a unique position. The absolute dependence of industry on electrical power means that its disconnection destroys industry's capacity to make money. In some cases—especially in the chemical and metallurgical industries—it may also destroy delicate continuous-process equipment.[27]

As a result, power companies' most obvious coercive mechanism, disconnection, was not a very credible threat, for reasons both political and economic. Cutting off power in retaliation for nonpayments was politically difficult because regulations adopted in 1992 mandated that the local authorities must give approval before any shutdown is carried out.[28] Although such approval was not impossible to win, it was given rarely and at best grudgingly.[29] Local authorities usually forced the power company to

---

[25] For a fuller discussion of this point, see chapter 5.

[26] The argument offered here parallels one earlier proposed in Jacques Sapir, "Inflation, stabilisation et dynamiques régionales en Russie: Analyse des trajectoires macroéconomiques et de leurs fondements micro et mésoéconomiques," École des Hautes Études en Sciences Sociales, Centre d'Études des Modes d'Industrialisation, Paris, June 1993, 42. Sapir drew on Thomas Schelling, *The Strategy of Conflict* (Cambridge: Harvard University Press, 1960), to explain with coercive deficiency and deterrence games what he saw as the prevalence of price restraint in Russian interenterprise relations in circumstances of mutual supplies of weakly substitutable goods.

[27] With regard to chemical industry, this factor was cited by a local power company in *Delo* (Samara), 12 November 1993.

[28] Interview with Samaraenergo officials, April 1994.

[29] *Kommersant*, no. 5, 15 February 1994, 31; interview with deputy governor for the energy and transport sectors, Samara Province, April 1994.

refrain from cutoffs while promising some subsidies and possibly invocation of the weak and virtually untested bankruptcy mechanism against those enterprises chronically failing to pay their bills.[30] Other utilities suppliers found themselves in a similar situation with respect to local authorities; it was reported, for instance, that some local administrations used special police units to prevent Gazprom from disconnecting its nonpaying customers.[31]

Even if political approval could be won for a cutoff of electrical power, there might be other reasons to avoid it. Enterprises without electrical power would not be able to earn money to pay back their debts, so the benefits would be minimal. Given that Russia's bankruptcy provisions were ineffective, power companies' chances of recovering their debts from shuttered enterprises' assets were all but nil. Therefore, power companies were inclined to attempt to disconnect the power of only those enterprises they viewed as likely to yield nothing but an endless stream of nonpayments. Samara power company officials, for instance, had gathered data on (much lower) world prices for the goods sold by one of their major debtors, in an effort to convince local authorities of the futility of blocking a power cutoff for this plant.[32]

For nonpaying customers with more prospects, some form of price concession made more sense than trying to implement a power cutoff. In some cases, the motivation for these concessions could be described in language familiar from any market economy. Electric power plants, like virtually any industrial firm, have a declining average cost curve—the more units of electricity they sell, the more cheaply each unit can be made (at least until sales reach the point where a new plant must be added, but in the shrinking Russian economy, this portion of the cost curve was not relevant). Thus it is often reasonable for them to price goods below current average costs to allow more sales and an eventual higher volume of production. In addition, firms that face limited competition usually practice price discrimination, seeking to charge customers the maximum that each can afford to pay. The fact that a firm is unable to pay its bill in money could be taken as good evidence that it is among those that should be offered a cheaper alternative.[33]

---

[30] Interview with official at Samaraenergo, April 1994. Cf. *Volzhskaia Kommuna*, 8 February 1994, 1. For a parallel story from Vladivostok, see *Novosti*, 12 October 1993, 2.
[31] *Monitor* (electronic newsletter of the Jamestown foundation) 1, no. 3, 13 June 1995.
[32] Interview at Samaraenergo, April 1994.
[33] The thesis that unrealistically priced interenterprise credit serves as a form of price discrimination and as a way of lowering prices to take advantage of declining average cost curves was proposed by Vladimir Kirillov, an analyst for the State Committee on Anti-Monopoly Policy (GKAP). See *Kommersant*, no. 48, 20 December 1994, 26–29. Western economists have also proposed price discrimination as an explanation for the use of trade credit in market economies.

Either an effort to cut costs by increasing sales or a desire to practice price discrimination could provide a motive, then, for giving a price cut to a customer that had accumulated nonpayments. In interviews, provincial power company executives did not articulate such a commercial logic in any detail (nor did they have the information necessary to implement it with any precision). They regarded nonpayments as their number one problem, were angry about cases in which nonpayments resulted from enterprises' hiding of revenues, and lobbied local authorities to be allowed to cut off debtors. Nevertheless, they did make differentiations between better- and worse-performing enterprises and suggested that too hasty a resort to a shutdown of nonpaying enterprises would mean the loss of needed customers. As executives in two different regions put it, to shut off enterprises with any prospects whatsoever would be "to cut off the branch we are sitting on."[34] A hard and fast distinction between concessions to incomplete or in-kind payments that resulted from the coercion of local authorities and those made to avoid destroying valued customers would be very difficult to draw. The most it seems fair to say is that local government intervention reduced, sometimes substantially, the bargaining power of electricity suppliers in their effort to maximize their receipts through an intuitive policy of price discrimination.

This language of maximization and prices is deceptive, however, because it implies decisions along a numeric continuum that was not an institutional reality for Russian power company officials. A weak bargaining position might explain the need to make it easier for impoverished customers to purchase electricity. It does not explain, though, why these concessions did not take the form of lower money prices. The answer lies in the institutional difficulty of such a formal price reduction. Local electric power companies had no flexibility in setting formal prices, which were established by provincial energy commissions. These commissions were not regular agencies but rather a committee that met as needed, consisting mostly of officials from the provincial government, as well as a representative from the local power company; major consumers also attended meetings.[35] The pricing structure they proposed was rudimentary, dividing consumers into only a few categories that were far too broad to allow for

[34] Interviews at Samaraenergo (April 1994) and Krasnoyarskenergo (July 1994). On the other hand, both power companies had made efforts—in Samara's case, even successful ones—to invoke cutoffs. (Existence of attempts to do cutoffs in Krasnoyarsk comes from a July 1994 interview with the head of the energy commission for Krasnoyarsk krai.) The head of the Samara energy commission also suggested that the power company had not pushed too hard for cutoffs, using the same arboral metaphor to explain why.
[35] Interviews with heads of energy commissions for Krasnoyarsk (July 1994) and Samara (April 1994) Provinces. The structure of the electric power industry had changed little by 1998; see the excellent survey in *Ekspert*, 13 April 1998.

effective price discrimination according to ability to pay. In Samara, for instance, all of industry was divided into only two categories, large consumers and small ones.[36]

Despite the representation of power consumers at commission meetings, its proceedings did not generate prices they could afford to pay in money, because demand factors did not have an institutional place in them. Prices were set to allow the power company a small formal profit based on its costs.[37] Adjustment of prices to what industry could afford could only occur in the context of discussions in the commission around what could be legitimately included in these costs. There was plenty of room for argument. As Fred Block has noted, "the seemingly objective facts of contemporary life are themselves shaped by accounting conventions."[38] This statement is nowhere more true than in the regulation of electric utilities, where cost is everywhere a far from self-evident notion. In specifying costs, Russian officials tried to make some allowance for the replacement of generating capacity, but given the huge uncertainty about future demand, such decisions were fairly arbitrary. Another reason the energy commission process tended to generate prices that were difficult for industry to pay was because household consumers were charged far lower prices, which had to be compensated for with higher industrial prices.[39]

In short, the formal price-setting process for electricity on the local level produced prices that were both rigid and higher than industry could afford. Forced by their weak bargaining position to make price concessions, but unable to do so simply by lowering money prices, local power companies tolerated reduced levels of payment or accepted payment in kind.[40]

So far, though, we have looked at only one side of the transaction. To substantiate this thesis that in-kind payment constituted a kind of price concession, we have to ask why debtors had goods to offer, and how their prices were determined. The goods power company debtors had to offer were usually goods that they had been unable to sell themselves. They too faced barriers to lowering prices as a means to promote sales, not because

[36] *Delo*, 12 November 1993, 1.
[37] *Kommersant*, no. 5, 15 February 1994, 31–32.
[38] Fred Block, *Post-Industrial Possibilities: A Critique of Economic Discourse* (Berkeley: University of California Press, 1990), 32.
[39] Interview with head of an industrial holding company, Vladivostok, November 1993. Plans to raise rates for household consumers had a long and contentious history thereafter. *Business-MN*, no. 18, 11 May 1994, 5; *Ekspert*, 13 April 1998.
[40] This argument is due in part to the Russian business weekly *Kommersant*, no. 5, 15 February 1994, 31: "by agreement with the local administration power supply enterprises can pull the plug on chronic non-payers. But this still only a threat, with a very limited sphere of action. Local administrations give such permission very rarely, and the main thing is that all the same one won't get the debt back this way. It is true that for liquidating the debt one can take production of the debtor. . . . And at present up to half of all payments are made with such barter."

their prices were fixed by a committee but because of accounting and tax regulations. In late 1992, Russia's Supreme Soviet passed a revision to the tax code that forbade enterprises to sell below "market" prices.[41] The point was to avoid the widespread tax evasion technique of declaring in tax documents a lower price for goods sold than actually applied. However, with no way to determine what market prices were for most goods, tax officials in practice applied a backup rule, almost certainly derived from Soviet pricing practice, of costs plus a fixed profit markup. (The inability to determine market prices should not be regarded solely as a reflection of the infirmity of Russian tax agencies. Even in developed countries, very few goods are sufficiently homogenous to trade on clear price-setting markets.) Enterprises that sold below the cost-plus-markup price were fined and charged taxes as if they had sold at the full price.

Although the demand that enterprises sell at a profit might seem uncontroversial, the pricing regulation created problems not only for those enterprises that would have been loss making in any event. An exceptional degree of arbitrariness was introduced by the issue of how to price assets inherited from the Soviet era. Regulations could force the inclusion of overhead and depreciation costs on equipment that was not being used, for instance.[42] The indexing of assets for inflation based on their meaningless Soviet-era historical cost likewise drove formal expenditures up. Finally, as in the case of electric power, price rigidity could interfere with the reasonable practice of charging some customers prices that were lower than average costs in an effort to promote sales.

Because of downward price rigidity, enterprises faced with lack of demand at the price their accounting departments determined often let goods accumulate in warehouses in hopes that inflation would eventually lower the real price sufficiently to allow buyers to be found.[43] Yet once inflation rates began to fall, enterprises needed another way of showing paper receipts satisfactory to the tax organs. Barter provided one answer to this problem, allowing some sales to take place that could not have happened in the official money economy. Unable to make sales at the prices they had set, enterprises offered their suppliers unsold goods. Faced with the choice of not receiving any payment at all, power companies were willing to accept payment in kind at the "price" determined by the fixed profitability markup over the cost of production.

[41] For the law and subsequent confirmations of this point , see *Normativnye akty po finansam, nalogam, strakhovaniiu i bukhgalterskomu uchetu*, no. 2 (1993): 35–36; no. 11 (1993): 54; no. 12 (1993): 25. The rationale and implementation of this regulation was discussed in an interview (July 1994) with officials of the tax inspectorate, Krasnoyarsk krai.

[42] Interviews in the industry department for Samara Province (May 1994).

[43] Interview with city government economic officials in Lesozavodsk, Primorye (August 1994).

The "price" of these goods was actually the amount of ruble-denominated electricity debt that would be canceled. Costs plus a markup represented a lower boundary set by the fact that these transactions must be official (and therefore follow the tax rules on pricing) if they were to do the paying enterprises any good in terms of clearing debts on their bank accounts or avoiding fines for late payment. However, power company officials interviewed in 1994 found it very hard to monitor or affect the prices at which they were transferred goods under barter payments. Krasnoyarsk electricity executives reported that they had discovered that many enterprises had multiple prices on their goods, with a special, higher one reserved for the power company. (A sawmill executive in the same province confirmed this practice.) The Primorye power company had no capacity to monitor goods prices, though in the summer of 1994 plans were in the works to create a new service to deal with this issue. In Samara, officials were under the impression that they accepted goods at the prices that other customers got them, yet complained of difficulties in selling them at full price.

The practice of making price concessions through accepting "overvalued" goods would not have had much significance if power companies had simply been able to sell the received goods at their "actual" money value. Yet in selling these goods, the cost-plus tax regulation meant that the power company had to apply an *additional* profitability markup over the usually already exorbitant price generated by the goods' original producers.[44] As a result, these goods became even harder to sell for money. Occasionally a power company, through its own commercial organization, was able to make a money sale that its customer could not. In such cases, goods had in essence been transferred to a marketing agent who could realize "economies of scope" in selling goods from a wide variety of producers unable to sell for themselves. As the head of the power company in Krasnoyarsk put it, "The quality of these products was perfectly good, and there was no reason we couldn't sell them. But selling them took time and commercial expertise that the factories couldn't command."[45] Samaraenergo also had a special commercial section to sell goods received in barter, whereas in Primorye this function was handled by the supply division.

But sales for money were difficult, given the high prices attached to goods accepted in payment for electricity. In the more usual cases where no sale was forthcoming at the official accounting-determined money

---

[44] Interviews at Samaraenergo (April 1994) and Krasnoyarskenergo (June 1994).

[45] Story and quote from Andrew Rosenbaum "A Land of Buried Treasure" *Euromoney*, no. 312 (April 1995): 147–151. A similar though less-organized system was already functioning during my visit in June 1994. For plans to introduce a similar system for the entire power network, see *Finansovye Izvestiia*, 17–23 February 1994, 2.

price, the price needed somehow to be "lowered."[46] Again, this lowering could not show up in the accounting. One method—difficult due to the lack of contract enforcement mechanisms—was to sell the goods on credit at terms that did not adequately reflect inflation. A second was to pass the goods on further through what one can call "price-ratification" barter—that is, essentially to follow the strategy of the enterprise that made the in-kind payment in the first place. Many potential trading partners were also stuck with goods they could not sell for money at the accounting price. When barter was carried out at the ratios between cost-plus-markup prices, which seems often to have been the case,[47] on paper both sides showed that they took in the necessary amount. (In one such deal in Krasnoyarsk, for instance, the power company accepted railroad ties in payment for electricity from a local sawmill and was later able to trade the ties for pipes the power company needed from a factory in the western part of Russia.) Although such mechanisms may have allowed markets creakily and partially to clear, they did not generate prices that were in any way useful in the planning of production.

Given the debility of the Russian tax authorities, some readers may be inclined to dismiss the foregoing argument on the grounds that it gives an implausible weight to accounting regulations in determining enterprise behavior. It is worth expanding on the evidence for such an effect. Although the regulation was cited in a number of widely separated interviews I conducted, especially by energy system officials unable to cut prices on goods they had received in barter, these interviews were not conducted according to a standard protocol and in any event do not constitute a survey. Publicly accessible evidence tends to be indirect, but convincing. Aside from critiques of the cost-plus rule by various public figures and government officials,[48] the regulation also spawned political action that is impossible to interpret without concluding that enterprises experienced

[46] These strategies are drawn from interviews with officials at Krasnoyarskenergo (June 1994); I should stress that they themselves did not think of barter as a way of lowering the price of the good. Rather, they simply bartered what they were unable to sell for money; they said that lowering the money price was not an option they could choose because of tax regulations. At Samaraenergo, the relevant official complained that his efforts to cut prices on goods taken as in-kind payment had been frustrated; he was hoping that he could convince delinquent customers to give him an IOU, which he thought he could then sell at a discount.

[47] Interviews at Samaraenergo (April 1994) and Krasnoyarskenergo (June 1994); interview with livestock feed factory director in Primorskii krai (August 1994); interview with Krasnoyarsk deputy governor for economic policy (June 1994); interview with Samara deputy governor for economic policy (May 1994) (in the last two cases the discussion concerned pricing for barter taxes). Since barter that took place at other ratios would in some cases be a tax violation, those I interviewed would not have been likely to mention it.

[48] For example, former economics minister Andrei Nechaev cited this regulation as a major economic problem in *Moscow News*, no. 35, 2–8 September 1994, 9.

substantial constraints on lowering prices below costs. (Indeed, the politics of price flexibility is a major theme of chapter 6 of this book.) For instance, enterprises organized loud joint public criticisms of accounting rules increasing amortization of inherited assets, arguing that higher on-paper production costs forced unsustainable price rises.[49] Ministries and committees responsible for sectors of industry also sought the right to sell for less than the cost of production in debates within the government; such demands resulted in the issuance of a presidential order that very slightly softened pricing rules.[50]

Given power companies' weak ability to punish firms for failing to pay their bills, and their partially coerced agreement to give price breaks through accepting payment in goods, one might wonder why any electricity bills were paid in money at all. The direct deduction of electricity bills from official bank accounts meant that to avoid paying for electricity was also to exit the officially visible money economy, which involved certain costs.[51] Without an official bank account, it was impossible to get a legal loan, and even subsidized loans that arrived on an "arrested" account were immediately transferred to creditors with direct deduction rights.[52] If enterprises did not value their official bank accounts, electricity payments would have dried up much sooner. Still, fewer and fewer industrial enterprises found that they could afford the benefits of an official bank account when the cost was paying the full money price for electricity (and taxes as well), and they dropped out of the visible money economy altogether. Their bank accounts accumulated creditor demands, on which high interest-rate penalties were assessed, making a return to the world of money ever more difficult. These institutional concomitants of the exit

---

[49] *Volzhskaia Kommuna*, 12 February 1994, 1. For exactly parallel complaints, see "Press Conference of the Representatives of the Oil Companies LUKOIL, SLAVNEFT, SIDANKO, SURGUTNEFTEGAZ and IUKOS." Federal News Service, 8 February 1996.

[50] *Kommersant*, no. 31, 23 August 1994, 60. The order allowed sale for money below production costs with special prior permission of the tax authorities once there are demonstrable failures at selling it at the markup price. Barter transactions must take place at the same price as recent money sales or, if there are none, at least at production costs.

[51] For an argument that exiting the official economy denies firms access to its benefits, see Jeffrey Sachs, "Russia's Struggle with Stabilization: Conceptual Issues and Evidence," *World Bank Research Observer, Annual Conference Supplement* (1994): 57–80.

[52] Interview with director of a machinery factory, Krasnoyarsk, June 1994. Sometimes, however, it was possible to combine the benefits of an official bank account with successful evasion of the power company's bill collectors. One common scheme cited by power company officials was the transformation of subdivisions into legally independent firms, with bank accounts of their own but no institutional relationship with the electric power company. Electricity debts stemming from the operations of the subdivisions accumulate on the bank account of the parent enterprise, which was kept empty. Interviews at Samaraenergo (April 1994) and Dal'energo (August 1994). For a published example, see *Moskovskie Novosti*, no. 19, 8–15 May 1994, 8.

from the world of money were another indication of the consequences of using an alternate means of payment to alter prices.

To summarize the arguments of this section: When nonpayments to electric power companies began to increase from the fall of 1993, power companies were usually unable to insist on payment because they were in a weak strategic situation.[53] The only threat they had available, to disconnect nonpaying customers, was likely to be blocked by local authorities and was in any event too damaging to be credible in many cases, since power companies could hardly have pursued a policy of destroying all their customers. Payment was made in money by firms that had made the decision that the benefits of retaining an official bank account outweighed the cost of paying electricity bills (and taxes) in full and on time. For the rest of firms with empty bank accounts, whether these stemmed from deliberate hiding of income or simply from the inability to make any sales, power companies conceded to reduced payments (and the accumulation of debts) or payment for electricity in kind. The "prices" for such goods in terms of electricity debt they canceled tended to be unrealistically high compared with what the goods would have brought if sold on the open market, if indeed they could have been sold at all at an acceptable price. Through these complicated processes, firms whose official (and often unofficial) monetary position consisted of nothing but debts continued operation through barter.

With the emergence of this barter of the bankrupt, Russia reached the second stage of its triple movement. In Polanyi's description of the double movement, central banking arose as a protective deviation from the application of the commodity fiction to money (i.e., a self-regulating gold market) because of the danger of deflation. The threat of a deflation lay in its institutional effects on productive organizations. Prices fixed in prior contracts and serving as the basis for choices of what to produce cannot fall instantly in response to a general change in the price level. These institutional barriers to rapid downward price adjustment meant that the transition to a lower price level, even if relative prices would eventually be restored, could be lethal for profitable firms. According to Polanyi, even before the nineteenth century, merchants regularly adopted alternate

[53] Anders Åslund, *How Russia Became a Market Economy* (Washington: The Brookings Institution, 1995), 211, suggests that "the energy enterprises, especially Gazprom, were the last to cut deliveries if they were not paid, because they counted on Chernomyrdin's help." Although it is true, as noted in the following, that the fuel and energy sector was relatively successful in lobbying for central assistance, it is a mistake to suggest that as a result energy enterprises were unconcerned about extracting payment. Immediate payment from a customer is *very* much to be preferred to the at best eventual and at any rate unreliable compensation from the state.

means of payment as a solution to this problem: "Token money was developed at an early to date to shelter trade from . . . enforced deflations that accompanied the use of specie [metallic money]."[54] In the nineteenth century, the rising importance of international trade led to a widespread embrace of the gold standard, and the creation of national central banks that performed on a grander scale the same function of defending business from deflation through creating alternatives to specie. Polanyi is silent, however, on why and how a national response to the danger of deflation replaced more local ones.

The barter of the bankrupt was also a response to the institutional consequences of downward price movements. In the case of Russia, however, the crude cost-plus-markup pricing rules that applied in different ways both to power companies and their customers gave a particular force and form to the institutional demand to show a formal profit over costs incurred at a prior price level. To make possible the numerical calculation of costs, arbitrary answers were given to fundamentally unanswerable questions about past (the proper valuation of equipment allocated under the Soviet economy) and future (the prospects of the Russian economy). Formal price reduction was not possible even when money-backed demand was not sufficient to pay the prices so generated. Alternate means of payment preserved formal prices. Unlike the national token currencies that Polanyi described, however, these alternate means of payment—the delivery of electricity or goods—were generated in local political arenas, in bargaining between power companies and their debtors shaped by the interventions of local authorities. The barter of the bankrupt did not affirm national integration under the aegis of the central bank, but rather called that integration into question.

Local and Federal Fiscal Responses to the Barter of the Bankrupt

Power companies trying to force delinquent customers to pay their bills in money ought to have had an ally in the state. The empty bank accounts of enterprises operating outside the visible money economy frustrated not only electricity suppliers but also the agents of the fisc. As states drive to expand their tax capacity, they tend to embrace the slogan "pay in money, or pay the consequences." As Joseph Schumpeter put it in a classic essay, "Tax bill in hand, the state penetrated the private economies and won increasing dominion over them. The tax brings money and calculat-

---

[54] Polanyi, *Great Transformation*, 193. For similar arguments on the functions of decentralized token monies before the nineteenth century, see Ron Michener, "Shortages of Money in Colonial New England: An Explanation," University of Virginia, 1983.

ing spirit into corners in which they do not dwell as yet, and thus becomes a formative factor in the very organism which has developed it."[55] A full explanation for the spread of barter must include not only reasons why parties to exchange chose this form of exchange, but also an account of why barter was not eliminated by the state.

We can begin this account by considering the situation of local authorities when faced with the decision of whether to authorize the shutdown of an enterprise not paying its electricity bills. They confronted a choice between eliminating an enterprise in serious trouble and forcing the power company to bear some costs. The latter choice was seen as feasible largely because electricity producers were perceived as relatively resilient in the face of nonpayments and barter. Some of the reasons for this resilience were the political factors analyzed more closely in the next section—the electric power sector had relatively strong political influence in Moscow, and in crisis situations central authorities were usually willing to supply emergency funds. But there were other reasons power companies were relatively resilient. First, the very low ratio of variable to fixed costs in the operation of power plants makes the short-term opportunity costs of supplying electricity for free quite low, though in the long term this amounts to a drawing down of the fixed investments in these plants. Second, electricity companies in the immediate post-price-liberalization period accumulated significant financial power. Indeed, local authorities and many employees of other industries often believed that power companies disproportionately benefited in the early stages of reform, when price rises, though regulated, nevertheless allowed power companies to pay very high wages. Thus, when power companies too began to face harder times with nonpayments, there was some sentiment that earlier gains compensated for later difficulties.[56] In at least a temporary and practical fashion there was some truth to this idea, since power companies had used their financial strength to build up their shares in the capital stock of local banks, which in some cases enabled the extraction of loans even from bankers who had become uncertain of the prospects for repayment.[57]

The relative financial resilience of electricity producers may explain why forcing them to bear the costs of nonpayments and barter was feasible, but it certainly did not compel such a choice. The roots of local leaders' great hesitation to sanction the shutdown of a nonpaying enterprise lay in

[55] Joseph Schumpeter, "The Crisis of the Tax State," in *The Economics and Sociology of Capialism*, ed. Richard Swedberg (Princeton: Princeton University Press, 1991), 99–140, at 108.
[56] For representative sentiments along these lines, see *Samarskie Izvestiia*, 12 March 1994, 1; *Delovaia Sibir'*, no. 21, 4–10 June 1993, 5; this was also a constant theme raised in my interviews in Vladivostok in the fall of 1993.
[57] See the figures on Dal'energo loans in *Krasnoe Znamia*, 28 September 1993, 1.

weighty political and practical considerations. In the pattern familiar from the long stream of literature stemming from Mancur Olson's *Logic of Collective Action*, an aggressive policy in support of electricity producers had many enemies with a minimum of collective action problems and few organized supporters.[58] As noted in the preceding chapter, Russia's directors' corpus was a spent force in national politics by 1993. But on the local level the shared opposition of the leaders of large industrial enterprises to high electricity prices and vigorous bill collection could rapidly give rise to at least a tactical alliance when required.[59] In Primorye Province, which inherited a weak and expensive power system from the Soviet period, opposition to a local administration that had given strong backing to the electric power company helped give rise to an exceptionally coherent alliance of industrialists, which managed to arrange the removal of the province's governor in the spring of 1993.[60]

Even if a somewhat stricter attitude toward electricity debtors on the part of provincial governors would have been politically feasible, it is difficult to see what reasoning would have pushed them to adopt such an attitude. The argument at the core of the literature on the "politics of stabilization" is that the suffering of the organizationally and politically visible victims of reform must be endured in the interests of the organizationally and politically invisible beneficiaries. Such an argument can appeal only to political leaders who can conceive themselves as representatives of the entire community to which the postulated eventual benefits of market reform would accrue. For leaders of subnational jurisdictions it is likely to be less than compelling.

This is especially true because local leaders were completely bereft of alternatives to the social and infrastructural services provided by enterprises that would be shut down.[61] Russia's extraordinary housing shortage made opportunities for labor mobility minimal, and the empty coffers of local budgets were unable to cope with present tasks, let alone with unemployment compensation.[62] Tolerating enterprise tax and bill evasion allowed enterprises to pay at least some salaries to their workers.[63] Moreover, the

[58] Mancur Olson, *The Logic of Collective Action: Public Goods and the Theory of Groups* (New York: Schocken Books, 1965).

[59] For an example in Samara Province, see *Volzhskaia Kommuna*, 8 February 1994, 1 and *Delo*, 11 February 1994, 1.

[60] The directors' discontent focused largely around prices, not collection of bills; that the anti-power-company bias of the new local regime also involved blocking shutdowns when the problem of nonpayments became more acute subsequently became quite clear (interviews in Vladivostok, October–November 1993, June 1994).

[61] Cf. Wallich "Intergovernmental Finances," 81.

[62] On the local budget squeeze, see ibid., 77.

[63] The mayor of Lesosibirsk in Krasnoyarsk Province made this point quite explicitly in a July 1994 interview; concern for the fate of employees was also cited by the assistant governor for

Soviet state had no reasons to make distinctions between public and private infrastructure, so that the sewage or heating of sections of major cities or entire smaller ones could be technologically inseparable from that of the industrial enterprises around which they were built. As a result, shutdown would mean massive and expensive problems for which there were no funds.[64]

All of this made local government willing to ignore or even facilitate firms' exit from the officially visible money economy and gave them strong reason to hope that current levels of final demand were artificially low and would at some point increase. In one of the provinces visited for this study, Samara, which had a highly militarized industrial economy, the administration official who would have had to give sanction to shutdowns believed that nonpayments were caused by the government's failure to pay for defense industry production it ordered in 1993. Shutdowns would thus attack the symptom rather than the cause of nonpayments and were "not a solution to the problem."[65] Key officials in a Siberian province investigated, Krasnoyarsk, were explicitly antimonetarist and believed that money should be printed to the level necessary to service the current level of nominal transactions in the economy. In the meantime, as a deputy governor put it, "Until the central government has corrected its line . . . it is necessary maximally to retreat from monetary circulation on the territory of the province, that is, to strengthen the mutual ties of enterprises, and try to carry out payments in kind [tovarnye vzaimoraschety]."[66] To the extent that barter on such motivations allowed production and sale of goods to continue, the view that final monetary demand was artificially limited became something of a self-fulfilling prophecy.

Relative power company resilience, fears of political opposition, unwillingness to suffer the burdens of a harsh policy when the benefits might accrue elsewhere, an absence of alternatives to the social and infrastructural services vested with enterprises under state socialism, and hopes that the economic depression would eventually pass, then, all contributed to local

energy and transport, Samara Province (May 1994), as a reason not to disconnect the power of those behind in their electricity debts.

[64] Interviews in Lesosibirsk, Krasnoyarsk Province, where the local power and heat generation capacity was on the territory of the town's major employer, August 1994; and Lesozavodsk, Primorye, where the town's sewage processing plant was on the premises of a major employer, July 1994.

[65] Interview with the assistant governor for energy and transport, Samara Province (May 1994). They have occasionally allowed shutdowns, as in Delo, 20 August 1993, 1; here local enterprises were trying to get government involved.

[66] Deputy governor V. D. Kuz'min, paraphrased in Krasnoyarskii Rabochii, 6 May 1994, 1. Kuz'min confirmed the accuracy of this quote and expanded on his monetary policy views in an interview (June 1994).

authorities' reluctance to allow the electricity cutoffs that would drive firms into the visible money economy or out of business. Whatever the motives, the policy of tolerating the barter of the bankrupt had important fiscal consequences. Tax officials were painfully aware that enterprises' in-kind receipts could not easily be taxed, even if officially recorded. Some idea of the magnitude of the problem is given by the huge growth in tax arrears (*nedoimki*) from the fall of 1993. Arrears were taxes officially assessed on the basis of a firm's records but which the firm has no money to pay. Both barter (when declared) and nonpayments produced arrears. At the end of the first half of 1994, arrears to the federal budget had reached 7.5 trillion rubles, an amount equal to a quarter of the tax revenues actually collected.[67] Because the tax authorities, like electric power companies, had the right automatically deduct payments from bank accounts, the growth of arrears was also a further indication of a widespread exit from the visible money economy.

Unsurprisingly, Russia's national authorities reacted to this situation with measures designed to improve tax collection, many of which were spelled out in a set of presidential orders on the economy in May 1994. Most of these measures concentrated on making it more difficult for enterprises to conceal money being held in banks.[68] However, a tax regulation in June gave fiscal authorities new powers to confiscate and sell property and production from delinquent enterprises. Although one newspaper described the order as "a return to federal taxes collected both in money and in kind," in fact the intent was to convert any confiscated goods into money. In practice, this meant the state was to attempt to succeed at selling for money goods their producers had been unable to sell. Available evidence on the implementation of this measure indicates that success was minimal.[69] The administrative difficulties involved were manifest. The volume of arrears to all levels of the budget system as of September 1, 1994, represented well over $39,000 per employee of the State Tax Service and State Tax Police. The conditions under which such a large volume of sales was to be made were not propitious. The measure called for tax authorities to attempt to sell production at the enterprises' cost-

---

[67] This figure somewhat understates arrears, since it refers only to the two most important taxes, the profits tax and the VAT. Actual tax receipts for the federal budget from *Finansy*, no. 9 (1994): 61; arrears data from *Segodnia*, 1 September 1994, 11. The scale of arrears may also be gauged by the fact that the minister of finance estimated the federal budget losses due to direct tax evasion to be much smaller than the losses from arrears. *Finansy*, no. 12 (1994): 4. For a clear explanation of arrears, see *Segodnia*, 5 July 1994, 12.

[68] For instance, enterprises were permitted to have only one bank account; debts subject to direct deduction could now be confiscated from hard-currency accounts of firms whose ruble accounts were empty, etc. The orders were printed in *Rossiiskaia Gazeta*, 25 May 1994, 4.

[69] For a survey of the problems implementing a very similar order signed one and a half years later, see *Finansovye Izvestiia*, 16 April 1996.

markup price, with permission to reduce the price after two months if no sales had been made. If warehouse space was unavailable, confiscated goods were to be stored on the premises of the tax-delinquent enterprise until they could be sold.[70] The head of the State Tax Service, Vladimir Gusev, stated in a speech published in November that even the threat of confiscating property had often caused enterprises to discover money to pay their tax debts; something over 1.3 billion rubles (around $600,000 at the time) had been collected in Tatarstan in this way. Gusev called for expanded use of this measure, but even if every other province and republic in Russia found it as effective as Tatarstan, this would have been only a tiny part of the total problem.[71]

Whatever the actual administrative outcome, the federal attempt to forcibly generate money income from tax delinquents operating outside the money economy followed the typical pattern of state-driven monetary consolidation. The response of local authorities was different in essence. For the reasons already indicated, local governments in the regions visited for this study (and, all evidence indicates, elsewhere in Russia), did not launch efforts to bring enterprises into the visible money economy for tax purposes. Instead, they moved to accept goods from those enterprises that could not pay their taxes in money. For local governments, such collection of taxes *in natura* was not a way station preceding a subsequent sale of these goods for money. Rather, local authorities' efforts focused on finding ways to make direct use of these goods, or to barter them for other goods locally needed.

Taxation in kind was organized largely by clearing operations (*zachety*) in which accumulated local tax arrears were canceled in return for the production of debtor enterprises. When possible, authorities made direct use of the goods taken in this way. The Krasnoyarsk administration, for example, used building materials accepted as taxes from local firms for construction projects financed by the budget.[72] In Samara, automotive fuels, fertilizers, and pesticides were accepted in taxes and distributed to farms in lieu of budget subsidies.[73] When goods available as in-kind tax payments could not be put to direct use, some way of exchanging them needed to be found; here the clearing operations become more complicated. Often

---

[70] The order (issued jointly by the Ministry of Finance, the Tax Police, and the State Tax Service) is described in *Kommersant-Daily*, 30 June 1994, 2 and *Segodnia*, 5 July 1994, 12. Before confiscating finished production, tax authorities were supposed to take various "luxuries" such as cars or office furniture "not directly involved in the productive process."

[71] *Finansy*, no. 11 (1994): 7.

[72] Interview with the deputy governor for economic policy, July 1994. For instances of local tax remissions in return for social services supplied by enterprises, see Wallich, "Intergovernmental Finance," 81.

[73] *Volzhkaia Kommuna*, 12 March 1994, 1.

tax arrears from the local power company were canceled in return for production from one of the power company's debtors for which the power company itself had no use. One province administration that had been unable to pay for medicine for a local hospital intended to solve the problem by retiring tax arrears due it from the local power company, which in return would supply medicine that it in turn had accepted in payment from one of its debtors.[74] Similar arrangements were encountered in two of the provinces visited for this study.[75]

These anecdotes illustrate how local administrations, unable to insist on money exchange practices, created some capacity to tax in kind and made use of this capacity to maintain critical local services. In so doing, they were drawn into arranging multilateral barter deals that made operation in the barter economy more practicable for local firms (by overcoming the problem of the double coincidence of wants required for a barter transaction). Local governments' ability to tolerate the operation of firms outside the visible money economy due to in-kind taxation capabilities thus provided a crucial facilitating circumstance for the increase of barter.

It is difficult to gauge the scale of local in-kind taxation at this early phase.[76] One indicator that its scale had become quite significant by late 1994 comes from the reaction of federal tax authorities. Most taxes in Russia were divided between local and federal budgets according to percentages that varied by the tax. In-kind taxes accepted by local governments counted only against the local portions of taxes, however, and thus were not shared with the federal budget.[77] By late fall, the head of the federal State Tax Service was beginning to express concerns about this practice.[78] In December 1994, new regulations were promulgated designed to give federal authorities better information on the scale of taxation in kind.[79]

---

[74] This example is reported by a tax official from Saratov, in *Finansy*, no. 10 (1994): 28.

[75] This system was most developed in Samara (interview at Samaraenergo, April 1994, interview with the deputy governor for economic policy, May 1994); and plans were in the works in Krasnoyarsk (interview at Krasnoyarskenergo; interview with deputy governor for the wood industry, June 1994). Primorye had also accepted taxes in kind (interview with tax inspectorate official, August 1994), but it proved impossible to ascertain the further fate of the goods accepted in this way.

[76] The only official interviewed in any of the three provinces who would guess at a figure was the deputy governor for economic policy in Krasnoyarsk, who estimated that 15 to 20 percent of Krasnoyarsk's budget income in the first quarter of 1994 was in kind (interview, July 1994).

[77] Tax inspectorate officials in Krasnoyarsk (July 1994) and Vladivostok (August 1994) reported that goods had been accepted only in payment of local portions of taxes.

[78] *Finansy*, no. 11 (1994): 5.

[79] See *Normativnye akty po finansam, nalogam, strakhovaniiu i bukhgalterskomu uchetu (prilozhenie k zhurnalu "Finansy")*, no. 2 (1995): 30–33.

The concern of federal tax officials over local in-kind taxation underscores the distinct situations in which central and local authorities found themselves with respect to the imperatives of promoting nonmonetary exchange. In his *Philosophy of Money*, Georg Simmel suggests that "independence," in contrast to autarkic nondependence, should be used to refer not to a lack of dependence on others in general, but to an absence of *concrete* dependencies on *particular* ways of providing for given needs.[80] Independence in Simmel's sense is a precondition for a single-minded pursuit of money income. The fiscal organs of an ideal-typical "independent" state are indifferent to the substance of the economic activity carried on by taxpaying organizations and individuals and are concerned only that it yield taxable money revenues. The collection and spending of tax revenue can be organizationally entirely isolated. What this implies is, as Max Weber noted, a "fully developed money economy" in which all that is necessary to the state's functioning can be purchased.[81]

Russia's local authorities found themselves in a situation very far from this ideal-type of Simmelian independence. Indeed, they were enmeshed in a thicket of concrete dependencies. The clearest example were power companies themselves, also in tax arrears due to nonpayments by their customers. No local government could take the attitude that it would simply dismantle and sell furnaces and power lines in response to an inability to pay taxes in money. Power companies were certainly a far end of what is clearly a spectrum of indispensability. Yet the leaders of Russia's provinces were inheritors to an economy built on the premise that no enterprise would ever cease production. As a result, large enterprises tend to cluster very close to this extreme of indispensability. Weber argued: "A political body based purely on deliveries in kind does not promote the development of capitalism. On the contrary, it hinders it to the extent to which it involves rigid binding of the structure of production in a form which, from a point of view of profit making enterprise, is irrational."[82] The in-kind taxation of local government did not bind local enterprise to unprofitable activities. It represented, rather, the rigid binding of local government itself to the foundations of the local natural economy. Local governments became not agents of monetary consolidation, but facilitators of the defense of productive organization embodied in the barter of the bankrupt.

[80] Georg Simmel, *The Philosophy of Money*, trans. Tom Bottomore and David Frisby from a first draft by Kaethe Mengelberg, 2d enlarged ed. (London: Routledge, 1990), 300–301.
[81] Max Weber, *Economy and Society: An Outline of Interpretive Sociology*, ed. Guenther Roth and Claus Wittich, 2 vols. (Berkeley: University of California Press, 1978), 1:351.
[82] Ibid., 199.

Moving Moscow: Regional and Sectoral Lobbying

The ingenuity of power companies and local governments in adapting to the barter of the bankrupt should not mask the huge problems with which it presented them. Despite the best efforts of those forced to organize barter trade, what Russians increasingly termed "live" money was still indispensable to make many purchases and, above all, to pay salaries. As enterprises accumulated tax and electricity payment arrears, any receipts arriving on their bank accounts were whisked away to pay their old debts. Power companies themselves fell into this situation as money payments to them shrank. Debts for wages mounted rapidly in tandem with the spread of barter. Measures to address wage problems through alternative means of payment, though common, were very distasteful. The governor of Krasnoyarsk, for instance, recommended that energy sector firms develop commercial operations to sell the goods of their debtors and proposed that they achieve "elimination of 50% of their debts to workers for salary through giving them consumer goods, food produce, and construction materials."[83] Krasnoyarsk's government also made a largely unsuccessful effort to convince schoolteachers to accept their salaries in sausages and other food goods paid as taxes by local producers. Some of the teachers, who had not been paid in several months, were willing, but worried about the "price" at which they would receive these goods.[84]

In light of the limits on local solutions, the need for live money fueled appeals to Moscow. Regional leaders made such appeals directly, as did the sectoral elites affected by their policies.

The pattern of regional lobbying was determined by the structure of the electrical power system each province inherited from the Soviet era, which set up particular political tasks that must be fulfilled if electric power is to be used as a source of subsidy. In Samara and Krasnoyarsk, which are home to hydropower plants, enormous investments in the energy sector were made in the Soviet era. Here the issue was one of ownership. The fate of these power stations as the national system was partially privatized in 1993 became the object of major center-regional controversy. The privatization scheme mandated that all power stations above a particular size should remain property of the federal system, whereas smaller and more out-of-date stations were to become local property.[85] Because the intent of the national power company was to set prices to reflect investment levels sufficient to reproduce systemwide capacity,[86] under this plan regions home to

---

[83] *Krasnoiarskii Rabochii*, 10 June 1994, 1.

[84] *Krasnoiarskii Komsomolets*, 4 June 1994, 1.

[85] The privatization program is described in *Kommersant-Daily*, 15 January 1993, 4.

[86] Interview with the deputy governor in charge of energy policy, Krasnoyarsk, July 1994. On the price policy implications of hydroplant privatization, see *Izvestiia*, 22 September 1993, 4.

large hydropower plants would not capture particular price benefits therefrom. The result would be higher prices for local electricity, feeding more nonmonetary price cuts.

As a result, local leaders in Samara and Krasnoyarsk fought to retain control over their hydropower plants. In Samara, though executive authorities discussed the need to acquire ownership of the local plant, they never seriously opened the battle for it. Instead, a strategy of projecting to Moscow an image of a loyal and proreform region paid off in a series of special orders from Yeltsin and the Council of Ministers that among other things mandated special low prices for Samara consumers on the output of the hydropower plant.[87] Krasnoyarsk authorities adopted a more aggressive approach of challenging the constitutionality of the privatization order that was to strip them of ownership of their much larger hydropower systems. After winning its case before the Constitutional Court, the province was able to work out a deal for shared ownership that retained substantial local control in price policy.[88]

Other regions with less fortunate inheritances from the Soviet period found that in the context of hardening lateral budget constraints, nonpayments to electrical power companies quickly raised bedrock problems of keeping the furnaces running. Regions that relied on fuel shipments from outside their borders were in an especially difficult position, as out-region coal mines and oil refineries were little interested in barter and increasingly unwilling to ship without payment in advance.[89]

Such regions, of which Primorye was one, were thoroughly dependent on central subsidies. In the latter part of 1993, the leadership of this province sought to combine a policy of defending debtor enterprises from

[87] On privatization of the hydropower plant, see *Delo*, 7 May 1993, 1; 10 November 1993, 13. On local leadership's lobbying and the eventual decision to reduce hydroplant power rates for local consumers, see *Delo*, 19 March 1993, 1; 31 December 1993, 9; *Volzhskaia Kommuna*, 22 March 1994, 1. For evidence of the Samara leadership's consistent proreform and pro-government image, see *ABV: Ezhenedel'naia Regional'naia Delovaia Gazeta*, 9–15 February 1994, 1; as an example, the governor seriously toned down the angry demands of local industrialists before agreeing to sign an appeal to the government they had drafted; *Volzhskaia Kommuna*, 8 February 1994, 1; *Delo*, 11 February 1994, 1.

[88] See *Delovaia Sibir'*, no. 13, 9–15 April 1993, 3; *Krasnoiarskii Rabochii*, 10 June 1993, 1; 25 June 1993, 1; *Izvestiia*, 22 September 1993, 4; interview with the head of the state property committee for Krasnoyarsk territory, June 1994.

[89] On barter, interview at Dal'energo (August 1994); Primorye had previously been able to barter fish for out-region fuel. On demands for money payment by out-region suppliers, *Krasnoe Znamia*, 20 June 1994, 1; 19 February 1994, 3. By contrast, Krasnoyarsk was able to fuel its coal-fired plants with local coal by organizing barter; interview with the assistant governor for economic policy, June 1994. Samara purchased natural gas for its furnaces by bartering cars from the giant VAZ plant (interview with assistant governor for energy policy, May 1994); by early 1994, VAZ's cars were increasingly hard to sell and the plan seemed likely to come under strain.

power company cutoff efforts while extracting money from Moscow on the basis of critically low levels of coal supplies.[90] Although Moscow regularly promised money to purchase coal, it appears to have delivered inconsistently at best, and suppliers stopped shipment in the face of nonpayments.[91] Moscow's orders to out-region suppliers to deliver coal without prepayment also appear to have been ignored.[92] As a result, the province struggled through a winter of brownouts and no hot water. All of this issued in a desperate local political struggle over whether to pursue more vigorous electric power debt collection to yield live money for purchase of out-region supplies.[93] Finally, in June 1994, the local governor—who as noted previously had come to power a year earlier at the head of a movement of industrialists united above all by anger at the high prices and aggressive debt collection of the power company—ordered the cutoff of any enterprises more than a month overdue in payments.[94] Interviewed in August, though, the head of the Primorye power company's bill-collecting department felt that even though the local administration had become more supportive of cutting off delinquents, there was little effect due to the absence of bankruptcy legislation. For the first eight months of 1994, the province's power company was paid only for about 64 percent of the electricity it supplied, and that payment was largely in kind, despite the fact that local energy prices had been frozen (in contradiction of regulations) for more than a year.[95] The energy situation in Primorye continued to be disastrous for the following four years.

The logic of the Primorye strategy was well expressed in a comment directed at a top government official: "The government can fire all the provincial governors, but no fuel oil will appear as a result. The risk of freezing the towns and villages will remain, however. And if this happens, the money will be found, and the fuel oil will be shipped. Why let things go all the way to a crisis?"[96] The danger of allowing power systems to fail seemed to be so serious as to make any commitment to such things as monetary restriction irrelevant.[97] But the upshot was merely to demonstrate how limited was Moscow's capacity to deliver reliably money where it had

---

[90] *Vladivostok*, 19 November 1993, 2; *Novosti*, 12 October 1993.

[91] *Utro Rossii*, 9 December 1993, 1; 22 February 1994, 1; *Zolotoi Rog*, 11 January 1994, 1.

[92] For the order, see *Segodnia*, 25 November 1993, 2.

[93] *Krasnoe Znamia*, 19 February 1994, 3.

[94] *Krasnoe Znamia*, 20 June 1994, 1.

[95] Calculated from information provided by Dal'energo.

[96] *Segodnia*, 25 November 1993, 2. In context, it is a little vague whether it was the governor of Primorye who uttered this phrase or some other governor; in any event, it expresses an attitude that the governor of Primorye would have found congenial.

[97] As economist Sergei Glazev put it, " . . . any government, even if it is monetarist three times over, will have to give money under the threat that there will be no light and no heat in Moscow." *Segodnia*, 11 December 1993, 10.

promised. When the lights went out in Vladivostok, Primorye's capital, it was a dramatic if distressing demonstration of the point that the practical problem facing the Russian state was not how to make a credible commitment to monetary restraint but how to make a credible promise to subsidize. Nevertheless, desperate for live money, many regions found few alternatives to asking for such subsidies.

Not only regional lobbyists pursued live money in Moscow's corridors of power; sectoral elites were also active in seeking live money for the enterprises they supervised. The problems raised by nonpayments and payment in kind raised for electricity companies gave rise to demands for subsidy articulated by the branch Ministry of Fuel and Energy (Mintopenergo). At a meeting in June 1994 on preparation for the coming winter, for example, Mintopenergo officials argued that nonpayments meant that central support would be needed to ensure enough money could be found to pay for winter stockpiles.[98] Under the leadership of Yuri Shafranik, former governor of oil-rich Tiumen Province who took over the Mintopenergo post in January 1993, the ministry mounted continual press campaigns to draw attention to the nonpayments problem, which as already noted, began seriously to affect the fuel sector even earlier than the electric power sector, since much of the former did not have direct deduction rights. As electricity nonpayments expanded the ministry broadened its lobbying to address this issue as well.

In general, Mintopenergo had some success in lobbying for subsidized credits for the enterprises it supervised, though in practice these credits were regularly not issued due to the reluctance of banks to accept responsibility for their repayment.[99] Even when credits did reach fuel and energy producers, this left them paying interest on loans made to compensate for customer nonpayments. As one oil industry executive put it, "They've made us into a source of indirect subsidies for the entire economy, and then they suggest that we take out a loan to improve our situation."[100] Increasingly, Shafranik's lobbying focused on convincing central authorities to hand out loans to nonpaying customers, which could use them to pay off their debts to the energy sector.[101] The energy sector's efforts to procure low-interest loans for its customers as well as its (forced) acceptance of nonpayments compensated for by federal government benefits demonstrated how the sector in effect became a lobbyist for the regional leaders whose actions helped to generate the nonpayments problem in the first place.

[98] *Rossiiskaia Gazeta*, 25 June 1994, 1.
[99] See chapter 3.
[100] The head of *Sibnefteprovod*, quoted in *Kommersant-Daily*, 12 January 1993, 1.
[101] Iu. K. Shafranik, A. G. Kozyrev, and A. L. Samsuev, "TEK v usloviiakh krizisa" (The fuel and energy complex in crisis conditions), *Eko: Ekonomika i organizatsiia promyshlennogo proizvodstva*, no. 1 (1994): 63–74.

An alternative to asking Moscow for new distributions of live money was to ask it for permission to retain live money otherwise destined for the federal tax coffers. Regional leaders sought permission to retain locally collected federal taxes to fund federal programs in their territory, though this proposal was sharply rejected by Prime Minister Viktor Chernomyrdin.[102] Sectoral leaders sought an easing of the arrests of enterprises' bank accounts to allow them to retain some share of live money earnings to use for wage payments. By August 1994, coal producers and wood processors, for instance, had been granted special rights to retain 50 percent of receipts on their bank accounts.[103] A top tax official complained in November that identical rights had been extended to "a number of important sectors."[104] After September 1994, all goods-producing enterprises were able to retain 30 percent of all money that came to their bank account to pay salaries for workers, before any taxes or other bills were deducted from their account.[105] (These temporary rights were to last only until the end of 1994 but were extended into 1996.[106] Debate on the priority of wage payments over tax and debts payments remained a major political issue through 1998, though with time one increasingly fought out in Parliament and the courts rather than within the executive branch.)

Moscow's intermittently positive response to lobbying for live money done at the national level—whether through requests for changes in power plant ownership allowing lower prices and less barter, direct subsidies, or pleas for an easing of confiscation of tax debts—represented the culmination of Russia's triple movement. Demands for protection from the institutional effects of enterprises' inability to make a formal profit had been transmitted from the local to the national political arena. As federal authorities made decisions on whether and to whom to allocate monetary subsidies, what was at stake directly was monetary policy. But the form and purpose of lobbyists' demands for money had been shaped by the failure of federal authorities to secure monetary consolidation in regions throughout Russia. The national politics of the cash register persisted, but these politics rested on and concealed a deeper and more fundamental struggle over rule and control in local arenas.

[102] *Rossiiskie Vesti*, 30 August 1994, 1–2.
[103] Interviews in Lesozavodsk and Luchegorsk, Primorye, August 1994.
[104] *Finansy*, no. 11 (1994): 3–7.
[105] "Ob ispol'zovanii predpriiatiiami material'nogo proizvodstva i biudzhetnymi organizatsiiami sredstv, postupaiushchikh na raschetnye scheta" (On use by enterprises in the material production sector and budget organizations of funds transferred to their bank accounts). Joint telegram of the State Tax Service and Ministry of Finance, no. 01–35/64, VP-6–13/349, 14 September 1994. Inforis.
[106] *Segodnia*, 16 January 1996, 3.

Conclusion

This, then, was Russia's triple movement. In its first stage, more and more of Russia's state-owned or newly private enterprises dropped out of the officially visible money economy as their bank accounts emptied, inventories of unsold goods gathered dust, potential creditors followed the newly audible counsel of their pocketbooks and refused to finance money-losing ventures, and the central government's ability to choose the recipients of its largess evaporated. Power company access to enterprise bank accounts was no longer an effective bill collection mechanism, and non-payments to electric power began to rise. In the second stage, the threat that nonpaying enterprises would have their power disconnected proved hollow, due to the devastating nature of the sanction and the interference of local authorities. At best, the threat of disconnection could extract in-kind payment at a price that was effectively much lower, though regarded as identical in the numerical world of tax collectors and accountants. Alternate means of payment protected enterprises that could not make a formal profit in terms of the rigid and arbitrary prices of the money economy from destruction.

Provincial governments could allow themselves to push the electric power sector into accommodating partial or in-kind payment. Although the spread of nonmonetary exchange raised fiscal difficulties, local authorities were able to organize in-kind taxation of electricity customers whose empty bank accounts signified their exit from the visible money economy. Provincial officials were also confident that the power sector would be relatively resilient in the face of difficulties. Their confidence stemmed in part from political factors: the strength of corporate organizations representing the fuel and energy complex and the perception of Moscow's unwillingness to permit wintertime collapse of systems that ensured heating to the population. And indeed, in the final stage of the triple movement, the federal government did regularly seek to satisfy, albeit partially and ineffectively, demands for the live money that the barter of the bankrupt could not completely replace.

Perhaps the most controversial aspect of *The Great Transformation* is Polanyi's invocation of "the principle of social protection." Though Polanyi suggests that this principle, like the competing principle of economic liberalism, is associated with "definite social forces," he insists that the clashes and alliances provoked by the monetary interests of these social forces are not enough to explain the rise of the protective response to the depredations of self-regulating markets. Indeed, arguments focusing on interest-driven class actions "all but completely obstructed an over-all view of market society, and of the function of [broadly understood] protectionism in such a society. . . . Ultimately, what made things happen were the interests of society as a whole, though their defense fell primarily to one section of the population in preference to another."[107]

This rather metaphysical image, in which the spirit of societal protection hovers over the social world until descending into one or another interest group, may seem outlandish in the context of contemporary political economy. Surely one cannot ascribe all deviations from the most consistent of market liberalisms to a universal urge for the "self-protection of society"; if this were adequate, the whole thriving school of comparative politics that focuses on the shaping of a variety of "market economies" under the impact of political struggles would be irrelevant. Indeed, even the movements for trade protection and against the deflationary strictures of the gold standard Polanyi cites as examples of the defense of society-wide interests have since been less mystically and quite convincingly analyzed in terms of the interests of social forces by Peter Gourevitch.[108] In our Russian parallel, industrialists' attempts to pressure local officials to block aggressive moves by debt collectors has, of course, a straightforward materialist explanation. Nor would it seem necessary to wrap the political logic of what Philip Hanson has called "Not-in-My-Backyard Stabilization" in glorious metaphysical raiment.[109]

Yet explanatory leverage can be salvaged from Polanyi's emphasis on an innate tendency to defend "the human and natural components of the social fabric."[110] Polanyi offers the insight that there is a social sine qua non, that, whatever the specifics of politics, the prospect of hideous social cataclysms will force a policy reaction out of all but the most rare and virulent of regimes. While one may debate whether the demise of, say, *Junker* agriculture ought to qualify for characterization in Polanyi's apocalyptic terms, it is possible to move his approach beyond an ethereal functionalism when the "social fabric" is *concretely institutionalized,* when bedrock tasks of social reproduction are the direct responsibility of identifiable organizations.

For Russian local administrations, the social fabric and the economic fabric are one. The absence of possibilities for labor mobility, the prevalence of one- or few-factory towns, and the intertwining of "public" and "private" physical infrastructures make "the defense of productive organization" emphasized by Polanyi as one aspect of the double movement a virtual imperative.[111] Local enterprise efforts at survival are coextensive with survival of critical sections of the local community. For local politics, then,

---

[107] Polanyi, *Great Transformation,* 152, 161–162.
[108] Peter Gourevitch, *Politics in Hard Times* (Ithaca: Cornell University Press, 1986).
[109] Philip Hanson, "Economic Change and the Russian Provinces," in *Transformation from Below: Local Power and the Political Economy of Post-Communist Transitions,* ed. John Gibson and Philip Hanson (Cheltenham, UK: Edward Elgar, 1996), 179–216.
[110] Polanyi, *Great Transformation,* 150.
[111] Cf. Wallich, "Intergovernmental Finances," 81.

the appeal to an ethereal principle of social protection is a huge but nonetheless forgivable oversimplification. In only one of the three cases studied here did provincial authorities even begin an attempt to force local enterprise to pay money prices for electricity, and this attempt ended with the political coalescence of industrialists and a change of local regime.[112] In the two other cases, local authorities protected established industrial enterprises from the effects of the formal price institutions to the maximum of their ability.

The idea of a social sine qua non can have no place in a world of numerical assessments of costs and benefits—it introduces an impossibility, like a division by zero. In the face of the incommensurable substantive economy, money retreated from the formal economy. As local administrations scrambled with ever-decreasing effectiveness to defend local industry from destruction, they found themselves condoning or even promoting the demolition of the price mechanism and a massive exit of industry from the money economy. This exit threatened the integration of the broader Russian economic and social space and left regions with vital dependencies on other parts of the country facing disaster as barter proved to have largely local purchasing power.

The prospect of this disaster began the final phase of Russia's triple movement. Even Moscow encountered the social fabric in concrete, institutional form when the fate of entire regional power systems was at stake. Initially, Moscow's solution took the form of distributing live money. But very soon, federal authorities too found themselves drawn into the nonmonetary exchange patterns that had begun with the barter of the bankrupt, a development they neither anticipated nor welcomed.

---

[112] In Primorye. For a similar functionalist account on the level of the country as a whole, see Peter Murrell, "What Is Shock Therapy? What Did It Do in Poland and Russia?" *Post-Soviet Affairs* 9, no. 2 (1993): 111–140. But here the oversimplification is no longer excusable, as the victory of the forces of loose money proved highly transitory.

CHAPTER FIVE

Monies Multiply, 1994–1996

... though the Bills grow scarcer, yet Goods of all sorts keep up their Prices: Nay, the scarcity of Bills helps to advance the Prices of Goods; for there being not a *Medium* to pay with, the Seller, if he must take other things in Exchange for his Commodities, will make his Price accordingly . . .

—"The Distressed State of the Town of Boston, Once More Considered," 1720

In the fall of 1994, as in the fall of 1993, the approach of winter was met in Moscow with apprehension. As officials discussed the looming battle with the elements in nationwide conference calls, the old language of the substantive economy, the same issues of production and logistics that Ligachev had dealt with a decade earlier, mingled with the new language of the formal economy—talk of money, debts, and payments that would have been irrelevant to the functionaries of the Communist era. In both 1993 and 1994, representatives of the energy sector, paid increasingly in kind or not at all, warned that they could not guarantee adequate stockpiles of fuel for heating and electricity. In both years, Prime Minister Viktor Chernomyrdin signed resolutions designed to prevent these problems of the formal economy from interfering with the functioning of the substantive economy. But where the 1993 resolution addressed debt problems with money, the 1994 resolution addressed them without money. In 1993, the government ordered the Central Bank to print new money and distribute it to affected enterprises. In 1994, the provision of fuel or electricity was allowed to count against present or future tax debts. Federal authorities also launched efforts to find chains of debts originating and terminating in the federal budget, so that debts could be offset against one another without issuing funds.[1]

In such subtle ways is sovereignty surrendered. The Russian government was no longer injecting money into industries operating with barter. It was entering the nonmonetary economy itself, abdicating the power Georg Friedrich Knapp had placed at the heart of his *State Theory of Money*: the power to specify the means of payment for taxes and legally contracted debts. The federal government's retreat from the ambition to give the means of payment it issued or closely regulated an exclusive status reflected the impasse the project of monetary consolidation had reached by late 1994. In an incredibly short time, huge numbers of enterprises had left the money economy for the sphere of barter, operating with empty bank accounts and rising tax debts, and the trend was continuing. Federal authorities at first tried to tackle the intensifying tax problem head-on, but given its enormous scale it was no surprise that fiscal organs could accomplish little by confiscating and selling the products of tax debtors. From early 1994, local governments had reacted to (and fostered) the spread of barter by setting up mechanisms to tax in kind. By the fall, federal authorities had little choice but to mimic them.

The entry of the federal government into the nonmonetary economy reflected the political and administrative stalemate of the project of monetary consolidation. This stalemate, however, led not to stasis but to extremely rapid change, as barter took on new forms and monies multiplied. Figure 4 gives some figures on the scale of barter, but barter was no longer the whole story.[2] This period also saw the emergence of an enormous variety of what were termed *quasi* or *surrogate* monies. Nonmonetary exchange was no longer an emergency local solution to local problems. It had become a nationwide practice pursued on an ongoing basis, generating new instruments.

[1] Compare Russian Government Resolution No. 1245, 16 November 1994, "O neotlozhnykh merakh po podgotovke narodnogo khoziaistva k rabote v osenne-zimnii period 1994–1995 godov" (On urgent measures to prepare the national economy for work in the fall-winter period of 1994–1995) with Russian Government Resolution No. 1054, 14 October 1993, "On merakh po obespecheniiu narodnogo khoziastva i naseleniia Rossiiskoi Federatsii toplivom, elektricheskoi i teplovoi energiei v osenne-zimnii period 1993–1994 godov" (On measures to ensure the supply of the national economy and the population of the Russian Federation with fuel, electricity, and heat in the fall-winter period of 1993–1994). Inforis.

[2] Figure 4 data are from *The Russian Economic Barometer* 7, no. 2 (Spring 1998). These figures are drawn from monthly surveys of an unchanging sample of 500 industrial enterprises, of which in the range of 160 to 200 respond. The figures are a simple average of the figures reported by respondents and are not weighted for sales, so they are more interesting for showing trends than for their magnitude. In fact, the figures may well be an understatement of the extent of nonmonetary exchange in industry, since they do not include exchange with surrogate currencies.

Figure 4. Share of sales through barter surveyed enterprises, February 1992–February 1998

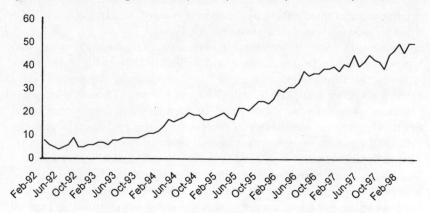

Paradoxically, as nonmonetary exchange became increasingly universal it also became increasingly particular. The proliferating new means of payment did not have general currency. Instead they moved within partially isolated circuits of exchange that rested on explicit accommodations among their members. These exchange circuits had their own systems of prices and existed in constant tension with the world of official money.

Central authorities' ongoing adaptations to the new world of nonmonetary exchange did not create it. Concessions to alternative means of payment were not the outcome of a politics of allocation fought out at the national level, but reactions to evolving exchange practices shaped in local interactions.[3] The triple movement described in the preceding chapter continued to operate, but it had new effects. Sectoral elites, demanding in the national political arena relief from the effects of barter practices born in local conflicts, were offered not money but assistance in arranging nonmonetary exchange. Meanwhile, the multiplication of monies led to a diffusion of the political realm, as monetary pluralism spawned and was in turn sustained by multiple political arenas in which contention revolved around the validity and formal valuation of nonmonetary means of payment. Negotiations between Moscow and provincial governments over taxation and expenditure became just one of these arenas in which the terms and the extent of the center's surrender of sovereignty over money were debated. However, central accommodation to nonmonetary exchange was uneasy at best. The federal government had a permanent need for rubles, the only means of payment easily transferred and accepted throughout Russian territory, and effectively the only way it could pay pensions for re-

[3] For the opposite position, see Daniel Treisman, "Fighting Inflation in a Transitional Regime: Russia's Anomalous Stabilization," *World Politics* 50 (January 1998): 235–265.

tirees and salaries for soldiers, doctors, teachers, and bureaucrats. To put nonmonetary exchange on a sustainable basis also involved intricate tasks of organization and monitoring that the federal government was never able to solve adequately. With time, the mounting fiscal and administrative crisis nonmonetary exchange created for the government, and the costs it imposed on powerful businesses, prompted the emergence of contending models for overcoming monetary fragmentation.

Examination of the politics surrounding these renewed efforts at monetary consolidation must await the next chapter, however, for it is the task of this one to explain the spread and ramification of the alternative means of payment that made them necessary. The transformation of barter unfolded so dynamically, I argue, because the practice of accepting goods in payment of debts had powerful but cross-cutting implications for the organization of exchange and control over pricing. As firms and bureaucracies quickly discovered, measures that made exchange easier also made control over pricing more difficult. Organizationally, barter complicated exchange because of the classic problem of the double coincidence of wants required for two parties to agree to an exchange of goods. Maximally fungible surrogate monies that substituted for direct bilateral barter served as a means around this problem. The pricing consequences of barter and surrogate monies arose from the need to give a formal monetary expression to nonmonetary operations. As actors in industry sought to exploit the discrepancy between obligations formally denominated in rubles and nonmonetary means of payment in order to pay lower prices, they created problems that could be contained only by making surrogate monies less fungible through restricting their use to closed exchange circuits. The fractured price system that resulted was itself of enormous consequence, disorganizing taxation and accounting and forcing even more firms out of the monetary economy.[4] I begin by explaining the trajectory that led from barter to circumscribed exchange circuits and then consider the way the proliferation of monies affected economic calculation and taxation. Against this background, the dilemmas raised for the federal government by its effort to enter the nonmonetary economy become clear.

Menger Versus Gresham: Trajectories of Exchange Practice

In 1893, Carl Menger proposed what is still the best-known account of the evolution of barter into money. Money emerges, Menger argued, due to the difficulties for barter exchange posed by the need for a double

---

[4] The view that the spread of nonmonetary exchange lay in distorted prices found its most articulate advocate in Petr Karpov of the Federal Bankruptcy Administration. See his interview in *Rossiiskii Neftianoi Biulleten'*, September 1997. See also Petr Mostovoi in *Ekspert*, 13 January 1997.

coincidence of wants. For barter exchange, purchasers not only have to find someone who is selling what they are seeking, but who wants to buy what they have to sell. Menger suggested that from an initial state of barter the most widely desired commodity would emerge spontaneously as a universally desired currency, since it would offer vastly improved convenience.[5] In the barter characteristic of the declining years of the Soviet Union, this argument was borne out, though multiple commodities (especially construction materials) served as currencies.

When barter began anew in post-Soviet Russia, Menger's dynamic once again came into play, pushing exchange beyond direct barter into various forms of surrogate money. Rendered in the "anthropological present," the trajectory takes the following path. It begins with two transactors—the state and a taxpayer, or two firms—one of which is creditor and the other debtor, as a result of the failure of the latter to pay a definite amount of money for a recognized obligation. At some point, the creditor makes a decision (whether based on strategic weakness, political pressure, or simply the need to maintain demand for its products) that accepting some less desirable means of payment, a de facto price cut, is preferable to continuing to seek a coercive recovery of the debt and ceasing sales to the debtor. Crucially, as we saw in chapter 4, an explicit price cut is barred by institutional factors. So the creditor begins to explore what the debtor is willing to offer for the debt—generally, unsold goods of the debtor's own production. Of course, the creditor simply may not need what the debtor has to offer. At this point the creditor begins to seek some way to assist the debtor in making a sale for something the creditor needs—preferably money, but goods if necessary. Thus the creditor takes on the tedious task of seeking chains of barter.

To make this task easier, chronic creditors with many debtors may begin to pay their own suppliers in debt instruments representing claims to their widely desired goods or services. These debt instruments are known as *vekselia* from the German noun wechsel, or bill of exchange. Wechsels that emerge from such a sequence, although formally obligations to pay a certain amount of money, are in practice exclusively used as promises to deliver products or services.[6] Since wechsels can be traded, their issue allows chronic creditors to avoid seeking ways to sell what they cannot directly consume. Debtors sell their own goods, accepting in payment their creditors' wechsels and transferring these wechsels back to the creditor in payment of the original debts. With time—or at least, so wechsel issuers intend—chronic creditors become simply sellers, their chronic debtors simply buyers, in a transaction in which wechsels serve as means of pay-

[5] Carl Menger, "On the Origin of Money," *Economic Journal* 2 (June 1893): 239–255.
[6] *Ekspert*, 14 April 1997. Some instruments Russians term wechsels do not emerge from such a sequence, but are simply sold for money on the open market like bonds.

ment. Menger predicted that widely demanded goods would take on the status of currency; wechsels allow the transfer of promises to deliver such goods rather than the goods themselves, but the motives underlying their issue are quite similar.

Relatively liquid wechsels solve the organizational problems of barter, but they raise new problems in the price system. Wechsels detach the de facto price reduction motivating barter from the concrete creditor-debtor relationship that originally motivated it. As a result, their very liquidity creates new dangers for their issuers. To allow them to serve as means of payment for what is formally a money debt, wechsels are assigned a nominal ruble value, and the issuers of wechsels agree to take them at this value on a par with money, in payment for their production (or services, taxes, etc.). The danger is that other customers of the wechsel-issuing creditor—including those quite able to pay their bills at full price, in money—will purchase wechsels at a discount from their face value and then use them to retire debts more cheaply. If this happens, wechsel issuers may find that their most impoverished customers continue to fail to pay their bills, while their richest ones pay them only in wechsels. This depressing scenario is a perfect illustration of "Gresham's law," which states the unsurprising principle that if two coins have the same nominal value but an unequal market value, the lesser-valued coin will be used to retire debts while the higher-valued coin will be hoarded.[7] "Good money" disappears from circulation, while "bad money" comes to dominate it.

If all wechsel systems were fated to succumb under the impact of Gresham's law, they would have disappeared quickly. Wechsel issuers, though, generally see the problem and take steps to preserve some of wechsels' flexibility while preventing their migration to customers who might be able to pay in money. The circulation of wechsels can be restricted to a limited number of parties, who make a prior agreement on the value at which wechsels will be accepted in payment. Such wechsel circulation schemes resemble a giro, which is a " 'payment society', in which the members agree to accept credit instruments of one or more of the members as media of exchange and as means of payment."[8] Sustaining a giro when the obligations that circulate might be sold to a secondary market at a discount requires very tight regulation, as will be seen shortly.[9]

[7] To my knowledge, Gresham's law was first related to Russian nonmonetary exchange by Kakha Bendukidze in *Segodnia*, 19 June 1996.
[8] L. Randall Wray, *Money and Credit in Capitalist Economies: The Endogenous Money Approach* (Aldershot, England: E. Elgar, 1990), 26.
[9] For the comparison of wechsel circulation to a giro, see Fedor Andreevich Gudkov, Aleksandr Viktorovich Makeev, Aleksandr Leonidovich Petrusha, and Galina Apollonovna Titova, *Raschety i Dolgi Predpriiatii: Prakticheskie Rekomendatsii po Rabote* (Payments and debts of enterprises: Practical recommendations for work) (Moscow: Bankovskii Delovoi Tsentr, 1997), 85–93.

The trajectory from debt to barter chains to wechsels to regulated giros was not universal. Some wechsel systems collapsed from Gresham's effects; some barter chains were never converted to wechsels in the first place. Several case studies serve to show the range of variation, illustrating as well how rapidly nonmonetary exchange grew to have a dominant role in key energy sector firms as well as in the finances of local government.

From Debt to Barter: Gazprom

The Russian natural gas industry is dominated by an enormous parastatal enterprise, Gazprom. Gazprom emerged out of the conversion of a Soviet ministerial structure to a "state concern" in the late Soviet period. Since a large share of Gazprom's domestic consumers are power generation companies, Gazprom could not help but be affected by the rise in nonpayments for electricity in the period from 1993 to 1994 (see the preceding chapter). It too reacted by accepting de facto price cuts in the form of in-kind payment, in part due to similar problems of strategic deficiency in dealing with its debtors and with the intervention of local governors to block shutdowns.[10] The company reported that in 1995, only 49 percent of gas delivered to domestic consumers was paid for. By early 1996, about half of the debt owed Gazprom by domestic consumers was owed by the power sector.[11] Debts from domestic consumers exceeded a year's worth of foreign sales.[12]

Gazprom sought to make purchases using the debts of its customers through organizing debt-offset transactions, which amounted to multilateral barter agreements. A number of commercial firms attached to Gazprom focused on arranging such transactions, which could be extraordinarily ramified. Consider the following example, drawn from a Russian business publication.[13] A Siberian gas-extracting subdivision of Gazprom, A, wishes to purchase equipment from a manufacturer in Petersburg. A's gas is regularly bought by the subdivision of Gazprom that manages the local pipeline, B, which owes A a great deal of money. A forgives B an amount of debt equal to the price of the equipment it wants to buy, but B itself has no dealings with the equipment manufacturer. So A must work its way down the

---

[10] A specific example of regional leadership intervention to block aggressive debt collection by Gazprom in Samara Province was reported in an interview at Samaraenergo, 14 April 1994; for Gazprom efforts to pressure nonpayers, see *Delo* (Samara), 18 February 1994, 1. For Gazprom's claim that regional leaders' interventions prevented shutdowns as a tool of debt collection, see *Segodnia*, 23 April 1996; complaints also sounded here about a federal government decision in November 1995 to restrict shutoffs of certain categories of consumers.

[11] *Segodnia*, 15 February 1996.

[12] *Segodnia*, 20 February 1996.

[13] *Delovaia Sibir'*, no. 26 (1995).

pipeline (to B's indebted customers, and to their indebted customers), until finally it acquires rights to a debt the Petersburg power company owes its local gas supplier. This debt A trades for the debt owed for electricity by the manufacturer in question, which is finally used to make the purchase of the equipment.

As early as 1995, according to one source, three-fifths of Gazprom's domestic receipts were in the form of such debt offsets (*zachety*); by late 1996, the company itself was reporting similar numbers.[14] Although Gazprom did not have a developed wechsel program as of mid-1996, the firm's own debts to suppliers were apparently traded in a sub-rosa secondary market at a substantial discount.[15] This market also gave rise to some Gresham's effects, as Gazprom's customers were able to achieve large savings on their gas bills by purchasing Gazprom's debts to other firms.

From Barter to Giro-Wechsels: Electric Power Companies

The rapid growth of in-kind payment for electricity, described in the previous chapter, was only a foretaste of what was to come. By 1995, 70 percent of electricity nationally was paid for in kind.[16] The national power system and semiautonomous local power systems began to seek ways to give the debt owed to them by their customers a documentary form, so they could accept these securities in payment rather than being forced to accept goods. However, it was clear that there was no likelihood of much demand for the commercial paper of firms unable even to pay their electricity bills. Therefore, the power companies sought to issue their own debt instruments, linked as closely as possible to facilitating the sale of debtor enterprise goods.[17]

Some power company wechsels collapsed under the impact of price disorganization, while others made a successful transition to a regulated giro. Perhaps the most prominent example of a Gresham's collapse occurred with the wechsels of Sibenergo, the power company for the Siberian region, in late 1995 and early 1996.[18] Sibenergo's wechsel scheme was an effort to substitute its own more broadly liquid debt for that of its main

---

[14] *Segodnia*, 19 June 1996; *Finansovye Izvestiia*, 8 October 1996.

[15] *Segodnia*, 19 June 1996; in a July 1996 interview, a high-ranking Gazprom financial officer did not deny the existence of this market.

[16] *Kommersant*, no. 5, 15 February 1994, 31; *Finansovye Izvestiia*, 30 January 1996. In general, sectoral information on the prevalence of nonmonetary exchange is scattered, and there is little evidence on the reliability of the figures.

[17] E.g., *Finansovye Izvestiia*, no. 7, 17–23 February 1994, 2.

[18] This account is based on *Ekspert*, 31 October 1995, 30–35; *Novaia sibir'skaia gazeta*, 16 February 1996, 4; and author's correspondence with an official of one of Sibenergo's subsidiaries, April 1996.

debtors, including its partially controlled daughter companies directly responsible for electricity supply in the Siberian provinces. Like most wechsels issued by industrial enterprises, Sibenergo's wechsels were never intended to be retired with a monetary payment to the bearer, but could be used only to pay for electricity. Sibenergo issued wechsels up to a substantial percentage of the debt owed to it. The company used the wechsels to make purchases, assuming that the wechsels would eventually return to it as payments for electricity from chronic debtors. Unfortunately, these circuits were rarely completed. Sibenergo pledged to accept the wechsels at face value and stated that its daughter companies would do so as well. Because the wechsels could be purchased for less than their face value, customers quite capable of paying full price for electricity quickly came to offer wechsels in payment of their bills. Since Sibenergo's daughter companies preferred to be paid in "live money" (i.e., rubles), they refused to accept the wechsels at par, leading to a collapse of their market value.

Transformation of wechsels into a regulated giro was perhaps more typical. The indispensable foundation of a giro was a stable, reciprocal agreement on valuation. Parties accepted a wechsel at a particular nominal value above what it would bring on the open market because they had assurances that they would be able to pass the wechsel on at a comparable rate. Unauthorized sale of wechsels for money to persons outside the giro represented a break in the network of reciprocal agreements. Though under Russian legislation, a wechsel represented a completely alienable and "unconditional monetary obligation," which must be paid to its bearer, issuers of giro-wechsels would often refuse to deliver goods against wechsels that had been sold on the secondary market. As a result, giro-wechsel systems could be recognized by the very large discounts at which the wechsels traded in formal markets. A typical example was the wechsel program maintained by the regional power company for the Tomsk province, Tomskenergo. Tomskenergo accepted the wechsel in payment only "as specified in a separated agreement," and wechsels' use for payments between third parties was also closely regulated by Tomskenergo. An official of the company summed the situation up this way: "The bulk of the wechsels circulate along a chain of mutual settlements (*vzaimozachety*) at their nominal value. There is a small share of the wechsels that go onto the secondary market. Why is their price there 20% [of face value]? This is not the affair of Tomskenergo."[19]

In form, the Tomskenergo wechsel plan was similar to many others, including one sponsored by the national power company, United Energy System (UES). Customers of UES were not (before 1997) final consumers,

---

[19] *Predpriiatie* (Tomsk), no. 80–81, 27 March 1997.

but rather regional power systems. UES issued wechsels to finance construction and investment and accepted these same wechsels only in payment of the regional power company's debts to it.[20]

Bank Giro-Wechsels

Commercial banks began issuing wechsels as early as 1994. Legally speaking, bank wechsels were similar to the banknotes circulated by "banks of issue" in the nineteenth century. A note-issue bank in the United States, for instance, would promise to pay a gold dollar to the bearer of its one-dollar note, in hopes that the promise would be convincing enough that the note would circulate at par. The longer the note circulated without being redeemed, the better for the bank. Like the deposit banking more familiar in contemporary times, banknote systems employed the fractional reserve mechanism. A bank could issue more notes than it had gold on hand, keeping only enough to ensure that it could redeem notes presented for redemption. The critical difference between notes and deposits is that in a deposit system, every payment to a third party is at least potentially a "redemption," requiring bank reserves, whereas this is not the case with notes. When bank deposits are used as a means of payment, the payee presents a claim on these deposits (e.g., a check) to the bank for payment. Unless the payee happens to be a customer of the same bank as the payer, the bank must pay out its reserves. When a note is transferred, no use of reserves is necessary. In essence, the payer transforms the payee into a depositor of the bank whose note is employed.

The wechsels of Russian commercial banks (most prominently, *Tveruniversalbank*, or TUB, which collapsed in mid-1996, but there were a number of others) were a promise to pay a certain number of rubles after a fixed date, and occasionally they also carried some interest.[21] Though banks had to carry some reserves against wechsels, they were initially reserved at a lower rate than deposits.[22] Whatever the legal circumstances, continued circulation of wechsels in transactions would allow banks to economize on reserves.[23]

---

[20] Author's correspondence with an official of one of Sibenergo's subsidiaries, April 1996. For some of the political implications of this system, see the following chapter.
[21] Unlike classical banknotes, TUB's wechsels were interest-bearing, but the rates were several times below market rates of interest on loans made in money. Author's correspondence with a wechsel broker, April 1996.
[22] Interviews at TUB St. Petersburg branch, June 1996. The banker in question did not regard the reserve differences as significant.
[23] For a clear, accurate discussion of wechsels that makes this point, see Erin Arvedlund, "Investors Join the Veksel Dance," *Moscow Times*, 30 September 1997.

For Russian banks, this meant that wechsels represented an opportunity to profit from helping enterprises move down the path from unpaid obligations to regulated giro circuits. Sometimes wechsels could be put into circulation when a creditor enterprise agreed to accept bank wechsels from its debtor in preference to receiving nothing at all. Often, however, the banks had to explicitly seek out chains of debt and broker an agreement in which all parties would agree to retire their debts by accepting a wechsel at face value.[24] Banks did not limit themselves to outstanding obligations, but also tried to set up new giros within which the bank's wechsels would be accepted.[25] Thus one Russian commercial bank noted that before issuing wechsels, regular practice involved "defining the list of enterprises who will be paid using the wechsel, and also the presumed sums and dates of payments," when necessary, with the help of bank personnel.[26] In this regard, wechsels were very different than nineteenth-century banknotes redeemable for gold, whose issuers hoped they would pass autonomously from hand to hand, secured by the reputation of the bank, at a value approximating that of the official means of payment as closely as possible.[27]

Careful arrangements regarding the payments to be made using the wechsel were needed to ensure that all parties agreed on the rate at which the wechsel would be accepted. As a vice president of a subsidiary of the national power company that arranged wechsel and debt-offset operations put it, "a wechsel is an indirect price regulator."[28] He provided a detailed description (reproduced in a slightly clarified form in figure 5) of how bank wechsels were facilitating relations between the energy company and a major metal firm. The scheme provides a striking example of the interaction of the Menger and Gresham dynamics in shaping regulated exchange circuits. Although the metal firm's direct suppliers were located in three different provinces, the fact that all of them used electrical energy made it possible to bring them into a single giro on the basis of an arrangement between the national power system, the metal plant, and the wechsel issuing bank. The detail in which the whole scheme is worked out also illustrates how explicit agreements were able to ensure a whole series of transactions at which the wechsel in question would have an agreed-upon value. According to the executive, bank wechsels were chosen in this case

[24] Interviews at TUB St. Petersburg, June 1996; *Kommersant*, 15 November 1994, 25.
[25] Interviews at TUB St. Petersburg, June 1996.
[26] Gudkov et al., *Raschety*, 131–132.
[27] On the clear prices and unmanaged circulation of banknotes, see Gary Gorton, "Reputation Formation in Early Bank Note Markets," *Journal of Political Economy* 104 (April 1996): 346–397.
[28] Interview in Moscow, June 1996.

Figure 5. Wechsel "giro"

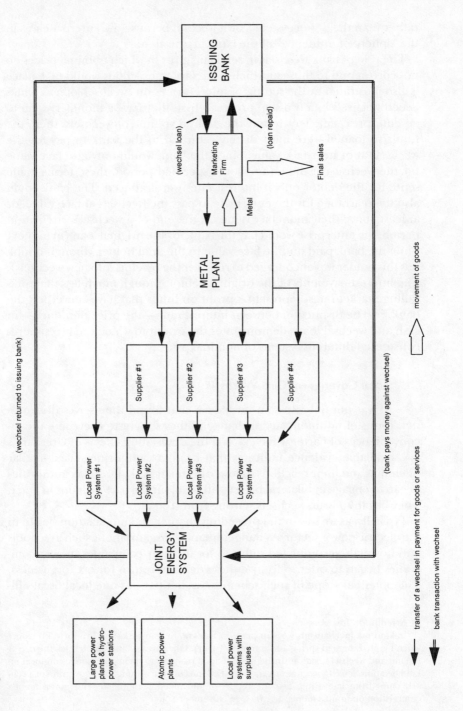

rather than the power system's own wechsel because the enterprise was in the "sphere of influence" of the bank in question.

The role of bank wechsels in servicing giros in which nominal prices do not correspond to those at which monetary transactions would take place is also illustrated by the setting of interest rates on "wechsel loans." Banks issued wechsels in a two-step process—first, they gave a monetary loan to an enterprise sufficient to buy the desired volume of wechsels; then, the funds so loaned were immediately returned to the bank to pay for the wechsels at or near face value. Since the bank would only give face value for the wechsels at the end of some specified period, these terms made sense for the debtor only if interest rates were reduced. The bank could also try to arrange for the enterprise to pass the wechsels at face value, or at least above their monetary value. At the end of a wechsel's circulation period, the enterprise would pay the bank for the original loan (in money) while the bank paid out the face value to the final holder (though doubtless this holder was encouraged to roll over the receipts into new wechsels). The interest payments of the original debtor, though much less than prevailing market rates, represent a profit on funds that have "never left the bank."[29] The distinction between interest rates—the price of money—on cash and wechsel loans demonstrates the extent to which the two spheres constituted different systems of nominal prices.

Local Government Giro-Wechsels

It was not only Russian businesses that found themselves driven to new forms of nonmonetary exchange as they sought to overcome the inconveniences of barter while evading the devastating effects of Gresham's law. Available evidence indicates that local tax authorities faced similar dilemmas and their reactions followed a similar path. Local tax authorities began to engage in bilateral barter and build simple barter chains in 1994. They began to issue wechsels starting from 1995.[30]

Typically, as we saw in the preceding chapter, in-kind taxation began in the electric power sector. As budget-financed organizations such as schools and hospitals accumulated debts to local power companies, power companies began to offer to forgive these debts in return for tax forgiveness. The potential scope of such schemes was limited—as one local fiscal offi-

---

[29] Arvedlund, "Investors."
[30] In-kind tax mechanisms were in place in Samara, Krasnoyarsk, and Primorye Provinces when I visited them in spring and summer of 1994. One can also attempt to track the rise of in-kind and wechsel taxation through the federal reaction to them. For worries on local in-kind taxation, see *Finansy,* no. 11 (1994): 5. Federal concern around local government wechsels dates from late 1995. See the report of the meeting of the federal government's commission on nonpayments, *Segodnia,* 23 November 1995.

cial wrote, budget-financed organizations "need a limited assortment of goods, primarily fuel and electrical energy."[31] Here, too, wechsels served as a means of overcoming the problem of the double coincidence of wants, although the wechsels employed to this end were various. They could be issued by the local government itself or by local banks under its control. Some regions chose to use wechsels issued by national banks, and still others attached themselves to wechsel programs organized by power or oil companies.[32] It proved possible to document that at least thirty-four of Russia's eighty-eight provinces had accepted wechsels in payment of taxes by mid-1996 (see table 4). Given the tone of discussion in the press, and the evident concern of federal authorities, one suspects that there may have been many more.

Some regional wechsel programs showed clear signs of Gresham's collapses. In Sakha, local officials, worried about the falling price of local government wechsels on the secondary market and the growing share of nonmonetary receipts, limited the amount of their own wechsels they would accept in taxes and tightened regulations on when they would accept corporate wechsels.[33] In Tatarstan, officials stopped accepting their own wechsels in taxes from firms selling alcohol, insisting on ruble payments instead; these firms had been paying 94 percent of their taxes in nonmonetary form.[34] Examples could be multiplied.[35] In other cases, like enterprise and bank wechsels, local government wechsels circulated among parties that had relatively precise agreements about wechsels' valuation and the kinds of obligation they could be used to fulfill. The resulting giro systems were to all appearances designed to ward off Gresham collapses. In Krasnoyarsk, for instance, users of the province's wechsels had to sign an agreement that they would not transfer the wechsels (issued by a local bank) to third parties without approval. If such transfers happened, the sellers would be fined double the value of the wechsel.[36] In Cheliabinsk, authorities replaced their wechsel system with a new system of "tax certificates" whose sale was entirely forbidden.[37]

[31] *Finansy*, no. 4 (1996): 12.
[32] On Nizhnii Novgorod, see "O primenenii vekselei AKB "Tver'universalbank" na territorii Nizhegorodskoi oblast" (On use of the AKB Tveruniversalbank wechsels on the territory of Nizhegorodskaia province). Nizhegorodskaia Province administration directive No. 1345-r, 10.10.95 . Inforis. For a plan to use power-company wechsels in payment of taxes in the Urals, see *Finansovye Izvestiia*, 10 October 1995.
[33] *V Mire Finansov* (prilozhenie k gazete "Respublika Sakha"), 7 May 1996.
[34] *Kommersant-Daily*, 20 December 1996.
[35] E.g., Barry W. Ickes, Peter Murrell, and Randi Ryterman, "End of the Tunnel? The Effects of Financial Stabilization in Russia," *Post-Soviet Affairs* 13 (April–June 1997): 105–133, at 125 n. 39; *Delovaia Sibir'*, no. 37 (1996).
[36] *Finansy*, no. 4 (1996): 13.
[37] *WPS Regional Press Survey*, 2 July 1997.

Table 4. Provinces known to have accepted taxes in wechsels

Province	Form of wechsel			Share of local budget revenue (%)
	Own	Bank	Other/unspecified	
Altaiskii	■			
Amurskaia		■		~7 (2/96)
Arkhangelskaia	■			
Buriatiia			■	
Cheliabinskskaia	■	■		
Chitinskaia	■			
Chuvashiia		■		
Iaroslavskaia	■			
Kabardino-Balkariia		■		
Kaliningrad		■		
Kemerovskaia	■			
Komi		■		
Krasnoiarskii		■		
Moskovskaia		■		
Murmanskaia		■		
Nizhegorodskaia		■		up to 5 (10/95)
Novosibirskaia	■			
Omsk			■	
Orelskaia			■	
Permskaia		■		
Primorskii		■		
Riazanskaia			■	~9 (10/95)
Sakha (Iakutiia)	■			13.8 ('95), ~25 ('96)
Samarskaia	■			
Sankt-Peterburg		■		
Saratovskaia	■			14 ('95)
Stavropolskii		■		
Sverdlovskaia	■			
Tambovskaia		■		
Tatarstan	■	■		33 ('95), 39 ('96)*
Tula			■	
Tverskaia		■		
Udmurtiia	■			
Voronezhskaia			■	

*Apparently including both wechsel and in-kind tax receipts.

Sources: Altaiskii: WPS, 21 July 1996. Amurskaia: WPS, 9 February 1996. Arkhangelskaia: WPS, 15 April 1996. Buriatiia: LDK, 4. Cheliabinskaia: WPS, 24 July 1996; Finmarket News and Commentaries, 27 September 1996 http://www.finmarket.ru/probe.ht; TUB. Chitinskaia: WPS, 8 April 1996, 4 July 1996. Chuvashiia: TUB. Iaroslavskaia: WPS, 26 February 1996. Kabardino-Balkariia: TUB. Kaliningrad: BiB, November 1995. Kemerovskaia: WPS, 5 August 1996; TUB. Komi: TUB. Krasnoiarskii: Finansy no. 4, (1996) 12–14. Moskovskaia: TUB. Murmanskaia: WPS, 4 November 1996. Nizhegorodskaia: "O primenenii vekselei AKB 'Tver'universalbank" na territorii Nizhegorodskoi oblasti." Nizhegorodskaia oblast' administration directive No. 1345-r, 10.10.95, Inforis. Novoskibirskaia: Seg, 2 November 1995. Omsk: LDK, 4. Orelskaia: Seg, 2 March 1996. Permskaia: WPS, 4 March 1996, 11 March 1996. Primorskii: WPS, 9 August 1996. Riazanskaia: WPS, 23 October 1996. Sakha (Iakutiia): VMF, 7 May 1996. Samarskaia: WPS, 26 February 1996. Sankt-Peterburg: TUB. Saratovskaia: KD, 24 January 1996. Stavropolskii: WPS, 31 July 1996. Sverdlovskaia: WPS, 31 July 1996. Tambovskaia: TUB. Tatarstan: KD, 24 May 1994; WPS, 27 October 1995, 31 July 1996, 16 August 1996. Tula: LDK, 4. Tverskaia: TUB. Udmurtiia: KD (on-line) 11 September 1996. Voronezhskaia: WPS, 24 July 1996.
Abbreviations: WPS: What Papers Say Regional Press Survey (http://koi.www.online.ru/rproducts/wps-pr-month/); LDK: Lider-daidzhest Kambio, no. 2 (in-house publication of Aktesptnyi Dom EES, Moscow 1995); TUB: Untitled report on Tver'universalbank's wechsel program, supplied by St. Petersburg branch; BiB: Biznes i Baltika on-line newspaper (http://www.neonet.riga.lv/BB/1995/11/0333/04/03330402.html); VMF: V Mire Finansov, prilozhenie k gazete "Respublika Sakha" (http://srv.yacc.yakutia.su/~resp/mirfin/n60/st21.html); Inforis:Inforis Russian legal database (http://www.inforis.nnov.su/infobase.html.k); Seg: Segodnia on-line edition (http://www.eastview.com/segodnia); KD: Kommersant-Daily.

Certainly it would be foolhardy to make strong claims for the representativeness of these case studies. Yet the pattern is too strong to regard them as scattered anecdotes. Their significance lies in confirming the fundamental hypothesis used to construct the stylized trajectory from in-kind debt payment to circumscribed exchange circuits: the initial barter transaction is motivated by the desire to reduce prices de facto while leaving them unchanged in nominal terms. Nonmonetary exchange began as a way around price rigidities. If wechsels were simply titles to goods that potential buyers could value at any formal price they wished, neither Gresham's collapses nor tight restrictions on how wechsels circulate could be explained. Unless nominal prices in the sphere of barter and wechsel circulation were higher than they would be if all parties were forced to use only official money, there would be no reason to expect Menger's dynamic to be limited. The distortion imposed by counting nonmonetary means of payment as formally equivalent to money could only cause massive difficulties, of course, for the calculation of economic advantage, and of taxes.

Calculation Without Money

As we have seen, ongoing circuits of nonmonetary exchange could only sustain themselves on the basis of a successful insulation from secondary markets where the obligations involved could be bought and sold for money. This insulation was, then, precisely an insulation from price-setting institutions that would have given a public, announced monetary value to these obligations. The absence of a public value for nonmonetary means of payment also complicated decisions about whether and at what "rate of exchange" to accept them. The general practice, to the extent that it could be judged, was to make use of rules of thumb. In the absence of clear price-setting mechanisms, numerical calculation was possible only if some relatively arbitrary choices were made. As a legal and accounting matter, the "monies of account" of the various giros were considered to be denominated in the same units. As a practical matter, of course, this apparent commensurability was false. But in the absence of price-setting markets, no rational procedure for conversion existed.

Many Russian firms adapted to the situation by setting differentiated "prices" at which different means of payment would be accepted.[38] These

---

[38] Multiple pricing practices can be verified in many advertisements posted by Russian firms to Usenet newsgroups. For instance, Message-ID <AAfZW5n4b4@spb.kemerovo.su>, posted to relcom.commerce.energy on 5 February 1996, gives prices that are approximately 5 percent higher in the case of wechsel or barter payment than for money payment. For more examples, see company reports supplied by Investext at www.securities.com.

multiple pricing schemes were probably illegal, at least through 1996.[39] But at least multiple prices made some effort to compensate for the effects of false commensurability on sales. The problem was much harder to address in accounting. Certain categories of inputs regularly paid for in nonmonetary form appeared to be a larger share of costs than they "really" were, but according to several accountants, what coefficient to apply to them was a mystery.[40] The usual adaptation appears to have been to seek to limit nonmonetary receipts to a fixed share of revenue. This, of course, was an equally arbitrary rule of thumb. The sort of difficulty involved in rational calculation in the presence of multiple imperfectly convertible monies can be underscored by the efforts of Western investment consultants to give appropriate financial analyses of Russian firms. Thus in an analysis of a large oil company, one Western firm chose to recalculate stated receipts using a 30 percent discount for all receipts received in kind.[41] Another foreign investment report noted that a metal firm evaluated one cash ruble as equivalent to two barter rubles.[42]

The most important systematic consequence of the price chaos brought on by monetary plurality concerned taxation. Firms' taxes were assessed on the basis of nominal receipts, whether these receipts were in monetary or nonmonetary form. Since nonmonetary receipts were "overvalued" (remembering that such gestures at a neutral, true standard of value mask the operation of arbitrary rules of thumb), their prevalence meant a raising of the effective tax rate. The share of taxes due to be paid out of receipts could and did regularly exceed the share of cash in receipts.[43] Taxpaying enterprises demanded that taxes also be accepted in nonmonetary form to compensate.[44]

The interaction of money-denominated calculating practices and nonmonetary exchange is especially well illustrated by the metal industry. From June 1993 to October 1995, the ruble appreciated almost five times against the dollar in real terms (in other words, the purchasing power of a dollar on Russia's internal market shrank to a fifth of what it had been).[45]

[39] According to a financial officer for the October Railway Division, St. Petersburg, interview June 1996.
[40] Interviews with accountants at a St. Petersburg machinery manufacturer and two major fuel sector firms in Moscow, June 1996, July 1996.
[41] "Russian Oil and Gas—Industry Report," Investext Report No. 2626347, 5 December 1997, www.securities.com.
[42] "Mechel—Company Report," Investext Report No. 1930063, 1 January 1997, www.securities .com.
[43] Kommersant, 15 November 1994, 25; Finansovaya Rossiia, 26 March 1998.
[44] Stenographic report of a meeting of the "Public Expert Council on Banking Activity, 'The Experience of Financial Institutes in Working with Wechsels,' " 16 April 1996. Supplied by S. I. Shevchenko.
[45] Russian Economic Trends, Monthly Update, November 1995.

Most of the appreciation occurred shortly after real interest rates became very high in the second half of 1993, but even from January 1994 to October 1995 the ruble appreciated by 100 percent. Russian metal producers, highly dependent on exports (especially given the collapse of the defense industry, which had been a key consumer), found that exports could only be carried out at a loss. As a result, they tried to compensate by raising their prices on the internal market. But, as one executive put it, "Our prices swelled, and at those prices one can't find a buyer with live money on the internal market—which meant barter operations."[46] The director of the country's biggest metal plant, the Magnitogorsk conglomerate, reported in January 1996 that with most suppliers 80 percent of payments were made in kind, complaining that the railroads would "only" accept 50 percent of their payment in kind.[47] Other major ferrous metal manufacturers also reported that very large shares of their receipts were in kind, and the situation appears to have been quite general in the sector.[48]

To keep cash receipts, these producers continued exporting, despite the fact that in formal terms export prices meant taking a loss.[49] To understand the logic of their behavior, let us consider a seemingly mysterious case in some detail. Magnitogorsk planned to export half of its 1997 production at a loss of 12.87 percent while selling the other half on the internal market at a profit of 27.31 percent. But the internal market sales were to be almost exclusively through barter and other nonmonetary forms.[50] Since domestic sales were to be in nonmonetary form, domestic purchases would be as well—since in barter, every sale was also a purchase. Therefore, the nominal prices at which receipts were earned and costs incurred on the domestic market would be higher than they would have been if Magnitogorsk were using rubles. Let us imagine that these costs and receipts were denominated in an alternate currency called the "bartle." The bartle's exchange rate against the dollar would be lower than the ruble's exchange rate, *and it is the bartle's exchange rate that would be relevant,* since costs would be incurred in bartles. Thus exports appear unprofitable because their profitability is calculated using the misleading assumption that bartles have an equal value to cash rubles. This language, of course,

---

[46] *Ekspert,* 11 December 1995, 36. "Izhorskie zavody," the plant in question, is both a producer of specialty steel and of construction and mining machinery.

[47] *Kommersant-Daily,* 23 January 1996, 11.

[48] For Severstal' (90% of receipts in kind) see *Segodnia,* 23 April 1996; for the West Siberian Metal Conglomerate (70% of receipts in kind) *Segodnia,* 17 October 1995. On the sector as a whole, see *Segodnia,* 22 February 1996.

[49] I first heard this explanation from Barbara Lehmbruch. For published examples, see *Segodnia,* 20 February 1997; *Segodnia,* 9 October 1996.

[50] *Rossiiskaia Aziia,* 21 May 1997.

implies a precision of calculation that would be impossible to attain in practice, since there is no institutional equivalent to the bartle. Nevertheless, the case of the metal industry shows how the need to show a formal profit can shift exchange to an in-kind basis. For exporters, this amounts to a localized "devaluation."

Another reaction to the problem of a strong ruble casting exporters back on a weak domestic market was simply for them to lobby for a weaker ruble, and the metal sector, at least, did this energetically.[51] But at least one proposal was voiced asking the government to accept tax payments in kind.[52] In context, this proposal appears as a suggestion that the over-assessment of taxes due to the misleading monetary denomination of in-kind revenue would be compensated for by paying taxes using production at an inflated price. As we shall see, this dynamic had far broader relevance.[53]

The Federal Reaction

The course of national policy on nonmonetary exchange was highly complicated, for much more than local government or industry, the federal government was torn between conflicting imperatives. The federal government experienced the evolution of debts into quasi money both as creditor and as debtor. Nonmonetary budget expenditure was a way of allowing an (unmeasurable) reduction in government obligations, but it was funded by nonmonetary budget receipts that represented (unmeasurable) tax breaks for those paying taxes in this form. The federal government was also especially vulnerable to Gresham's effects, since it was unable successfully to organize its own giros or to enter those of others—the detailed monitoring that would have been involved was simply far beyond its organizational capacity.

The first and, in many ways, most consequential federal government reaction to the spread of nonmonetary exchange was worked out in the final days of August 1994 by the newly created Operational Commission on Perfecting the System of Payments and Settlements, henceforth referred to as the nonpayments commission. This commission was created to craft a response to the expanding problem of tax and energy debts described in the preceding chapter. Over the four years of its existence, the commis-

---

[51] *Kommersant-Daily,* 23 January 1996, 11.

[52] *Segodnia,* 23 April 1996.

[53] On the way that distorted prices lock enterprises into continued use of money surrogates, see V. Klistorin and V. Cherkasskij, "Denezhnye Surrogaty: Ekonomicheskie i Sotsial'nye Posledstviia" (Money surrogates: Economic and social consequences), *Voprosy Ekonomiki* (October 1997): 52–57.

sion would essentially become the government's main agency dealing with monetary pluralism in a relatively systematic fashion. Initially, the commission was headed by Oleg Soskovets, a vice premier usually seen as a representative of industrial interests and the metal sector in particular. In its first measures, the committee focused on nonpayments to the energy sector and to the budget.[54] The policies the commission endorsed operated in two directions. On the one hand, there was a limited effort to improve price flexibility by allowing firms to sell for less than their cost of production under sharply defined circumstances. The commission also approved (and quite probably brokered) a "cartel agreement" in which railroads, coals firms, the state committee for the metal industry, and the national electric power network agreed to mutual price restraint.[55] Enterprises participating in the arrangement were explicitly granted the right to sell lower than production costs to other participants.

At the same time, the initial decisions of the committee relied on—and contributed to—nonmonetary means of overcoming price rigidity. The participants of the cartel arrangement were allowed to postpone tax payments that arose as a result of their debt offsets, presumably because these would not generate monetary receipts. The commission also expressed approval of the efforts of local authorities to organize debt-offset operations and gave explicit endorsement to bank giro-wechsels. Moreover, the commission began to implement similar measures on a federal level, carrying out bilateral offset operations with the sectors involved in the cartel agreement that canceled taxes owed against debts from the budget.

Another consequential decision taken by the commission in late 1994 was the creation of the federal government's own giro-wechsels, the so-called treasury obligations. The treasury obligations paid a desultory (at the time) 40 percent per year, far less than the rate of inflation. They were not, in fact, government bonds at all, but rather closely resembled bank wechsels. Commercial banks even administered the treasury obligations market. According to a deputy finance minister, this was regrettable but unavoidable in the absence of federal bureaucracies capable of handling the program. The government clearly recognized that financing budget expenditures with treasury obligations constituted a de facto reduction of these expenditures. In the words of a Ministry of Finance official, "financing expenditures with [treasury obligations] given their present interest rate is one of the means of economizing on funds, which we are forced to

---

[54] Accounts of the commission's early measures in the next two paragraphs are drawn from *Rossiiskie Vesti,* 23 September 1994, 1–2; *Kommersant,* 20 September 1994, 4–5, 46; and *Kommersant,* 23 August 1994, 60.

[55] Prime Minister Chernomyrdin singled out the cartel agreement for praise in *Rossiiskie Vesti,* 30 August 1994, 1–2.

do. Yes, this is not very fair, so the [treasury obligations] are divided proportionally between all the sectors."[56] At the end of their period of circulation, the Ministry of Finance retired the treasury obligations by paying out money or, for approximately half the volume, by granting tax forgiveness to budget debtors. To ensure that the treasury obligations would not lead to Gresham effects (their sale on the secondary market at a discount to purchasers who wanted a cheaper way to pay their taxes), the Ministry of Finance paid out only on those treasury obligations that had already been accepted in payment by at least six enterprises.[57]

The federal government entered the nonmonetary economy by adopting exchange mechanisms already prevalent. Both of the forms of nonmonetary payment the commission encouraged in August and September 1994 (mutual offsets between firms themselves or between firms and the government, and the use of bank-administered wechsels) had precedents either in the private sector or in local taxation practice.[58] The trend to nonmonetary taxation developed throughout 1995, in earnest from the year's last quarter. In February 1995, the head of the State Tax Service sent a letter to local organs encouraging them to find ways to "cancel debts to the budget with in-kind payment."[59] During the summer, large oil companies began paying tax bills by supplying fuel to farms and military bases. In the fall, the Ministry of Finance began to organize major offset operations with electric power companies, forgiving tax debts in return for forgiveness of debts owed by budget-financed organizations to the power companies.[60]

The scale of the in-kind taxation sustained through these two mechanisms was substantial. Although detailed data on the composition of federal tax revenues are hard to come by and complicated to interpret, a general picture can be gleaned from public statements of leading officials and occasional reports in the press. In 1995, approximately 19 percent of federal tax income was in a nonmonetary form.[61] In 1996, this share had

[56] *Kommersant,* 14 February 1995, 19.
[57] Ibid., 18.
[58] Ickes et al. ("End of the Tunnel," 125) argue that "*vekseli* [*sic*] are a private sector development mirroring government non-monetary innovations at the federal and local level." But the historical development actually ran in the opposite order.
[59] "O neudovletvoritel'nom polozhenii s obespecheniem postuplenii v biudzhet platezhei za prirodnye resursy," (On the unsatisfactory situation regarding securing the transmission of natural resource payments to the budget) Russian Federation State Tax Service letter from 23 February 1995, No. BG-6–02/97. Inforis.
[60] *Kommersant-Daily,* 3 October 1995, 2 (translated in *Eastview Press Press Digest,* 3 October 1995).
[61] *Finansy,* no. 3 (1996): 4. Rory MacFarquhar (personal communication) reports that tax income as defined in Russia does not include some forms of budget revenue, such as customs, and it is often difficult to tell what categories of revenues are included in any given claim about budget income. All figures cited here seem to refer to the narrow notion of tax revenue but they should in any event be regarded as indicative rather than definitive. Another

risen to 33 percent, and by 1997 it had reached around 40 percent.[62] These figures are broadly consistent with month-by-month data given by one source for 1996 and half of 1997, which show the share of nonmonetary federal budget revenue ranging from a low of zero in January 1997 to a high of 64 percent in March 1997.[63] In 1998, the government once again pledged to eliminate all forms of nonmonetary taxation, though it continued to accept nonmonetary payments, which it used to pay off budget debts from 1997.

Taxing in nonmonetary form was not easy for the federal government. It was never able to engage in the detailed monitoring of circulation needed to prevent Gresham effects. The purchase or sale of the two successors to the treasury obligations—"treasury tax offsets"(*kaznacheiskie nalogovye osvobozdeniia,* or KNOs) and the misnamed "monetary offsets" (*denezhnye zachety*)—was sharply limited. Regulations specified that only firms that had a preexisting tax debt could pay taxes with these instruments, in order to avoid their use by firms able to pay taxes in money. Nevertheless, Russian firms displayed impressive inventiveness in overcoming these restrictions.[64] Budget organizations whose purchases were to be financed with KNOs often preferred cash to goods and found it simpler to sell the offsets at a discount, for cash, to firms looking to reduce their tax.[65] The finance director of one of Russia's major oil companies, for example, claimed in the summer of 1996 that the firm was paying 100 percent of its taxes using offsets.[66] Given the figures on the composition of federal budget receipts, there is no reason to assume this was unusual.[67]

major difficulty with interpreting such figures is that the Russian federal budget has rolled over substantial debts from year to year; income in the form of offsets that cancel these debts is often applied to previous years' revenues. The figures quoted in the text are calculated from figures on total revenues, regardless of the annual budget to which they pertain.

[62] "Informatsiia o predvaritel'nykh itogakhh ispolneniia federal'nogo biudzheta na 1997 god i zadachakh po ispolneniiu federal'nogo biudzheta v I kvartale 1998 goda" (Information on the preliminary results of the execution of the federal budget in 1997 and tasks for the implementation of the federal budget in the 1st quarter of 1998). (Unpublished Russian government memorandum to the State Duma, 1998). A very similar figure for 1996 can be derived from a Russian tax service report, though the underlying absolute figures on revenue are somewhat different: Denis Mikhailov, "Nalogi, Kotorye My Sobiraem" (The taxes we collect), *Nauchnyi Park*, 25 February 1997.

[63] *Finansovye Izvestiia*, 21 August 1997. These figures seem to report only budget revenue for the year in question, not nonmonetary payment accepted against debts of prior years.

[64] *Ekspert*, 23 December 1996; interview with a broker dealing in such transactions, Irkutsk, August 1997.

[65] Interview with a broker dealing in such transactions, Vladivostok, August 1996. See also Ickes et al., "End of the Tunnel," 125.

[66] Interview in Moscow, July 1996.

[67] For even higher estimates of nonmonetary taxation in the summer of 1996, see *Segodnia*, 14 August 1996.

The danger of a Gresham's collapse was not the only complication facing federal authorities at the transition from barter to an exchange-facilitating currency. Any issue of debt intended to be used as a means of payment, when this is done by the state, inevitably shades over into money issue—as both the treasury liabilities and tax offset episodes illustrate. In effect, both the KNOs and the treasury liabilities were ways of ratifying decentralized creation of means of payment in interenterprise debt. Leaving aside the government's own commitment to fighting inflation through monetary restriction, the issue of these quasi monies in any event tended to bring objections from the International Monetary Fund (IMF).[68] In July and August of 1996, for example, in part under pressure from the IMF and in part simply because of its own realization of the difficulties brought on by the prevalence of offsets, the government made a sharp turn against them. In July, the government simply stopped accepting offsets in payment of taxes.[69] In August, Prime Minister Chernomyrdin pledged that offsets would be rapidly eliminated.[70] In fact, there were at least two replacements that were not substantially more monetary in character.[71]

It is important to dispel the notion that the succession of federal government quasi monies was simply the hide-and-seek statagem of a government trying to evade limits on monetary issue imposed by the IMF.[72] Rather, nonmonetary taxation had, as it were, a "supply" side and a "demand" side, both created by the proliferation of alternative means of payment and the price distortions they entailed. Nonmonetary means of payment generated formal money receipts but no actual money to pay taxes, leading to tax arrears.[73] Tax arrears led to arrears on budget expenditures. The motivation to supply quasi monies thus came from the government's desire to reduce its de facto obligations under the budget while fulfilling the budget in nominal terms. The motivation to demand

[68] For instance, regarding the treasury liabilities: "Apparently, the experts from the IMF could not comprehend the Ministry of Finance's explanation about the dual nature of the [treasury liability], combining in itself the features of a security and the by-definition interest free issue of money by the treasury." *Kommersant,* no. 11, 28 March 1995, 75.

[69] For the IMF pressure, see *The Washington Post,* 20 August 1996, C03; change in policy from interview with broker, Vladivostok, August 1996 and Russian Ministry of Finance Order No. 373 of 22 July 1996 from Inforis.

[70] *Segodnia,* 23 August 1996.

[71] *Finansovye Izvestiia,* 6 February 1997; *Ekspert,* 13 October 1997.

[72] Ickes et al., "End of the Tunnel," 125.

[73] Although it was not entirely clear what share of tax arrears could be ascribed to nonmonetary exchange, it appeared to be very large. A State Tax Service analysis of VAT collections in the first half of 1997 attributed 40 percent of the growth in arrears to nonmonetary payment, with another 50 percent of this growth due to interenterprise nonpayments that may well have represented only the first stage of a barter transacaction. B. A. Minaev, "Analyticheskaia zapiska o postuplenii naloga na dobavlennuiu stoimost v biudzhetnuiu sistemu za ianvar'-iun' 1997" (State Tax Service of Russia, 17 July 1997, State Tax Service web site).

nonmonetary taxation came from firms whose high nominal receipts in alternative means of payment caused an inflation of their tax obligations. Nonmonetary taxation allowed inflated tax payments to compensate for inflated tax assessments. In this regard, the political and economic circumstances of the first decisions on federal nonmonetary taxation (those of August and September 1994, discussed previously), which seemed directly designed to compensate industry for the inflation of its tax obligations by nonmonetary exchange and nonpayments, are quite telling.

Nonmonetary Taxation and Fiscal Federalism

Regional authorities also played an important role in pushing the federal government to nonmonetary forms of tax collection. This role can be seen through a brief analysis of the center-regional dimensions of tax arrears. As noted in the preceding chapter, provincial governments were the first to react to tax arrears through accepting nonmonetary payment. And although data on the composition of local budget revenues is even scarcer than that on composition of federal budget revenues, what information is available universally indicates that local budgets take in a substantially greater proportion of their revenue in kind than the federal budget. In late 1994, the Ministry of Finance ordered that local governments begin collecting data on how much of their revenue took a nonmonetary form, but this data had not been published by early 1998.[74] As late as March 1996, the federal treasury had to carry out a special survey to get approximate figures: it suggested that about 40 percent of local and 20 percent of federal revenue was in kind.[75] The Organization for Economic Co-operation and Development has reported data on thirty-three subjects of the federation for 1996.[76] In these regions, about 50 percent of consolidated budget revenue and 60 percent of provincial budget revenue took a nonmonetary form. (Since the consolidated budget includes the provincial budgets, these figures obscure the differences between the two budget levels; roughly, the figures imply that 40 percent of federal taxation was in nonmonetary form). In all but seven of these regions, regional nonmonetary receipts were more prevalent than consolidated budget nonmonetary receipts.

---

[74] *Normativnye akty po finansam, nalogam, strakhovaniiu i bukhgalterskomu uchetu (prilozhenie k zhurnalu "Finansy")*, no. 2 (1995): 30–33.
[75] *Segodnia*, 26 April 1996.
[76] Seija Lainela, "Money Surrogates and Regional Financial Markets in Russia" (paper presented at the 29th National Convention of the American Association for the Advancement of Slavic Studies, Seattle, November 21–23, 1997). Lainela (personal communication) has said that these numbers were drawn from a survey done by the Ministry of the Economy.

These differences had important consequences for fiscal federalism. All Russian tax collection was carried out by federal agencies (the Tax Inspectorate, the State Tax Service, and the Tax Police). As a result, though regions often threatened to withhold monetary revenue from central authorities, they were able to make good on such threats only exceedingly rarely.[77] The Tax Inspectorate had the responsibility for dividing revenue in accordance with the proportions that were supposed to go to the federal and to the regional budget. (The proportions were set by legislation and, in many cases, by arrangements worked out between the individual subjects of the federation and federal authorities, including the president.)[78] When tax receipts were in money, this mechanism worked relatively automatically and reliably. However, in the case of nonmonetary receipts, such division was not automatic. A nonmonetary collection counted at its nominal price toward the tax receipts of the authorities that authorized it. When a region authorized a large number of in-kind or monetary surrogate payments, its share of nominal tax receipts exceeded the share legally allotted to it. This was not an unambiguous bonus for the region, since any monetary receipts would be applied toward the federation's share of taxes. As a result, regional governments' ability to pay salaries could decline, and their revenues would be "overvalued" compared with federal revenues. Nevertheless, to the extent that regions were more successful in arranging nonmonetary taxation, they received a higher share of budget income.

Though central fiscal authorities complained that regions were collecting in-kind taxes not split with the center on a number of occasions, it is hard to gauge the scale of the phenomenon.[79] A State Tax Service report on VAT collections noted only a slight diversion in the first half of 1997 through this mechanism.[80] And the relative federal and regional shares of arrears remained approximately constant in the period from 1994 to

[77] Public talk at Harvard University by Alexei Lavrov, fiscal federalism expert for the presidential administration, 7 April 1997.
[78] Philippe Le Houerou, *Fiscal Management in Russia* (Washington, D.C.: World Bank, 1996); Philippe Le Houerou and Michael Rutkowski, "Federal Transfers in Russia: Their Impact on Regional Revenues and Income," *Comparative Economic Studies* 38 (Summer–Fall 1996): 21–46; and Stephan Barisitz and John Litwack, "Fiscal Federalism in Russia: Evolution, Problems and Prospects" (paper presented at the 29th National Convention of the American Association for the Advancement of Slavic Studies, Seattle, November 21–23, 1997).
[79] *Kommersant-Daily*, 29 May 1996; press conference with head of the State Tax Service Alexander Pochinok, 23 April 1997, reported by Federal News Service; author's interview with Alexei Lavrov, Russian Federation presidential administration adviser on fiscal federalism, April 1997; *Segodnia*, 26 April 1996; *Finansy*, no. 11 (1994): 5. For analytic mentions of the problem, see Yuliya Latynina in *Ekspert*, 12 January 1998, and Barisitz and Litwack, "Fiscal Federalism," 4.
[80] Minaev, "Analiticheskaia zapiska."

1997. However, when data on the regional prevalence of nonmonetary taxation is compared with data on arrears in 1996, a strong suggestion emerges that diversion was large, and the relatively stable division of shares between the levels concealed a more-complicated process of federal adjustment to local taxation practices. Judging by government figures on arrears to the federal and consolidated budgets, the federal government believed it should have received around 60 percent of the taxes collected, but in fact it only received 43.6 percent.[81] This diversion could be linked to local governments' refusal to transfer the federal share of taxes—but all evidence indicates that this was quite rare. The case that nonmonetary taxation explains diversion is strengthened by the fact that in provinces where a high share of federal budget receipts was in nonmonetary form, there was less diversion. In provinces where a higher percentage of local than federal taxes was collected in nonmonetary form, there was more diversion.[82] Although the nature of the data do not admit of a fuller investigation, these correlations lend credence to federal government complaints that local government taxation was leading to a shift in revenues away from federal authorities. In February 1996, the Russian minister of finance defended nonmonetary taxation as necessary to finance key budget expenditures and called for a vigorous continuation of the policy. Moreover, he called on regional governments to become more actively involved in arranging in-kind taxation—"since without their participation such work is virtually impossible to conduct."[83] It was likely that behind this statement was a complaint that the receipts of local in-kind taxation were not shared more readily with the center.

How this highly mediated competitive tax rate reduction between central and local authorities looked to enterprises on the ground was described by a Moscow banker at a parliamentary hearing on wechsel legislation in the summer of 1996. Complaining that both federal and local authorities were using nonmonetary budget finances to reduce their effective expenditures, he noted that this would not be so annoying if the nonmonetary instruments could be used to pay taxes. "If this situation is somehow soluble on the level of the local budgets, say, in Moscow province, where Tveruniversalbank wechsels and a number of others can be used to

[81] Calculated from "A Statistical Look at Russia's Regions," *Russian Economic Trends*, January–March 1997.
[82] Calculated from "A Statistical Look," and Lainela, "Money Surrogates." For each region, a diversion index was calculated based on the difference between the share of receipts the federal government expected to be remitted and the share of receipts actually remitted. This was then correlated with the figures specified in the text , calculated from the OECD data on shares of nonmonetary receipts to the provincial and consolidated budget for each province. The correlation was in magnitude approximately .33 in each instance.
[83] *Finansy*, no. 3 (1996): 8.

pay taxes, for the federal budget this problem is not solved at all." He suggested that the reaction of enterprises funded out of the federal budget was to artificially become a debtor of the federal budget, so that the federal government would agree to accept nonmonetary tax payment instruments, thus reducing taxes to compensate for the reduced budget payments.[84]

A second way that center-regional tax competition was mediated through nonmonetary taxation was through the process of devolution of federal tax collection and expenditure to local authorities.[85] Tax devolution involved an agreement linking the collection of federal tax revenue in a territory to its spending in that territory for particular purposes specified in the federal budget but that would not otherwise be funded due to budget shortfalls. Nonmonetary mechanisms ensured that the funds would be spent as agreed and not automatically transferred out of the region. These mechanisms appear to account for a substantial portion of funding of the so-called federal transfers due to most provinces to support their budget revenues. In late 1996, a reportedly huge share of regional transfers was funded through mutual offsets.[86] In October 1997, the federal government agreed to allow the federal share of the VAT collected in a province to be used to pay federal budget debts to the province due under the revenue support program.[87] But substantive examples are more informative. In Moscow, for instance, 50 percent of overdue taxes to the federal budget were directed to fund subway construction that had been scheduled for finance from the federal budget.[88] A slightly more complicated example involved the federal pension fund. A bank in Nizhnii Novgorod used its wechsels to purchase crude oil from firms in Tiumen' Province and delivered the oil to a Nizhnii refinery. The Tiumen' oil firms used the wechsels to pay their pension fund obligations; the federal pension fund then transferred the wechsels to the Nizhnii province fund in lieu of payments that had previously been due but not forthcoming. The bank was then able to pay out cash for pensions by selling the refined oil.[89] An especially intricate form of devolution involved Chita Province, deep in Siberia, in the sale of goods from Belorussia. The receipts from these sales would accrue to the region in place of transfers due it from the fed-

---

84 Stenographic report from "Public Expert Council."
85 I thank Rory MacFarquhar for finding the right word for this.
86 *Finansovye Izvestiia*, 21 August 1997.
87 Issues in the Execution of the Federal Budget for 1997. Resolution of the Government of the Russian Federation from 11 October 1997. *New in Russian Legislation*, 22 October 1997.
88 *Segodnia*, 17 April 1997. For an identical report from Cheliabinsk, see Clifford C. Gaddy and Barry W. Ickes, "Russia's Virtual Economy," *Foreign Affairs*, September–October 1998, http://www.foreignaffairs.org/issues/9809/gaddy.html.
89 *Kommersant*, 18 February 1997.

eral budget. The federal budget, in turn, would arrange to pay Belorussia's debts for gas, presumably by forgiving taxes due from Gazprom.[90]

The point of such rococo schemes was to ensure that given shortfalls in funding by the federal budget and the pension fund, what payments were made would be directed to particular recipients. The regions, as the federal budget's creditor, accepted nonmonetary payment of obligations. In a broader frame, such incidents represent efforts to convert the budget into a giro, in which the collection of revenue and its valuation would be closely tied to how it would be spent. It is worth noting in passing how such a nonmonetary budget fundamentally eviscerates democratic oversight of the budget process and collective decision making about where to direct scarce resources in the case of shortfalls.[91] In terms of center-regional tax competition, devolution demonstrates how regional facility in nonmonetary taxation pulls federal authorities toward similar measures.

Conclusion

The spread and transformation of nonmonetary exchange, this chapter has argued, was driven by actors pursuing their advantage in a difficult environment. Forced by circumstances to cut prices, but unable to do so in nominal terms, firms embraced barter. Faced with the labyrinthine complexities of organizing barter, firms sought to avoid them by creating quasi monies. When quasi monies led to a loss of control over pricing by offering discounts to those who had no need of them, firms restricted their circulation. As the nominal equivalence and factual distinction between rubles and alternate means of payment inflated tax obligations, firms demanded that they be taxed in the form they received their income. Central and local bureaucrats aiming to maintain taxation and spending took many similar measures, on similar reasoning. There were attempts on all sides to exploit those accepting nonmonetary means of payment at their nominal value, and attempts to resist this exploitation. Fragmentation of the price system made it harder to define economic advantage precisely, but as a result it was pursued all the more vigorously.

The implications of this vision of the origins and transformation of barter become clearer if it is contrasted with other proposed arguments, which generally offer accounts of the uses of barter's nontransparency that have plausible application to particular cases but cannot account for the

---

[90] *Delovaia Sibir'*, 18 October 1996. Cf. the catalog of Chita Province's strategies for extracting budgeted transfers from the center in *WPS Russian Regional Press Bulletin*, 12 February 1997.

[91] This point is also made in Gaddy and Ickes, "Russia's Virtual Economy," and by Oksana Dmitrieva in *Segodnia*, 16 October 1996.

general pattern described here. Kathryn Hendley and her colleagues suggest that barter is driven by tax evasion, since it allows firms to avoid automatic confiscation of taxes and some categories of debts from bank accounts.[92] But off-the-books cash in rubles or dollars would serve the same the purpose, while avoiding the manifest difficulties of barter. Levels of barter have also shown no tendency to decline even in periods when rules on automatic debt confiscation have been relaxed.[93]

If barter does not exist to facilitate tax evasion, perhaps its purpose is to conceal theft. Some Russian officials and journalists offer an explanation along the lines of what Althusser once called "*la solution par la clique.*"[94] On this view, nonmonetary exchange, as well as nonpayments, were designed to allow firms' directors to personally benefit from the arbitrariness both provide in deciding at what price goods will be accepted in payment, or even whether payment will be made at all.[95] There is no question that arbitrariness in pricing in-kind transactions, as well as the possibility of determining when and which monetary substitutes will be accepted in payment of taxes or debts, creates innumerable opportunities for kickbacks and sweetheart deals. However, this kind of *cui bono* functionalism seems to confuse consequence with cause. If nonmonetary exchange were merely a kind of virus of corruption, which escaped from a vial somewhere near the initial meetings of the Soskovets nonpayments commission, there would be nothing systematic about the phenomenon—no enduring sectoral differences, for example. Nor would such things as the lobbying of enterprises and regional governments for rules allowing firms to retain a share of monetary receipts for salary payments make any sense, since money transactions ought to be shunned. In Russia's chaotic environment, those inclined to theft and graft and possessed of decision-making power in business or the fiscal bureaucracy had ample opportunities for enrichment without building a mighty machinery of nonmonetary exchange.

A third and more recent approach suggests that barter and other forms of nonmonetary exchange conceal not tax evasion and not theft, but a "vir-

---

[92] Kathryn Hendley, Barry W. Ickes, Peter Murrell, and Randi Ryterman, "Observations on the Use of Law by Russian Enterprises," *Post-Soviet Affairs* 13 (January–March 1997): 19–41, at 36.

[93] Hendley and colleagues also discuss some more elaborate tax avoidance schemes that involve concealing income through nonmonetary exchange. Barter again does not seem the simplest way to solve the problems in question; but in any event, it is manifest that huge amounts of nonmonetary exchange were in fact declared as income by enterprises, since this was a main source of arrears.

[94] Quoted in Philippe Van Parijs, "Functionalist Marxism Rehabilitated: A Comment on Elster," *Theory and Society* 11 (July 1982): 497–511.

[95] *Ekspert*, 13 January 1997. This point of view was a successor to the earlier claim that firms allowed nonpayments in return for kickbacks to directors. *Kommersant* 13 September 1994, 2–5.

tual economy" built on a pervasive system of subsidies to firms that consume more than they produce.[96] Clifford Gaddy and Barry Ickes argue that barter is a way for value-subtracting firms to conceal their value-subtraction by overpricing their goods. They are sustained in this behavior by value-adding natural resource exporters, who accept overpriced goods in payment because they can pass them on to tax authorities at nominal value and because they regard the costs of subsidizing uncompetitive industry as a necessary political payoff for the right to continue exports. The pretense involved comes home to roost, however, when it becomes clear that overpriced goods cannot be used for wage payments and budget outlays that must be in money. As a result, a web of chronic debts emerges, reflecting an underlying shortage of rubles to pay obligations. When the "virtual" nonmonetary economy is compared to the "real" economy that would result from cash prices, the underlying structure of subsidies and the origins of chronic debt problems in value subtraction is revealed.

By linking nonmonetary exchange to rigid prices (albeit prices made rigid by firms' desire to pretend that they add value), the virtual economy argument achieves a significant advance over other alternatives. The simple model Gaddy and Ickes present compactly relates the problem of wage and tax arrears to the false equalization between monetary and nonmonetary receipts. Nevertheless, the virtual economy model rests on flawed foundations that make it deeply misleading in both political and economic terms.

The agents striving to maximize their advantage in nonmonetary exchange did not have easy access to what Gaddy and Ickes misleadingly call "real" prices. The key to the sociological-institutional theory of money defended in the introduction to this book is the abandonment of an unreflective notion of economic value as an objectively existing numerical entity that can be more or less precisely measured by money prices and accounting procedures. Practices of monetary exchange and calculation constitute value, rather than measuring it.

But Russia's loss of monetary sovereignty fragmented the institutions giving form and coherence to economic value. Hardheaded capitalist business practices, like charging different consumers different prices according to their ability to pay, were constrained by Russia's rigid price system, but practiced in spite of it through switching to alternate means of payment. Unmeasurably distorted prices were propagated along chains of exchange stretching through the tax system. All of this is not evidence of the

[96] Clifford Gaddy and Barry Ickes, "A Simple Four-Sector Model of Russia's 'Virtual' Economy" (Washington, D.C.: The Brookings Institution, May 1998), and Gaddy and Ickes, "Russia's Virtual Economy." Gaddy and Ickes's arguments became available as this book was being prepared for publication.

concealing of value subtraction by agents given to self-deceit. It is evidence of the creation of multiple realms in which value was given a local meaning—just as it is by different national currencies. Unlike separate national currencies, however, the boundaries between Russia's multiple monies were not sustained by central banks and different national legal frameworks. Instead, they were imperfectly policed by the agents organizing them, in constant struggle with legal and accounting frameworks that insisted on a false commensurability across realms. The value subtraction that Gaddy and Ickes detect is equally the effect of an illegitimate comparison across monetary realms. The number of lire that Italian firms pay their workers is greater than the number of pounds that British firms pay their workers, but this is not an indication that the Italians are pretending to make a profit. At most, depending on the exchange rate, they might be accused of a competitive devaluation. Some of those drawn into Russia's self-isolating giros might have preferred that the obligations that circulated within them trade at a higher "exchange rate" against the ruble, but they had lost this political battle in the arena that mattered. There was still business to be done.

By 1996, discontent with this fractured monetary space and the constant crises it generated was rising. The fiscal disaster facing the government concentrated attention on the difficulties of nonmonetary exchange and raised questions about its use of taxation in kind and through money surrogates. Federal officials began to attack the nonmonetary fiscal practices of regional governments and complained that in-kind and wechsel taxes meant that the provinces were failing to remit revenues due to the federal government. Gresham collapses of wechsel systems called into doubt the long-term viability of this solution to the problem of the double coincidence of wants. At the same time, certain large Russian businesses were finding the prevalence of nonmonetary exchange increasingly onerous, for reasons to be explored in the next chapter. In this environment, new projects for monetary consolidation emerged, gathering supporters and opponents and revealing the political terrain created by five years of economic upheaval.

CHAPTER SIX

The Politics of Monetary Consolidation, 1996–1998

No State shall . . . make any Thing but gold and silver Coin a Tender in
Payment of Debts . . .

—Constitution of the United States, 1787

In the late summer of 1786, farmers in western Massachusetts began a series of protests against aggressive enforcement of debts they owed, protests that were eventually to grow into what is known as Shays' Rebellion. According to the historian David Szatmary, repayment pressure had its origins with merchant wholesalers from the eastern part of the state, who were in turn being pressed to repay debts to their English suppliers.[1] These debts had to be settled in specie (gold or silver). Specie was extremely scarce, due both to substantial new specie taxes imposed by the Massachusetts government in an effort to settle war debt and to a massive trade deficit brought on in part by discriminatory British policy in the aftermath of the Revolutionary War. Wholesalers who had extended credit to retailers pushed them to repay this credit in specie; retailers, in turn, asked for specie payment from their farmer customers. Previously, relations between farmers and retailers had typically not had a monetary character. Even if they had store debts denominated in money terms, farmers had regularly paid for their relatively limited purchases in

---

[1] The account that follows is based on David P. Szatmary, *Shays' Rebellion: The Making of an Agrarian Rebellion* (Amherst: University of Massachusetts, 1980).

their own produce or through performing work.[2] Given the new specie tax burdens, farmers were in no position to pay back their debts when these nonmonetary options were denied, leading to a wave of debt prosecutions that affected astounding percentages of the rural population.[3] In response, a farmers' movement, under the leadership of Revolutionary War veteran Daniel Shays and calling itself the "Regulators," began mass actions to shut down debtors' courts and called for the issue of paper money and for "tender laws" that would allow taxes to be paid in kind. What ensued serves as a parable for Russia's struggles over means of payment more than two centuries later.

The Regulators met with a heavy-handed reaction from the Massachusetts government, headed by wealthy banker James Bowdoin. Although the government agreed to accept some in-kind payment for tax debts that had been overdue for more than two years,[4] it refused to issue paper money or to sanction the postponing of debt collection procedures until after new elections. Instead it suspended habeas corpus and threatened Regulators with jail.[5] By early 1787, the Regulators' protests led to a brief military struggle, handily won by a Massachusetts army hastily raised with funds donated by leading Boston merchants. Christened "Shays' Rebellion" and probably rather exaggerated by Federalists who had been seeking an occasion to demonstrate the need for a powerful national government, the incident became a major influence on the adoption of the U.S. Constitution, including the decision to vest key military and monetary powers with federal authorities.[6] For present purposes, however, Shays' Rebellion is more interesting as an instance of a conflictual and politically negotiated relationship between monetary and nonmonetary means of payment. The Regulators did not demand that their debts and taxes be reduced in nominal terms. Rather, they demanded the possibility of a different means of payment.

---

[2] Ibid., 31. Farmers were not the only ones affected by the specie shortage. Debts in the period were not only "book debt" with stores but also more negotiable promissory notes. Promissory notes allowed many people to be both debtor and creditor, but as calls for specie intensified this decentralized credit money system began to crumble, leading to many debt prosecutions, not always effective. Jonathan M. Chu, "Debt Litigation and Shays's Rebellion," in *In Debt to Shays: The Bicentennial of an Agrarian Rebellion*, ed. Robert A. Gross (Charlottesville: University Press of Virginia, 1993), 81–100.

[3] Some nonmonetary options for repayment did persist, though apparently on substantially worse terms. Ibid., 96.

[4] Rock Brynner, " 'Fire Beneath Our Feet': Shays' Rebellion and Its Constitutional Impact" (Ph.D. diss., Columbia University, 1993), 85.

[5] Ibid., 89.

[6] Szatmary, *Shays*, 120–134; Brynner, "Fire," 136–179; Stephen E. Patterson, "The Federalist Reaction to Shays' Rebellion," in *In Debt to Shays: The Bicentennial of an Agrarian Rebellion*, ed. Robert A. Gross (Charlottesville: University Press of Virginia, 1993), 101–118.

This demand had ample precedent. Ron Michener has investigated a number of periods of "monetary shortage" in Massachusetts in the pre-Revolutionary era.[7] These periods involved, among other things, "debt collection problems," both for private debts and for taxes, and "widespread resort to shopnotes (shopkeeper I.O.U.s), credit, and barter in place of cash transactions." During monetary shortage, prices quoted in specie were substantially lower than the nominal prices quoted for payment in other kinds of goods. Michener offers several explanations for this phenomenon, including the following:

> . . . the use of overvalued shopnotes and produce as a means of payment provided an important way of mediating between debtors and creditors. The fiction of high nominal values helped debtors. Obligations could be met with shopnotes and produce, and the possible legal and social consequences of defaulting on debt were largely avoided. Insofar as falling cash prices made full repayment of debts unlikely, the use of overvalued shopnotes and produce might be said to have aided creditors as well.[8]

Michener also notes that in several periods of monetary shortage, colonial authorities made provision for the payment of taxes in goods, establishing fixed prices at which different kinds of goods would be accepted. Often these prices were substantially higher than those the goods could have brought on the open market. One can reasonably suggest that the motivation of fiscal authorities was similar to that of creditors described in the preceding passage. Nonmonetary payment in both cases was a kind of repressed deflation—nominal values were preserved through a change in the medium of payment. Debt collection problems, low specie prices, and a switch to nonmonetary means of payment were all prominent during the run-up to Shays' Rebellion.[9] From 1785, though, unlike earlier periods of monetary shortage, government and merchants did not go along with the relaxation of the price system.

Analogies between the politics of monetary consolidation in a continental postsocialist industrial economy of the late twentieth century, with its cities of millions, and the predominantly agrarian society of late-eighteenth-century Massachusetts, with its villages of hundreds, are not likely to be analytically fruitful. To the student of post-Soviet Russia, the history of Shays'

[7] Ron Michener, "Shortages of Money in Colonial New England: An Explanation," University of Virginia, 1983.
[8] Ibid.
[9] Patterson, "Federalist Reaction," 107–109; Jonathan Smith, "The Depression of 1785 and Daniel Shays' Rebellion," *William and Mary Quarterly, Third Series* 5 (January 1948): 77–94, at 79.

Rebellion is of no use as a comparative case, but as parable it is quite illuminating. By late 1996, Russian approaches to the problem of monetary consolidation had begun to coalesce, as a result of the prevalence of the fracturing of the internal market and the Gresham effects described in chapter 5. Russia had its Bowdoins, intent on upholding the sanctity of nominal debts by whatever means necessary, and its Shaysites, struggling to subordinate the abstraction of numbers fixed in contracts to the concreteness of established modes of production and exchange. Between these two forces, as in our Massachusetts parable, no middle ground was to be found. For if demonetization is the only way to relax the price system, Bowdoin and Shays have no difference to split: one or the other must win. Compromise is tantamount to surrender. Yet the shades of Bowdoin and Shays did not stalk the Russian political landscape alone. A third force sought to find a way to make monetary consolidation possible on the basis of a negotiated nominal deflation. If it had spiritual ancestors in 1786, history does not record them.

This chapter investigates the character of contending projects for monetary consolidation (provisionally identifiable as neo-Bowdoin, neo-Shays, and conciliationist) as of spring 1998. It inquires into their political fortunes and prospects, and thus into the social forces on which they rested and the other projects in which they were implicated. The reference to "social forces" may seem to prejudge some important questions, insofar as it already implies the presence of stable and identifiable groups, capable of forwarding projects characterized by at least some degree of ideological coherence. In Russian politics as often portrayed in journalism (webs of corruption, agglomerations of personalistic relationships) it would make no sense to speak of social forces. Yet monetary disarray proved to be a kind of social X ray, identifying, perhaps not least to themselves, previously obscured social actors. The forces that produced the triple movement—center, region, and sector—were important players in the politics of monetary consolidation as well; yet it proves necessary to take account of contending bureaucracies in the "center" and the emergence of powerful new banking groups with interests of their own.

As I will argue in the epilogue, the unusual character of Russian monetary circumstances, in particular the coexistence of modern central banking and nationwide state bureaucracies with barter and giros more medieval in flavor, make it difficult to find appropriate comparative referents. Thus in defining approaches to monetary consolidation, we must rely on the more general typological approach adumbrated in chapter 3. There it was suggested that a monopoly on the definition and terms of creation of the means of payment can be pursued through macro strategies, intimidation or ratification, and micro strategies that simplify the use of the preferred means of payment or complicate the use of alternates.

Table 5. Projects for monetary consolidation

Justification for monetary consolidation	Macro strategy	Micro strategy
Hard-state liberal	Intimidation	Complication (fight alternative monies)
Productivist	Ratification and regulation	
Home market	Intimidation	Simplification (facilitate use of state money)

Three projects composed of these techniques (summarized in table 5) were being forwarded by the late 1990s. These can be termed the *productivist* (Shays), *hard-state liberal* (Bowdoin), and *home market* (conciliationist) projects. The first of these labels, the productivist approach, covers a family of proposals that would have the state ratify and regulate the creation of giro-wechsels of the sort that were described in chapter 5. Thus, although productivist approaches would put a firmer legal basis under giro-wechsel arrangements, they would not bring about a thoroughgoing monetary unification. Advocates of productivist approaches did not in general form a unified front, since the question of whose giro-wechsels will be ratified can prompt conflicts among supporters of different versions. The hard-state liberals advocated a continued tight monetary policy combined with repressive measures against enterprises operating outside the money economy. Firms chronically unable to pay their electricity and other bills in money should be shut or drastically reorganized under new leadership. In the home market approach—so named for the character of its political backing, as will become apparent in the following—nonmonetary exchange would be eliminated through transforming the implicit price reductions involved into explicit ones, allowing money transactions through obviating the need for "the fiction of high nominal values."

The three models rested on contrasting views on the causes of nonmonetary exchange, the appropriate economic role of the state, and the character of taxation. The productivist approach located the origins of nonmonetary exchange in a shortage of money to lubricate production. It implied a vision of the state as coordinator of the substantive economy. Taxation would be inseparable from the organization of production and exchange through chains and networks of firms bound by a variety of mutual obligations. Thus productivist approaches were associated with support for a directive state industrial policy focused on making things rather than making money. For hard-state liberals, the state was no more than its reputation. Nonmonetary exchange stemmed from the state's reputation for indulgence and willingness to accept taxation in kind or in money surrogates. Taxation should be an arm's-length monetary transaction, with evasion deterred through fear of detection and punishment. Industrial policy should be shunned as leading to a resurrection of soft budget constraints. Finally, the home market approach saw nonmonetary exchange as deriving from nominal prices set at a level beyond what the market would bear. It needed a state that would create a regulatory environment permitting explicit price reductions to replace barter, which would allow taxation to become an arm's-length monetary transaction. Industrial policy should involve negotiated price adjustments among private actors, not directive planning by the state.

The extent to which the different approaches were bound up with different visions of the state highlights how the politics of monetary consolidation is a politics of sovereignty. It also has important methodological consequences, since it implies that there is no single arena to which one can look to see how political contention around monetary consolidation was playing out. That is, the approaches were competitors, but this competition was often indirect, due to the distinct institutional fora relevant to each. By and large the projects were not prosecuted and resisted in the legislative arena, but in various parts of the federal bureaucracy, in the parastatal energy sector firms, or on the provincial level. Thus, the conflict between these approaches can only be appreciated through an examination of the separate efforts to forward each.

In the case of productivist projects for monetary consolidation, the most significant struggle was a center-regional one involving local authorities' right to issue wechsels. Regional authorities were able to play on divisions in the federal bureaucracy and also sought to push their case in Parliament. They were opposed by hard-state liberals as well as banks who preferred to issue any such wechsels themselves. In the case of the hard-state liberal model, one key arena from 1995 onward was the government's non-payments commission, supplemented from the fall of 1996 by the Emergency Tax Commission. The difficulties this model encountered were more in the form of a cumulation of case-by-case problems with implementing a tough policy than in organized political opposition. Finally, the home market model was at the center of debates on natural monopoly reform, for which the government had commissions and designated agencies from late 1996; these reforms were supposed to involve the rail, gas, and electric sectors, although only the last two are treated here. In the case of the gas sector, the home market model was able to make political headway after defusing conflicts with hard-state liberals, whereas in the case of electrical power reform, efforts led to polarization on center-regional lines that collapsed into a battle between centralizing hard-state liberalism and localizing productivism.

The balance of the chapter deals with each of the approaches to monetary consolidation.

Productivist Monetary Consolidation

Most of this section discusses conflicts over regions' issue of giro-wechsels, but some miscellaneous proposals to ratify and regulate giro-wechsels may be briefly summarized first. Often, these proposals advocated Central Bank money issue tied to the issue of wechsels by private parties, along the lines of the application of the Real Bills doctrine in the 1920s (see chapter 1). But while 1920s practices are sometimes cited in defense of such an approach,[10] the meaning of turning to a Real Bills–based policy of ratification and regulation of private credit issue would be quite different. Wechsels of the 1920s serviced commercial transactions, and their nominal value was meaningful in the context of a price system unified by a single means of payment. The nominal value of the wechsels of the 1990s reflected rigid definitions of production costs, obscuring their commercial value which derived from the exchange circuits within which they functioned. Schemes to tie money issue to wechsels were thus descendants of the transmuted form of the Real Bills doctrine born of the Credit Reform, not of the orthodox capitalist practices of the 1920s. Classical wechsels are a monetary obligation, discounted by banks or a central bank because of their reasonably certain link to a future sale, for money, of the goods represented by the wechsel.[11] Since the wechsels of Russian industrial firms represented an obligation to supply goods, not money, discounting them would be tantamount to using money as a lubricant of production. In essence, the policy would be a decentralized version of 1992's clearing operation (see chapter 3). By putting live money in the hands of enterprises operating with money substitutes or barter, productivist ratification would raise tax revenue, but the attitude of hard-state liberals to such arguments was summed up by the phrase of a government expert: "There's absolutely nothing to be gained from the practice of the early years of reform, when the state senselessly gave loans to enterprises, and they paid taxes punctually."[12] A variation on this theme was the stillborn proposal of the national electrical power company that the state issue "marked money" that would be designated for payments for electricity.[13]

In the context of a Central Bank committed (from mid-1993 or at the latest the fall of 1994) to a policy of tight money, efforts to convert wechsels into money through rediscounting were stymied. Accordingly, most proposals for productivist monetary consolidation involved state recognition of giro-wechsels. Contention centered around their legitimacy and

[10] *Ekonomika i Zhizn'*, no. 40 (1995).
[11] Discounting refers to making a loan on the security of a wechsel. See chapter 1.
[12] *Segodnia*, 28 February 1996.
[13] *Segodnia*, 1 March 1996.

who could issue them. The legal regulations for wechsels had a curious origin. The Soviet Union became a signatory to an international convention on bills of exchange in the 1930s and promulgated a regulation implementing international wechsel standards, according to which wechsels were an unconditional monetary obligation. Though this regulation was naturally entirely irrelevant to Soviet domestic trade, it was still on the books in 1991, when it was rediscovered and endorsed by the Russian Parliament at a time when it was seeking to be seen as a promoter of market reform. These regulations formed the basis for post-Soviet wechsel issue.[14] But because of wechsel users' need for tight regulation to prevent Gresham's effects, the regulations were often ignored in practice. In particular, wechsel issuers would refuse to pay them off in money, offering goods instead. This created the basis for a conflict over new wechsel legislation.

Around August of 1995, officials from the Siberian Agreement regional alliance association approached the Federal Commission on the Securities Market (known by its Russian initials as the FKTsB) with a proposal for new "paperless wechsels" that would circulate under the control of a single electronic clearing center—essentially a giro chamber. This proposal represented an effort to achieve federal legitimation for local government practice of closely managed giros as an alternative to direct in-kind taxation. Its forwarding by the Siberian Agreement represented part of a reactivation of regional cooperation on the backdrop of growing barter. After the collapse of the Soviet Union, interregional organizations formed to manage barter in the late Soviet period (cf. chapter 2) had generally entered a decline, continuing essentially as groups for joint lobbying of the center on shared interests (which could be rare) and as a way of aggregating provincial governors so that federal government representatives could meet with them in groups. The paperless wechsel proposal, designed to create a cross-province capacity to manage nonmonetary exchange, exemplified the way in which nonmonetary exchange promoted subnational integration.[15] Indeed, at least two other regional associations launched wechsel programs.[16]

The Siberian proposal highlighted the kind of divisions within the federal bureaucracy that Timothy Frye has insightfully analyzed.[17] The FK-

---

[14] *Delovoi Iuridicheskii Zhurnal,* 15 July 1995.

[15] This is very clear in the remarks of the Siberian administrator of the wechsel program, in "Press-Konferentsiia Predsedatelia Goskomiteta Po Rynku Tsennykh Bumag Dmitriia Vasil'eva (Leninskii prospekt, 9, 27 avgusta 1996 goda, 13.00) (Press-conference of the chair of the state committee on securities Dmitrii Vasiliev)." From *Vestnik Upravlenii Pravitel'stvennoi Informatsieii.* For other interregional barter managed through the Siberian Agreement, see *Delovaia Sibir',* 31 May 1996.

[16] *Rossiiskie Regiony,* no. 29, 1997 (special issue); *Finansovye Izvestiia,* 23 October 1997.

[17] Timothy M. Frye, "The State and the Market: Governing the New Russian Economy" (Ph.D. diss., Columbia University, 1997).

TsB, already battling other bureaucracies over the extent of its jurisdiction, became a champion of paperless wechsels. The Central Bank, which saw wechsels as a monetary matter, ferociously resisted them. In this the bank was seconded by tax authorities and the nonpayments commission, which first began to take a dim view of wechsels in the fall of 1995. They were especially concerned about regional wechsels, on the scale of which very little information was available. Officials expressed the fear that wechsel issue would complicate the fighting of inflation.[18] In October 1995, the Central Bank and the Ministry of Finance telegrammed local governments with the statement that existing budget regulations did not allow regions to issue wechsels, though this warning seems to have had little effect.[19]

Fencing between the Siberian Agreement–FKTsB alliance and their opponents in the Central Bank and the "financial block" of the government continued for the next two years. The hard-state liberal forces decided to pursue their agenda through passage of a new law, on which drafting began in late 1995, that would forbid regional governments to issue wechsels and would forbid paperless wechsels specifically.[20] Meanwhile, the FKTsB promulgated its paperless wechsels regulation in March 1996, perhaps in an effort to preempt the Parliamentary process.[21] In Parliament, Siberian Agreement representatives put forth their own version of the law that would legitimate local issue of giro-wechsels.[22] The battle between the two versions would not be resolved until the end of 1996.

For its part, the Central Bank took aggressive action to forestall the spread of paperless wechsels. In August 1996, it issued an instruction forbidding commercial banks to perform any operations involving paperless wechsels.[23] It also organized the creation of a self-regulating organization, the Association of Wechsel Market Participants (AUVER)—adopting a stratagem for maintaining its jurisdiction that had previously been used by the FKTsB to consolidate its regulatory authority over the stock market.[24] Initial participants in AUVER were in the main large, Moscow-based banks.[25]

[18] *Segodnia*, 23 November 1995.
[19] "On the Issue of Obligations by Executive Branch Organs," (O vypuske obligatsionnykh zaimov organami ispolnitelnoi vlasti) Telegram No. 05–01–04, 10/25/95. Inforis.
[20] *Finansovye Izvestiia*, 21 November 1995.
[21] Federal Commission on Securities and the Securities Market of the Government of the Russian Federation, Resolution No. 5 from 21 March 1996. Inforis.
[22] *Kommersant*, 16 April 1996.
[23] "On the Possibility of the Issue and Circulation of Paperless Wechsels," (O vozmozhnosti vypuska i obrashcheniia bezdokumentarnykh vekselei) Central Bank telegram of 5 July 1996. Inforis.
[24] On the similar, earlier actions by the FKTsB in the stock market, see Frye, "Governing."
[25] *Ekspert*, 21 October 1996.

The Siberian Agreement nonetheless continued to press its case and began operation of the paperless wechsel system in September 1996. At a joint press conference of the FKTsB and the leadership of the Siberian Agreement, Novosibirsk governor Vitalii Mukha argued that approval of the plan was a bellwether event: "This is the first time that such document, a quite serious document, about state building . . . has appeared, the first time when the subjects of the Federation and the center have united to resolve common problems."[26] However, Mukha's sentiments proved to be premature. In December, the lower house of Parliament (the Duma) passed the bill in a version congenial to the Central Bank, including the ban on paperless wechsels and on regional government wechsels in general. The law was then overwhelmingly rejected by the upper house, the Federation Council, composed of regional lawmakers and governors, where Mukha could count on the support of his provincial colleagues. However, under the Russian constitution, the Duma had the right to pass bills over the Federation Council's objection in a veto-override-like procedure, which was invoked in March 1997. The final law was essentially a restatement of the earlier regulations, with the addition of a ban on regional government wechsel issues.[27]

The passage of the law was not the end of the story. Regional governments in many cases were able to continue the issue of giro-wechsels under other names, or to make use of the wechsels of local enterprises. Even paperless wechsels were resurrected in a form putatively consistent with the new law.[28]

The wechsel law incident should not be regarded as merely a struggle between the Central Bank and the financial block of the government, on the one hand, and the FKTsB and the Siberian Agreement on the other. In the course of prosecuting the struggle, the Central Bank was also discovering a community of interest with bankers who hoped to dominate the local circulation of giro-wechsels. Large banks' participation in the Central Bank–sponsored AUVER can be regarded as an indication of this community of interest. In early 1996, as the struggle over wechsel regulations was beginning to take shape, a leading banker operating on the wechsel market stated that setting up wechsel plans with local administrations would be a top priority for banks in the coming year.[29] Such deals were indeed struck in great numbers over the following year, and the banning of local government wechsel issue could only have accelerated the trend.[30]

---

[26] "Press-Konferentsiia."

[27] Segodnia, 19 December 1996; Delovoy Ekspress, 31 January 1997; Kommersant-Daily, 25 February 1997.

[28] Rossiiskaia Azia, 23 April 1998; Segodnia, 15 October 1997; Ekspert, 12 January 1998.

[29] Finansovye Izvestiia, 16 January 1996.

[30] Finansovye Izvestiia, 18 July 1996.

The wechsel law incident revealed the weakness of the political base for a regulated ratification of wechsels other than those of banks. Despite overwhelming support in the Federation Council and an ally in the federal bureaucracy, the Siberian Agreement was not able to carry the issue. Denied de jure recognition of their wechsels, the regions retreated to legal tricks and reconstructing their giros on a basis more resistant to Gresham effects.

Hard-State Liberalism: The Battle for Tax Collection

As noted in the preceding chapter, in late 1994 the federal government took a relatively accommodating posture to nonmonetary exchange. From January 1995, however, the federal nonpayments commission was taken over by Anatolii Chubais. Chubais, who had designed Russia's privatization program, was perhaps the most vigorous advocate of hard-state liberalism in the Russian government, and he made the commission one of the centerpieces of his postprivatization efforts to "continue reform."[31] He used the commission as a platform for a sharp attack on nonmonetary exchange, focusing on its consequences for taxation. As Chubais declared at a commission meeting in October 1995, "the state is not only the army and defense. The state is the budget."[32] Chubais dismissed the argument that tight monetary policy caused barter and nonpayments, consistently advancing the argument that nonpayments in general, and nonpayments to the budget in particular, resulted quite directly from criminal behavior by enterprise directors, who according to Chubais took kickbacks from customers for shipping them goods without payment.[33] In this the commission was supported by the Federal Bankruptcy Administration, headed by Petr Mostovoi, who similarly argued that nonmonetary exchange practices were a cover for malfeasance.[34]

By fall 1995, Chubais had identified a list of forty-one debtors he believed to owe half the balance due to the budget, and he began trying to force them to pay back taxes.[35] His successes were at best very mixed. Although it is certainly true that heavy political fire was directed against the Chubais commission for its activity, it is equally true that the commission as often had to retreat in the face of economic as political reality. Many of the tax payments made by those key debtors that did submit to the commission's demands were in kind.[36] Nor could the commission, faced

---

[31] Craig Mellow, "Paper Promises Save Russia from Debt Debacle," *Euromoney*, no. 309 (January 1995): 54–56.
[32] *Ekspert*, 11 December 1995, 38.
[33] Ibid.
[34] *Ekspert*, 13 January 1997.
[35] This history of this episode is detailed in *Segodnia*, 16 January 1996, 3; see also *Ekspert*, 11 December 1995, 38.
[36] See *Ekspert*, 24 October 1995, 34, and 12 November 1995, 38.

with the fact that coal producers were regularly not receiving payment for their production, even begin to assert that they must pay their tax bills or pay the consequences.[37] Chubais eventually drafted a plan allowing tax debtors to restructure their debts, which went into effect in January 1997.[38]

The impression that the commission's difficulties in eliminating non-monetary exchange were not so much the product of the political manipulations of those whose corrupt interests it served as of systemic phenomena was reinforced after the hard-state liberal approach to the issue received a new impetus in the fall of 1996. By then, Gresham effects due to nonmonetary federal taxation were devastating federal receipts; in the summer of 1996, nonmonetary receipts approached half of revenue. At the same time, with the end of Yeltsin's election campaign, the IMF took the opportunity to push a much stricter line on tax collection. The confluence of these two circumstances explains the Russian government's adoption of a series of extraordinary tax collection measures from the summer of 1996. The extent to which those behind this effort saw reputational effects as critical was dramatically underscored in the creation of a special tax-collecting commission named to coincide with Lenin's secret police, the Vecheka. (In case anyone missed the pun, the heads of both successor agencies to the KGB were appointed as members of the commission.)[39] The reasoning behind such measures was not that each tax debtor would be individually coerced—this was clearly unfeasible—but rather to create enough fear of coercion among those not coerced that they would begin to seek to make ends meet in money (and thereby to pay their taxes) on their own. The state must make it clear that even if many firms may go under in a money economy, they may not go outside of it. A headline from a Russian paper indicated the end-point of this line of thinking: " 'Terrifying Measures' being prepared for tax debtors; even beat cops will be collecting taxes."[40] Apparently, the powers of the police proved to be insufficient: less than a year later, a high-ranking government official of hard-state liberal views suggested that tax debts be sold on the open market, since then their recovery would pass into the hands of *organized crime groups,* who could choose any collection methods they preferred.[41]

This perhaps can be dismissed as rhetorical excess, though it is very revealing of the way in which a reputational vision of the state differs from, say, a bureaucratic one. Or such statements could simply reflect frustration at the lack of success of the hard-state liberal program. Over the first full

[37] *Segodnia,* 30 November 1995.
[38] *OMRI Daily Digest,* 25 January 1996.
[39] *Segodnia,* 12 October 1996; *Ekspert,* 21 October 1996.
[40] *Moskovskie Novosti,* no. 29 (21–28 July 1996): 13.
[41] Interview with Alfred Kokh in *Ekspert,* 12 May 1997.

year of existence of the Vecheka, tax debts that went to the federal budget (not including late fees) grew by nearly 61 percent, far in excess of inflation.[42] Payments extracted from tax debtors investigated by the Vecheka often were in the form of offsets, as enterprises sought to compensate for the inflated nominal prices on their nonmonetary receipts, or simply did not dispose of money receipts sufficient to permit payment of debts in this form.[43] A committee that performed a detailed investigation of 210 of the largest tax debtors noted that on average, only 27 percent of their income took a monetary form.[44]

In rhetoric, hard-state liberalism seemed to leave little room for politics—for building a coalition behind the improved tax collection, government services, and facility of transactions that a monetized economy would bring. It reduced politics to political will, to the state representing itself as the general interest—understood in post-Olsonian fashion as precisely that interest which is unorganized. The hard-state liberal approach also ruled out any political accommodation with the regions, whose critical role in nonmonetary exchange has already been noted, for accommodation could be viewed as weakness. Yet one should not conclude that the hard-state liberal model of monetary consolidation was entirely without a political constituency. The insistence that nominal debts must be paid in money meant in practice that virtually any enterprise could be bankrupted. And this, in turn, could mean the transfer of its ownership. The initial wave of privatization in Russia, carried out from 1992 to 1994, had tended to entrench insiders at most enterprises.[45] Insistence on monetary payment of debt could serve as a means to lever them out. In January 1997, the government adopted Resolution 254, allowing firms with tax debts to retire their payments due to the budget by issuing new shares of stock to be sold on the open market.[46] The regulation was authored by Vladimir Potanin, a member of what has been called the Russian banking oligarchy: eight large commercial banks, headquartered in Moscow. From the mid-1990s, these banks had engaged in empire-building acquisitions of industrial assets in the provinces, forming "financial industrial groups."[47] With

---

[42] "Materials for the Briefing by V. D. Popov, Head of the Department of Forced Confiscation of Tax Arrears," State Tax Service web site at www.park.ru, 20 February 1998.

[43] Interview with Petr Karpov in *Rossiiskii neftianoi biulleten'*, September 1997.

[44] *Russkii Telegraf*, 31 January 1998.

[45] Joseph Blasi and Andrei Shleifer, "Corporate Governance in Russia: An Initial Look," in *Corporate Governance in Central Europe and Russia*, ed. Roman Frydman, Cheryl W. Gray, and Andrzej Rapaczynski, vol. 2 *Insiders and the State* (Budapest: Central European University Press, 1996), 78–108.

[46] *Ekspert*, 10 March 1997. Also see Potanin's earlier comments on the need to remove present manager-owners in *Ekspert*, 9 December 1996.

[47] Juliet Johnson, "Russia's Emerging Financial-Industrial Groups," *Post-Soviet Affairs* 13 (October–December 1997): 333–365.

their dominant position in domestic holdings of money, the eight banks stood to benefit from any transfer of ownership made possible by the enforcement of nominal debts.

That a coercive solution to tax difficulties might amount to a transfer of assets to power Moscow financial groups was illustrated by the efforts to collect overdue taxes from Nizhnevartovskneftegaz, a large oil company. In the face of large overdue tax debts, the government decided to invoke bankruptcy proceedings against Nizhnevartovskneftegaz in June.[48] Its director, Viktor Palii, claimed at a press conference that the fiscal organ's pressure on his company was carried out entirely in service of one of the big eight banks (Alfa-group), which hoped to buy out his firm.[49]

It is neither feasible nor necessary to assess the claim that decisions on redistributing property to pay off tax debt were deliberately designed to ease the expansion of the empires of the eight banks, or of a particular bank.[50] A coercive attempt at monetary consolidation, undertaken on whatever motivation, would intersect with particular business projects. A coercive solution to nonmonetary exchange could seek the political support of large Moscow banks and would institutionalize their dominance over the economy in exchange, budget finance, and production. In light of the extraordinary concentration of money and money exchange in Moscow, and the prevalence of nonmonetary exchange outside Moscow, one can speak of two different economic realms.[51] Bringing the nonmonetary economy forcibly into the monetary one would institutionalize the power of those who dominate the latter. The early results of the hard-state liberal approach did not suggest, however, that federal authorities were in any position to achieve such results.

Natural Monopolies Reform

A third forum in which struggles over monetary consolidation were fought out was the area of natural monopolies reform. Natural monopolies in the Russian context came to be a proper noun referring to the rail-

[48] Reuters report from Moscow, 17 June 1997.
[49] "Press Conference with Nizhnevartovskneftegaz Company General Director," Federal News Service, 1 July 1997.
[50] Nor am I implying that the hard-state liberals did not have quarrels with the big banks, or certain of them. Indeed, there were efforts to use Resolution 254 against Potanin-controlled firms once he left the government. *Kommersant-Daily*, 9 December 1997.
[51] Peter Rutland has termed this situation a "dual economy." Rutland, "The Russian Elite and the Challenge of Regionalism" (paper presented at the American Association for the Advancement of Slavic Studies Annual Conference, Seattle, November 21, 1997). On the growing concentration of the Russian banking sector, see Juliet Johnson, "Regional Development of the Financial Sector in Russia" (paper presented at the American Association for the Advancement of Slavic Studies Annual Conference, Seattle, November 21, 1997).

ways (subordinated to the railways ministry, MPS), Gazprom, and the electric power sector. It was in policy discussions around these sectors that what were labeled earlier as "home market" arguments for a reduction in formal prices to allow them to be paid in money were most often heard. Some impulses in this direction were noticeable as early as 1994. As discussed in chapter 5, in the fall of 1994, the national electric power and coal companies, the railway ministry, and the state metallurgy committee signed an agreement on mutual price restraint and received permission to make sales to one another at less than the cost of production. This agreement seems to have fallen apart quickly. However, the collapse of this so-called cartel agreement was followed by a series of government resolutions mandating price restraint on the part of the natural monopolies (rail, electricity, and gas), first through price freezes and then by limiting price rises to a fixed coefficient (.7 or .8) of wholesale prices more generally. The motivation for such decisions, apparently, was to avoid "provoking nonpayments" through overly high prices.[52] In other words, because natural monopoly prices would fall relative to the price level, such measures could be viewed as efforts to transform the repressed deflation represented by nonpayment and nonmonetary payment into an open deflation, opening the way for money payment. They were singularly unsuccessful. Nonmonetary payment for gas and electricity on the domestic market continued at very high levels (70–90 percent).

In the second half of 1996, the situation changed, in part in the context of a widening agenda on the part of the IMF. The IMF began to demand natural monopoly reform along the lines worked out by Western economists who had argued that virtually no monopolies are "natural."[53] According to this view, to implement a market in gas and electricity, it is necessary to separate distribution from production of energy, allowing independent producers to compete with one another. Although the IMF had put natural monopoly reform on the agenda, in practice the issues contested regarding policies in these sectors of the following year and half were usually distant from this plan to transform them into markets. Rather, what was central was a renewed emphasis on organizing a nominal deflation of prices to allow monetary payment.[54] In January 1997, a

[52] *Segodnia,* 14 November 1995.
[53] Harold Demsetz, "Why Regulate Utilities?" in *Chicago Studies in Political Economy,* ed. George Stigler (Chicago: University of Chicago Press, 1988), 267–278.
[54] Ben Slay and Vladimir Capelik, "The Struggle for Natural Monopoly Reform in Russia," *Post-Soviet Geography and Economics* 38, no. 7 (1997): 396–429, note that reforms in the 1996–1997 period "focuse[d] primarily on reducing prices in these sectors, and improving tax discipline and cash-flow management." Rather than seeing this as a distraction from the main issues of creating market competition in these sectors, it would be better to see eliminating barter and other forms of nonmonetary payment as the key government priority.

government expert on bankruptcy began to argue that the only way to overcome systemic distortions in nominal prices was to organize sharp reductions in energy prices.[55] In March, Boris Nemtsov, a former provincial governor, joined the government and took on responsibility for natural monopoly reform. From the outset, his program was simple: "we are planning to sharply lower energy prices for customers that can pay, and at the same time payments will be made in money and not with this idiotic barter."[56]

Over the next year, the nominal deflation model proved far more politically successful in the gas sector than in the electrical power sector. Indeed, Gazprom had been making its own efforts to be allowed to charge lower prices in return for money payment from the fall of 1996, on the argument that lower prices would allow more money payment and thus more tax payment.[57] Although price reduction was not passed quite in the form Gazprom had hoped, the firm did receive permission to cut deals with its debtors to forgive part of the debt in return for payment, *and to pay taxes only on what was actually received in such deals*. Essentially, this concession allowed Gazprom to pay taxes based on money receipts rather than on the inflated receipts that stemmed from the use of nonmonetary mechanisms. The concession was, however, weakened, by the statement that no such deals with debtors could be concluded at lower than the cost of production and delivery of the gas; this seems to have had its origin in concerns of the tax authorities.[58]

The explanation for Gazprom's desire to eliminate nonmonetary exchange can be found in the changing importance of the internal market to the firm. Gazprom was reacting to the staggering increase in the real exchange rate of the ruble against the dollar. The scale of this increase is illustrated by the fact that in 1996, the purchasing power of Russia's export receipts on the domestic market was approximately a tenth of what it had been in 1992 (see figure 6), and this despite the fact that the dollar value of exports had risen by more than half over the same period. Exporting looked increasingly insignificant next to sales to domestic consumers—if these consumers could be brought to pay in rubles rather than in kind. Gazprom officials demonstrated great awareness of the importance of the domestic market by 1996. In February 1996, the firm made available figures demonstrating that nonpayments of Russian consumers were greater than firm's exports.[59]

[55] *Finansovye Izvestiia*, 21 January 1997.
[56] *Delo* (Samara), 3 June 1997.
[57] *Vestnik Upravlenii Pravitel'stvennoi Informatsiei*, 3 October 1996; *Nezavisimaia Gazeta*, 3 October 1996.
[58] *Rossiiskaia Gazeta*, 22 October 1996.
[59] *Segodnia*, 20 February 1996.

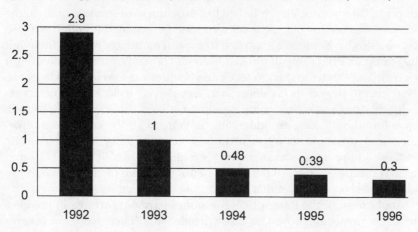

Figure 6. Purchasing power of Russia's exports on its domestic market, 1992–1996 (1993 = 1)

A study by a Western investment firm estimated that Gazprom's domestic sales were worth about 30 percent more in dollars than its sales to Western Europe in 1996, despite the fact that domestic prices were on average about half of foreign ones.[60] In early fall, the head of the firm's *export* division expressed his "hope that Russian customer's ability to pay would gradually grow, since in principle the internal market should be the main one for Gazprom."[61] Gazprom director Rem Viakhirev was more direct: "the internal market is the most profitable one for us, even in today's prices."[62]

Such declarations were not just slogans. Gazprom launched a complete reorganization of its domestic sales structure, replacing its eight key distributors with more than five dozen new local branches, one for each individual province in which it did business. The new structures gave Gazprom's sales apparatus a regional structure corresponding to Russia's administrative divisions. As the company explicitly stated, this structure was designed to facilitate bargains with local governments to bring about monetary rather than in-kind payments for gas.[63] Viakhirev himself traveled when necessary to conclude such deals; in January 1997, for instance, he went to Sverdlovsk. By December of the same year, Gazprom seems to have had formal agreements with all sixty-two provinces it served.[64]

---

[60] Salomon Brothers, "Rao Gazprom—Company Report," 17 September 1997, Investext Report No. 2585971, www.securities.com.
[61] *Nezavisimaia Gazeta*, 10 October 1996.
[62] *Ekspert*, 13 January 1997.
[63] *What Papers Say*, 21 January 1997.
[64] "Executive Branch Day by Day," Bulletin of the Press Service of the Governor of Sverdlovsk, no. 1, 1997; *What Papers Say*, 20 December 1997.

Gazprom's effort to monetize its receipts through nominal reduction of its prices thus became closely linked to a program to promote growth on the internal market through alliances with local governors. This effort was also consistent with Nemtsov's approach to natural monopoly reform. Initially it appeared that the campaign had a hard-state liberal cast, especially after it won a manifestly temporary victory when Gazprom agreed to take a large foreign loan to pay off its tax debts in money despite its lack of monetary receipts.[65] After some high-volume public conflicts, however, compromises were found, reflecting an underlying agreement on the causes of nonpayment and nonmonetary payment and the need to eliminate it. Emblematic of these compromises was an explicit presidential order licensing Gazprom to lower its price up to 40 percent for customers that paid in money, without the tax consequences that had previously followed such measures.[66]

Application of the lower-prices-for-money-payment formula in the electrical energy sector proved far more problematic. There were two reasons for this. First, unlike Gazprom, the electrical energy sector had no substantial exports. The increased dollar value of (actual and potential) domestic market receipts was irrelevant to the firm. Suggestions by the firm's leadership that money be printed (or, if not money, at least special "energy rubles" that would have amounted to state-sanctioned giro-wechsels tethered to energy payments) demonstrated the indifference of United Energy System (UES) to the possible effects of such measures on the external value of the ruble.[67] The absence of exports also meant that the company had no outside source of funds with which to support a program of growing the internal market through lower prices. As a result, when UES leaders did suggest price decreases (as in the fall of 1996), they did so only in the context of proposing a renewed cartel agreement that would lower the costs of their inputs and the prices of their outputs simultaneously.[68] Similarly, the firm was unable to embrace Gazprom's strategy of achieving post hoc price reduction through reducing the value of outstanding debts to it—since this would have left the firm without funds to pay its own creditors. Instead, the firm's leadership up until early 1997 focused on winning government acquiescence to in-kind taxation (in the form of debt netting) and relaxed rules on the immediate confiscation of money receipts for overdue taxes.[69]

The second reason that monetization through nominal deflation proved politically more difficult in electrical energy than in gas was the rel-

---

[65] *Kommersant-Daily*, 7 June 1997.

[66] *Ekspert*, 21 April 1997; *Kommersant*, 1 July 1997.

[67] *Ekspert*, 24 February 1997.

[68] *What Papers Say*, 26 October 1996. Gazprom was also part of this effort, but unlike UES, continued to push to be allowed to lower prices even outside a joint price restraint framework.

[69] *Rossiiskaia Gazeta*, 21 December 1997.

atively decentralized ownership structure . When electrical power generation was privatized, generators were split into two categories. The largest and most modern, generating the cheapest energy, went to the national parastatal company, UES, which also retained ownership of large transmission lines and the dispatcher organizations responsible for coordinating interregional energy balance.[70] At the same time, almost every province formed a local power system, which retained responsibility for local energy transmission and ownership of the generally older and more expensive generating plants not incorporated into UES's ownership structure.[71] UES also held substantial ownership in provincial power systems (known individually as Sverdlovskenergo, Mosenergo, etc. and collectively as the "AO-Energos"). As we saw in chapter 4, this privatization plan was heartily resented by local leadership, which waged a generally though not exclusively unsuccessful battle to retain the best generating plants. As a result of this division, some provinces became "energy deficit" provinces and had to supplement local generation with purchases from UES. Other, "energy surplus" provinces, could sell energy above what they produced for their own needs through UES. Atomic power plants remained fully state-owned and subordinate to the Ministry of Atomic Energy. They too were supposed to sell electricity through UES. Seconding this regional fragmentation of ownership was a regional fragmentation of regulation. Prices for energy sold by the AO-Energos were set by local energy commissions, generally headed by vice governors and including representatives of both producers and consumers.[72]

This regional division, which was created just as nonmonetary exchange was emerging, proved to have important consequences for the effort to monetize electricity receipts. In April 1997, Nemtsov arranged for the appointment of a close associate, Boris Brevnov, as chief executive officer of UES. Brevnov's major priorities were to improve payment discipline and monetize UES's receipts. He pursued this policy through a mixture of coercion and nominal price reductions for money payment. In practice, both policies were directed against the financial interests of the AO-Energos.

[70] *Kommersant-Daily*, 15 January 1993, 4.
[71] The problems of doing appropriate cost calculations for electrical power networks are everywhere exceptionally technically intricate—even when solved by "the market," this is a market very carefully constructed and managed by state authorities. One particular difficulty is determining the boundaries of the unit for which costs are to be calculated. Some generators are best adapted for running at constant levels of load—this is true of Russian coal-fired plants, for instance. Others, like hydropower plants, are best suited for responding to rapid fluctuation in the demand for power. As a result, although one can speak of the generation costs of a particular plant in a (relatively) straightforward manner, the costs of a power delivery system are a matter in which the conventional nature of accounting rules are especially pronounced.
[72] *Ekspert*, 13 April 1998.

On the coercive side, Brevnov took steps to stop Gresham effects brought on by UES's wechsel program. These typical giro-wechsels, administered by a quasi-independent firm with close ties to the company's leadership, could be used only to pay for interregional electricity transfers and the AO-Energos' so-called subscriber fees for the services rendered by the national network.[73] Although UES had guaranteed the acceptance of these wechsels, Brevnov ordered that these guarantees be revoked. Wechsels would be accepted in payment only for about 70 percent of debts incurred before August of 1997, and only if accompanied by monetary payment for the balance. This amounted to a sharp post hoc increase in the rates AO-Energos were paying for UES's services, and a transfer of ready-money receipts to UES. Brevnov continued the coercive approach to monetization with threats to fire local AO-Energo chiefs who failed to improve collection. His style recalled a Bolshevik Governor Bowdoin.

> On January 5–6 we gathered all regional power companies and the first thing we did was to give them quarterly payment collection assignments. I used the same method of transparency and publicity. I showed the general directors a table containing their norms of payment collection. We started from the average level and decided to collect not less than 30 percent from each regional company in the first quarter. I told them that this table did not contain a "Objective Factors" row. I told them that it was a public table.[74]

The other half of the policy of monetization involved nominal deflation in return for money payment. In practice this proved to be exceptionally difficult because of the regional fragmentation of the power sector. In essence, UES did not control the prices that needed to be lowered. UES itself made sales only in the context of transfers to "energy deficit" regions. Within each region, prices on sales to final consumers were regulated by local energy commissions, who had to take as a baseline the higher costs of locally owned energy producers, even if this led to a level of prices that prompted nonmonetary payment. Brevnov's solution was to allow large final consumers direct access to the UES-run "wholesale market" for electrical energy, and then to offer substantial (30 percent) discounts for payment made in money, rather than in kind.[75]

This policy amounted to an effort to pry those customers capable of paying in money away from the regional power systems, increasing the pres-

[73] *Segodnia*, 19 August 1997. Details of the wechsel plan from correspondence with an official at a UES subsidiary, April 1996.
[74] "Press Conference with RAO EES Rossii Chair Boris Brevnov," Federal News Service, 29 January 1998.
[75] *Nezavisimaia Gazeta*, 3 July 1997. This plan was specifically allowed by government order.

sure on them to monetize their remaining receipts. As Nemtsov explicitly stated, the wholesale market plan would attract the "7–8% of enterprises presently paying in money."[76] This implied not just a shifting of revenue from the provincial power systems to UES, but simultaneously moving the taxes on this revenue from provincial budgets to the federal and Moscow budgets. Thus the plan made enemies among local governors as well as the heads of local power systems, who would lose the revenue of their most reliable customers. (Gazprom, by contrast, promised to pay the taxes on Mezheregiongaz revenues where they were collected.)[77]

In January 1998, the political costs of Brevnov's strategy became clear when the former CEO of UES, Anatolii Diakov, made an effort to push Brevnov out as head of the company. The Diakov–Brevnov conflict was intense and colorful, involving mutual allegations of corruption that created the impression that what was at stake was a personal rivalry, or a battle between those nostalgic for a planned economy and new managers with a financial outlook. Behind the shouting match and mudslinging, however, was the stark fact that Brevnov had alienated the managers of virtually all the AO-Energos. At a government meeting to assess the results of Brevnov's half-year at the head of the company, not a single AO-Energo head spoke positively of him.[78] Diakov's key backers in his bumbling attempt at a palace coup after the meeting were almost all heads of regional power companies. Though Diakov was rapidly overruled by the Ministry of Fuel and Energy, arguments over who should head the company continued through the spring. Brevnov made some hasty efforts to shore up his regional support, but these were evidently not enough; he resigned in March 1998.[79] In the summer, Anatolii Chubais became Brevnov's permanent replacement, pledging to continue efforts at monetizing the companies' receipts and to bring the AO-Energos to heel by subordinating them more directly to the national power company.[80] There was no particular reason to assume he would be any more successful.

One reason for Brevnov's weakness was that his flagship program for creation of a national wholesale market failed to show results. This was not only because of resistance to the shift of the small (if vital) share of payments for electricity that were done in money from regional coffers to central ones. The reform also threatened the structure of local in-kind taxation. Wholesale consumers of electricity would be the firms whose products were most widely demanded and thus easily exchanged in barter

[76] *Segodnia,* 1 July 1997.
[77] *What Papers Say,* 21 January 1997.
[78] *Rossiiskaia Gazeta,* 29 January 1998; *Ekspert,* 9 February 1998.
[79] *Rossiiskaia Gazeta,* 13 February 1998.
[80] *Ekspert,* 22 June 1998.

operations. When these firms purchased power from local power companies, provincial administrators could bring them into barter chains. If they were to purchase their electricity from out-region suppliers, however, this possibility would cease. Therefore, the effort to shift large consumers to the wholesale market threatened not just regions' monetary revenue, but also their "fiscal apparatus" for in-kind taxation. The nature of this threat was particularly clear in the case of railways. As early as October 1996 the railways were allowed by presidential order to buy their energy directly from the wholesale market. Yet in January 1998, the head of the Federal Energy Commission had to report that this decision was being "torpedoed by virtually every provincial governor," due to worries both about the loss of revenue and about the loss of relatively fungible goods for barter.[81]

Regional leaders' resistance to the creation of a national and money-based energy market that would severely damage their capacity for local in-kind taxation demonstrates once again how barter exchange promotes subnational integration while promoting national disintegration, and how money exchange promotes subnational disintegration while promoting national integration. The effort to bring enterprises into a national market for electricity was inherently and inevitably an effort to detach them from the local in-kind economy, with concomitant implications for the ability of local governments to sustain these economies. As Brevnov himself put it, "Barter relations and in-kind payment cannot be equated with market relations. Barter leads to disintegration. The development of the wholesale market is connected with money payments."[82]

Conclusion

The debates over the wechsel law, tax collection, and natural monopolies reform revealed the protagonists of the battle over monetary consolidation and something of the arenas in which they did combat. In part, the tableau resembled that of Shays' Rebellion as presented at the outset of this chapter. In the role of the Regulators, determined to ensure that the payment of nominal debts in gold did not destroy a way of life resistant to monetary calculation, we have the regional governors and the interregional associations, seeking central government sanction for their efforts to manage local economies in the service of goals not defined in monetary terms. Governor Bowdoin and the narrow merchant and banker alliance behind him, standing for specie debt payment at all costs, found their successors in the Emergency Tax Commission and the limited group of

[81] *Ekspert*, 19 January 1998.
[82] *Segodnia*, 16 October 1997.

bankers that stood to benefit from the redistribution of assets that a coercive monetization of debts would bring. Brevnov's efforts on behalf of the national power system at the expense of local ones displayed the same spirit.

Unlike in 1786, however, in 1996 to 1998 these two forces fought to a stalemate. In the national arena, hard-state liberals were able to block provincial government efforts to win backing for institutions that would essentially allow the regional tax systems to coordinate local production, sales, and prices. On the other hand, whether or not this defeat meant anything significant for actual practice (as opposed to legal status) on the local level was another matter entirely. Meanwhile, efforts to force firms that operated outside the money economy either into liquidation or into returning to the world of money were equally ineffective. Neither hard-state liberalism nor local productivism was able to win a decisive victory.

The development of the third project for monetary consolidation, the home market model, was the most interesting. In the case of Gazprom, the switch to a focus on the domestic market was accompanied by a coordinated campaign to establish province-by-province alliances with local governors. In the case of UES, the effort to use lower money price to lure the best customers of local power systems into a national money economy failed completely in the face of regional resistance. Here, too, policy seemed to be moving in the direction of province-by-province deals with governors. What was not clear was whether this pattern of bilateral agreements represented the natural monopolies conceding to the terms on which regional nonmonetary economies were organized, or whether these agreements would be the first step toward bringing about monetary consolidation on a home market model.

When this book was completed, it was simply too early to tell which model of monetary consolidation would prevail, nor was it clear how the enormous financial crisis that broke out in August 1998 would affect the players. Although the wechsel law incident appeared to demonstrate that regional prospects for institutionalizing their giro arrangements were dim, the battle between the coercive and home market models was still unfolding, and their contradictions becoming more apparent. The foundering of coercive monetization in electrical energy and through tax enforcement did not bespeak a federal capacity to break local defense of the in-kind economy. Gazprom's negotiated model had likewise not given the desired results, though the company announced further price cuts in the spring of 1998. In government, no single policy had emerged. In miniature, the key tension could be seen in December 1997. When Minister Without Portfolio Yevgeni Yasin identified allowing firms to sell for less than their formal cost of production as the top priority for economic policy, he was immediately countered by State Tax Service head Alexander Pochinok, who argued that this would lead to huge tax evasion.[83] Whether the federal state would come to see its fiscal interest in promoting monetary exchange, and on this basis sanction a negotiated nominal deflation, or whether it would conceive its fiscal interest in projecting a reputation for hardness, and on this rationale seek the support of Moscow-based financiers in breaking the power of local authorities, remained very much an open question.

With the emergence of clear contending projects for monetary consolidation, one can also speculate what the victory of any of them would mean for the integration of Russia's internal market and the structuring of the political arena. If local governments continued to maintain their isolated giro exchange systems on the basis of central legal sanction, any eventual growth would depend on a thoroughly local industrial policy and would likely be export oriented. Unfortunately, the more likely outcome would be the gradual erosion of the local infrastructure and eventual collapse into thoroughgoing deindustrialization. Banks might dominate the organization of this fragmented, shrinking nonmonetary economy, but this would not be a platform on which they could build long-term strength. As for the home market and coercive approaches to monetary consolidation, they differed in their attitude to regional efforts to sustain their economies through nonmonetary exchange. The home market model would base monetary consolidation on negotiated agreement with local leaders, temporarily subsidized by export receipts in hopes of eventually achieving domestic growth. This would make national economic integration and a unified money the product of ongoing and eventually institutionalized consultations between national and local executive bodies, maintaining Parliament in a secondary position and curbing, as well, the empire-building aspirations of the large Moscow banks. The agents and axis of national economic integration would be the infrastructural organizations inherited from the Soviet era, not the Moscow-based banks produced by the new circumstances. Nationwide business movements transcending existing sectoral structures would be unlikely. Finally, if coercive monetary consolidation were to prevail, it would mean institutionalizing the dominance of Muscovite financial structures and breaking the power of local authorities. The federal fisc and a finance-dominated big business would be closely allied and centered in Moscow; alternative centers of financial power or industrial policy would be unlikely.

In chapter 4, I argued that the origins of the nonmonetary economy lay in a "triple movement"—a defense of the susbstantive economy from the formal economy, intially implemented by regional governments, but then sustained by the national government under pressure from regional and

[83] *Moscow Times*, 23 December 1997.

sectoral lobbying. Each of the contending projects for monetary consolidation offered a different answer to the dilemma of the triple movement. The various versions of productivist monetary consolidation took the triple movement least seriously, locating its origins in an unwarranted separation of the process of money issue from production and exchange. Once this mistake was corrected, the need for the triple movement would quickly disappear.

The hard-state liberals, by contrast, showed signs of perceiving the root of the triple movement in an imperfectly unified internal sovereignty that could only be overcome with the decisiveness of a Bowdoin. A project to conquer sovereignty by depriving the provinces of the ability to accept non-monetary means of payment appeared to be coalescing. The implication would be that national integration would have to be reconstructed from the ground up on the basis of thorough central dominion of the financial system.

For advocates of the home market model, the triple movement represented something different—not a hindrance to national integration but rather the form of national integration that Russia already possessed. Rather than rebuilding from the ground up, the approach was to work with what exists. Rather than being the object of a tug-of-war between central and regional authorities, the nationally integrated sectors should strive to become the fulcrum of their cooperation. The structures that make Russian national integration a substantive reality might also take on the mission of making Russian national integration a formal reality through the generalization of monetary calculation. The triple movement would not be evidence that all must be started anew, but instead an indicator of where to start.

The generalization of monetary calculation will not in any event be an easy task. Hard-state liberals hold the depressing and plausible conviction that the Soviet economic system—with its partitioned monies, unsystematic prices, and imperative for reproduction of existing organizations at all costs—created a substantive economy that will never be able to function as a by-product of formal calculation of market opportunity. On this view, as long as local and even national authorities are constrained to tax in what the economy produces, rather than coercively producing an economy that can be taxed, Russia will be doomed to stagnation and decay.

Friends of Russia can only hope that this conviction is mistaken. The fascination that the phenomenon of money exchange held for Simmel lay above all in its curious mixture of subjectivity and objectivity—each exchange prompted by purely subjective personal desires and yet precisely measured in numbers that seemed to transcend all personality in a perfect objectivity. "Society is a structure that transcends the individual, but that is not abstract. . . . Society is the universal which, at the same time, is concretely alive. From this arises the unique significance that exchange . . . has for society; exchange raises the specific object and its significance for the individual above its singularity, not into the sphere of abstraction, but into that of lively interaction which is the substance of economic value."[84] If lively interaction is the substance of economic value, then economic value is a human creation. Humans make money—in the conventions and institutions they create to define and regulate it—and in so doing, they give a meaning to economic value. There are of course better and worse ways to structure the conventions that permit formal economic calculation and money exchange. But perhaps recognition of the irreducible element of arbitrariness in the social construction of economic value can reveal possibilities that too ready a resort to the numerical metaphors of profit and loss would obscure, and allow Russia's abstruse clashes over accounting rules and exotic financial instruments to appear not as subjectivity run riot, but as inevitably and therefore properly contentious collective efforts to design a *useful* objectivity.

[84] Georg Simmel, *The Philosophy of Money*, trans. Tom Bottomore and David Frisby from a first draft by Kaethe Mengelberg, 2d enlarged ed. (London: Routledge, 1990), 101.

EPILOGUE

Russian Monetary Consolidation in Comparative Perspective

By the summer of 1998, more than six years of vigorous struggle over the shape and policies of monetary institutions had
produced no decisive outcome. These years had, however,
brought about a major transformation in the character of the political aims
of key economic actors. Conflicts over how the central government's
money should be distributed no longer had even the derivative role they
had played in the first years after price liberalization. The new conflicts
were conflicts over institution building. The "directors' corpus," so prominent in 1992, was no more than a memory, destroyed along with the Soviet payment institutions that had sustained it. The triple movement
politics of 1993 to 1995 persisted, but in changed form. Provincial governments continued to use nonmonetary exchange as a way of making ac-
commodations to local demands for protection from the destructive
effects of the rigid price mechanism, and to push some of the costs of this
policy onto organized sectors of industry whose political clout in Moscow
helped them bear the burden. But provincial governments also sought,
however ineffectively, to win legal recognition for the monetary powers
they regularly employed, and to reinvigorate interregional alliances as a
means for managing ongoing nonmonetary exchange. For their part, the
energy sectors could no longer count on monetary compensation for the
costs of nonmonetary exchange. At best they might win the temporary aid
of the fiscal organs in putting together chains of barter; at worst, they might

have to fight off one of the periodic campaigns of hard-state liberals to force them to pay all their taxes in money. In very different ways, leaders in these sectors reacted by seeking to bring a new predictability to their relations with local authorities so as to strengthen their position at the national level. Inside the central government, different approaches to monetary consolidation competed, but there was no part of bureaucracy that saw continued ad hoc adaptations to nonmonetary exchange as tolerable.

With monetary consolidation firmly at the center of Russian politics, it might seem reasonable to look to comparative analogs for guidance as to how it might turn out. Under the ordinary intellectual and historical circumstances in which the study of comparative politics is practiced, the concept of monetary consolidation could be used to describe a settled historical outcome and organize an explanation and narrative of divergence across cases. The student of Russia's still-unfolding transformation needs to approach the problem of comparative analogs from a somewhat different angle. What is needed is guidance in how to describe the dimensions along which "outcomes" might vary, rather than explain the outcome itself. Unfortunately, finding useful comparative analogs for Russia's monetary disarray poses immense challenges. Other postsocialist countries have seen extensive use of alternative means of payment, but their experience is too little chronicled and their outcomes too unsettled to be of much use in achieving purchase on the prospects for Russia. Thus one is driven to seek historical analogs. Unfortunately, the processes whereby money's definition and issue have come to be monopolized by central state authorities have received very little attention in comparative politics literatures on state building and political development.[1] As for economists, those interested in the possibility for private provision of the means of payment under a system of "free banking" have excavated important historical instances of decentralized monetary systems, but by and large they have focused on the advisability and feasibility of eliminating the state's monopoly on money rather than on historical explanations for its origins.[2] A

---

[1] Recent path-breaking exceptions are Kiren Aziz Chaudhry, *The Price of Wealth: Economics and Institutions in the Middle East* (Ithaca: Cornell University Press, 1997), and Richard Franklin Bensel, *Yankee Leviathan: The Origins of Central State Authority in America, 1859–1877* (Cambridge: Cambridge University Press, 1990).
[2] Many of the most important readings in this vein are collected in Lawrence H. White, ed., *Free Banking*, 3 vols., *The International Library of Macroeconomic and Financial History* (Aldershot, England: E. Elgar, 1993). The free-banking focus on monetary stability has inspired at least one theory of the state monopoly on money, which links it to states' need to have seigniorage available for use in wartime. See David Glasner, "An Evolutionary Theory of the State Monopoly over Money," in *Money and the Nation State: The Financial Revolution, Government and the World Monetary System*, ed. Kevin Dowd and Richard H. Timberlake (New Brunswick: Transaction, 1998), 21–46.

somewhat separate historical literature by economists has grown from debates around the quantity theory of money and is usually concerned with political and institutional history only as it bears on this issue.[3] Nor is there a thematically unified literature by historians on which to draw, though there are many studies with more or less bearing on the issue.

The difficulties of finding a source base for comparative investigation are, of course, ultimately practical ones. Far more significant is the fact that the process through which the developed states achieved monetary consolidation (largely in the nineteenth century) occurred in the context of the use of metallic media of exchange (silver and gold). The direct challenge involved was achieving regulatory control over the creation of credit money on a gold or silver base through the fractional reserve mechanism. Credit could be created through the now-familiar mechanism of deposits, or through the then-popular mechanism of issuing notes backed by a promise to pay out gold and silver. The credibility of these promises was often quite difficult to ascertain and led to substantial regional fragmentation of credit monies. However, this sort of monetary pluralism is of a very different character than that which emerged in Russia. As a result of the use of metallic monies, monetary consolidation in the nineteenth and early-twentieth centuries occurred in a context of constant systemic risk. The use of relatively fungible reserves meant that even when credit monies created on their base were regulated in regionally diverse ways, problems in one regionally partitioned system of credit money quickly propagated to others. The failure of a single bank issuing gold-backed notes threatened the reserves of other note-issuing banks. Such crises were regularly transmitted across national borders as well.[4] Indeed, since the use of metallic media of exchange was more or less worldwide, decisions about the regulation of the monetary system were inseparable from decisions about managing the terms of domestic integration with the international economy.[5]

The potential of systemic risk associated with the fragmented but usually metal-based monetary arrangements of the nineteenth century was not

[3] Michael Bordo, "Explorations in Monetary History: A Survey of the Literature," *Explorations in Economic History* 23 (October 1986): 339–415 is an exhaustive introduction.

[4] For one of innumerable examples of the international transmission of financial crisis due to the wide use of gold reserves, see the account of the Panic of 1837–1838 in Bray Hammond, *Banks and Politics in America from the Revolution to the Civil War* (Princeton: Princeton University Press, 1957), 451–499. For a broader perspective on events somewhat later in the century, see Giulio M. Gallarotti, *The Anatomy of an International Monetary Regime: The Classical Gold Standard, 1880–1914* (Oxford: Oxford University Press, 1994), 165–169.

[5] A sense of this intimate relationship can be gained from Gallarotti, *Anatomy*, 141–180. See also Karl Polanyi, *The Great Transformation: The Political and Economic Origins of Our Time* (Boston: Beacon Press, 1965), 201–208.

present in the Russian situation of the late-twentieth century. Russia's means of payment were of limited fungibility and regionally and organizationally fragmented. The repercussions of the collapse of any particular quasi-money system were limited. Similarly, though there were, of course, links between Russia's thoroughly monetized foreign trade and the quasi-monetary and nonmonetary exchange prevalent on the internal market, they were of a much less direct character than in the case of fragmented but metal-backed credit monies.

In this light, given the thoroughgoing localism of Russia's alternate means of payment, it might seem plausible to argue that an enlightening comparative analog for Russia's monetary consolidation should be sought not in the nineteenth century, the era of nation-states and national markets, but somewhere closer to the sixteenth century, in the eclipse of manorial economies and the transition to capitalism and a monetized economy. Such a comparison would not be without precedents. Katherine Verdery, for instance, has advocated the study of the "transition from socialism to feudalism."[6] Michael Burawoy and Pavel Krotov argue that the collapse of the Soviet state cleared the field for the activities of a pre-capitalist "merchant capital" in which exchange is parasitic on existing structures of production, rather than transforming them.[7] Kenneth Jowitt employs a different sociological idiom, but with similar comparative import. Describing the Soviet enterprise, with its nonmonetary production goals and its drive for self-sufficiency, as an *oikos* in Weberian terms, he argues that it is thus the font of a premodern mechanical social solidarity in the Durkheimian sense.[8] Finally, and most directly for our topic, the Russian journalist Yuliya Latynina, the leading press expert on nonmonetary exchange, lost no opportunity in the latter half of the 1990s to portray quasi monies and barter systems as a recrudescence of feudalism.[9] Such positions would imply that applying theories of what Polanyi termed "the discovery of society" to postsocialist Russia would simply be anachronistic and unilluminating, since Russia would not have a society in this sense. In Polanyi's stylized historical sequence, Russia would stand prior to the elimination of subnational barriers to markets, waiting for its unification

[6] Katherine Verdery, "A Transition from Socialism to Feudalism? Thoughts on the Postsocialist State," in *What Was Socialism, and What Comes Next?* (Princeton: Princeton University Press, 1996), 204–228.

[7] Michael Burawoy and Pavel Krotov, "The Soviet Transition from Socialism to Capitalism: Worker Control and Economic Bargaining in the Wood Industry," *American Sociological Review* 57 (February 1992): 16–38.

[8] Ken Jowitt, *New World Disorder: The Leninist Extinction* (Berkeley: University of California Press, 1992), 127–139, 289–290.

[9] For examples, see *Izvestiia*, 13 March 1997, and *Ekspert*, 12 January 1998.

through a mercantilist policy understood in the manner of Schmoller or Hecksher.[10]

It cannot be gainsaid that a feudal comparative referent would have certain advantages. In particular, it would underscore the tax difficulties raised by nonmonetary exchange. Although regionally fragmented credit monies on a metallic base of the nineteenth century did have fiscal implications, these were rarely important issues for monetary consolidation in general.[11] Taxes could always be collected in specie. A feudal analogy, by contrast, would invite comparisons to the rise of Schumpeter's tax state, and his argument on how, "[t]ax bill in hand, the state penetrated the private economies and won increasing dominion over them. The tax brings money and calculating spirit into corners in which they do not dwell as yet."[12] Further, we would be free to invoke Weber's insight that the dissolution of the manorial system was brought about by the combined effort of state-builders looking for monetary tax revenue, outside capitalists looking for new spheres of activity, and manor insiders who perceived the market opportunities a new monetary order would make available.[13] Indeed, such considerations have been important in discussing the Russian state's reaction to the fiscal crisis brought on by nonmonetary exchange.

Nevertheless, however evocative, the analogy with feudalism is strained. It should not be forgotten that socialist industrial enterprises were *industrial* enterprises, built as part of an economy national in scope. Autarky, however constant a tendency, was a much more relative notion than in any preindustrial society. Individual industrial enterprises could never be fully self-sufficient, and much bureaucratic politics was devoted to finding the level of organizational aggregation that would in fact ensure enough autarky to give relatively reliable production. It was often the case that an entire ministry behaved as an autarkical unit, transferring supplies among its

---

[10] Gustav von Schmoller, *The Mercantile System and Its Historical Significance, Reprints of Economic Classics* (New York: A. M. Kelley, 1967); Eli F. Heckscher, *Mercantilism*, trans. Mendel Shapiro, Revised 2nd ed., 2 vols. (London: George Allen & Unwin, 1955).

[11] This is essentially because taxes could always be assessed in gold. There were some nuances. In the United States, for example, virtually all federal government tax revenue before the Civil War came from customs duties collected in gold (Hammond, *Banks and Politics*, 451). Internal taxes were the province of the states. In some states this contributed to monetary fragmentation, since these states drew revenue from their equity share in local banks of issue and wished to block competition with them. John Joseph Wallis, Richard E. Sylla, and John B. Legler, "The Interaction of Taxation and Regulation in Nineteenth-Century U.S. Banking," in *The Regulated Economy: A Historical Approach to Political Economy*, ed. Claudia Goldin and Gary D. Libecap (Chicago: University of Chicago Press, 1994), 121–144

[12] Joseph Schumpeter, "The Crisis of the Tax State," in *The Economics and Sociology of Capialism*, ed. Richard Swedberg (Princeton: Princeton University Press, 1991), 99–140.

[13] Max Weber, *General Economic History*, trans. Frank H. Knight, with a new introduction by Ira J. Cohen ed. (New Brunswick, NJ: Transaction, 1981), 92–114.

subordinate enterprises over vast distances to avoid complicated dealings across ministerial boundaries.[14] The formal resemblance of the guiding spirit of such activity to that animating Weber's *oikos* should not obscure its very different geographical scope and the technological and organizational underpinnings involved. Russia's politics of monetary consolidation, as the preceding chapters have shown, has depended critically on the articulation between the national and the local political and administrative arenas, especially through descendants of such ministries. In a truly localized manorial economy, these forms of articulation could not exist.

Aside from such economic factors, it also should be stressed that the reach of the late-twentieth-century Russian state, for all of its notorious infirmities, was incomparably greater than that of absolutist states in the manorial era. To take the most relevant example, when manorial economies were transformed, central banking was not yet even a gleam in a monarch's eye. The Bank of England, for example, was only founded in 1694 and did not begin to resemble what we now consider a central bank for some time thereafter, whereas the manorial system was eclipsed well earlier.[15] At most, "national" governments in the manorial era claimed often tenuous monopolies on minting coins and specifying units of account, which given the importance of credit money is quite different from a monetary monopoly *tout court*.[16] Russia's monetary pluralism, in contrast, developed despite the nationwide presence of the Central Bank, which had representative offices in every province. Similarly, the bureaucratic capacity of Russia's nationwide tax services, however derisory from the perspective of outside observers, would have been awesome to an absolutist monarch. The mere fact that many Russian enterprises subscribed to Internet databases carrying the latest tax and commercial regulations (even if they read them indifferently) illustrates how misplaced any sustained analogy between the postsocialist transition and feudalism would be.[17]

One final difficulty in choosing an appropriate comparative referent for Russia's monetary consolidation is the changing definition of money over

---

[14] For an excellent discussion of the tendency to autarky in the Soviet economy, see Nikolai Shmelev and Vladimir Popov, *The Turning Point: Revitalizing the Soviet Economy* (New York: Doubleday, 1989), 114–128.

[15] H. V. Bowen, "The Bank of England During the Long Eighteenth Century, 1694–1820," in *The Bank of England: Money, Power and Influence 1694–1994*, ed. Richard Roberts and David Kynaston (Oxford: Clarendon Press, 1995), 1–18.

[16] Herman Van der Wee, "Monetary, Credit, and Banking Systems," in *The Cambridge Economic History of Europe.*, vol. 5, *The Economic Organization of Early Modern Europe*, ed. Edwin E. Rich and Charles H. Wilson (Cambridge: Cambridge University Press, 1977), 290–393.

[17] On enterprise use of Internet legal databases, see Kathryn Hendley, Barry W. Ickes, Peter Murrell, and Randi Ryterman, "Observations on the Use of Law by Russian Enterprises," *Post-Soviet Affairs* 13 (January-March 1997): 19–41.

time, what Richard Sylla has termed "monetary innovation."[18] The key transitions may be summarized in a stylized way: a plurality of coins can prompt sovereigns to claim a monopoly on minting them; but control over the minting of metal coins may be rendered secondary by the growth of banks that issue notes on a coin reserve; and a monopoly on banknote issue can be rendered secondary by the growth of fractional reserve deposit banking. Russia's case, in which control over fractional reserve deposit banking is rendered secondary by a proliferation of closed barter circuits and the absence of unified power to make and enforce decisions on what will be counted as payment of a debt, does not seem to have a historical precedent.

Nevertheless, the next few pages present a brief comparative investigation of two countries, Italy and the United States, in the era in which primary contention was centered on regulation of the issue of banknotes. Thus the time period involved begins in the first half of the nineteenth century for the United States and the second half of the nineteenth century for Italy. Both countries, in the periods under discussion, had national states that sought, with greater or lesser intensity and success, to extend their authority and jurisdiction at the expense of subnational rivals. Thus, although neither the antebellum U.S. federal government nor the post-Risorgimento Italian state forms a precise analog to the Russian government—which inherited the trappings of a nation-state's power as the result of the collapse of the Soviet Union—at least it can be said of all the cases that there was a national government that faced internal challenges to the scope of its authority.[19] Italy and the United States also faced, again to varying degrees, the issue of national market unification characteristic of both early and late developers in the nineteenth century, when transportation technologies and nationwide legal authority made such an integration seem feasible.[20] And the fracturing of economic space by multiple banks of issue, though for reasons already described not entirely parallel to the fragmentation created by Russia's localized barter circuits, may hold a similar political import.

The major distinction between the politics of monetary consolidation (used now in the specific sense of the centralization of banknote issue) in

[18] Richard Sylla, "Monetary Innovation in America," *Journal of Economic History* 52 (March 1982): 21–30.
[19] Because a drive for monetary unification was part and parcel of the movement for German unification in the nineteenth century, the German case is less interesting in this regard.
[20] On the political significance and dynamics of building a national market, see Kiren Aziz Chaudhry, "The Myths of the Market and the Common History of Late Developers," *Politics & Society* 21 (September 1993): 245–274; Chaudhry, *Price of Wealth*; and Kiren Aziz Chaudhry and David Woodruff, "Political Origins of Market Institutions" (paper presented at the Annual Meeting of the American Political Science Association, Washington, DC, 1997).

Italy and the United States is that in Italy, contention over this issue was relatively disconnected from the politics of national market integration, whereas in the United States the two issues were far more closely linked. Both countries experienced what might be called a "Listian moment," involving the simultaneous unification of the internal market and its defense against foreign competitors. In Italy, however, this impulse was much weaker and soon overtaken by an outward focus on the part of business interests, whereas in the United States. the national market-building project came to fruition in the policies the Republican Party instituted when in control of government during the Civil War. As will be discussed next, these contrasting fortunes of the Listian project had consequences both for the eventual origin of central banking in both countries and for the constitution of key social forces.

Italy's unifying "Risorgimento" was mostly accomplished between 1859 and 1861. This process was led from the Piedmont on the French border, the center of the Kingdom of Sardinia, and unification initially had the form of annexation to Sardinia. The Kingdom of Italy was formed in 1861 and continued to annex new territory until 1870. The newly incorporated areas had been controlled by a variety of foreign powers, local monarchies, or recently victorious liberal or nationalist revolutionaries. They also had their own economic arrangements, including a variety of banks of issue. In the Piedmont, well before the Risorgimento, Prime Minister Cavour had orchestrated the emergence of a single dominant bank of issue, closely linked to the state: the Banca Nazionale degli Stati Sardi, or BNS.[21] Once annexations of territory began, the BNS hoped to secure a monopoly on banknote issue throughout united Italy. Through buying out existing competitors and preventing the emergence of new ones, the BNS was relatively successful in northern Italy. However, in central and southern Italy, the BNS was not so successful, despite the backing of Cavour. By 1861 it had become clear that political means were not going to bring the BNS its desired exclusive position. It adopted the official-sounding name of Banca Nazionale nel Regno d'Italia (BNR) and turned to a long-running campaign of aggressive competition against its Tuscan, Neapolitan, and Sicilian competitors, including organizing runs against their reserves.[22] The government, meanwhile, continued efforts to set up a single bank of issue

---

[21] Paul M. Howell, *Capitalism in the Risorgimento: Joint-Stock Banking and Economic Development in the Kingdom of Sardinia, 1843–1859* (New York: Garland Publishing, 1992); Gianni Toniolo, *An Economic History of Liberal Italy*, trans. Maria Rees (London: Routledge, 1990), 47.
[22] This account draws especially on Luigi De Rosa, "Unity or Plurality? Italian Issuing Banks, 1861–1893," *The Journal of European Economic History* 23 (1994): 453–475; see also Valeria Sannucci, "The Establishment of a Central Bank: Italy in the Nineteenth Century," in *A European Central Bank? Perspectives on Monetary Unification after Ten Years of the EMS*, ed. Marcello De Cecco and Alberto Giovannini (Cambridge: Cambridge University Press, 1989), 244–279;

by brokering a merger between the BNR and its Tuscan competitors and drafting a bill that would give the merged bank exclusive responsibility for handling government accounts. The Neapolitan bank (Bank of Naples, or BN) was able to block passage of this bill in Parliament in 1865.

In 1866, a financial crisis led to the suspension of convertibility; at this point, pressure on the BN was eased since "the government needed the support of all the issuing banks in the country, including the Bank of Naples."[23] Inconvertibility lasted until 1881. Initially the BNR was given the exclusive right to issue government fiat money as well as legal tender status for its own notes, but monetary fragmentation persisted. Both banks and various nonbank institutions issued notes. Government regulatory capacity was too weak to control the volume of notes in circulation and to ensure that all note-issuers were reliable, and this meant that "there were [some] notes circulating all over the country and others confined to more limited areas."[24] Apparently concerned by this fragmentation, and needing to draw on all the major banks for funds to reduce the budget deficit, the government arranged for passage of a new law in 1874 that organized six banks of issue into a consortium that issued money with legal tender.[25] Members of the consortium were also allowed "to issue banknotes in any province where they had a branch or where a local bank acted as their agent, making it possible to overcome the regional limitations of the issuing system."[26] In point of fact, however, government regulation of the consortium banks was quite weak, as revealed most dramatically in the Banca Romano crisis of 1893, when it developed that this bank of issue had printed substantially more notes than had been authorized. This and associated events led to the collapse of a number of major banks.

Why did Italy preserve a system of multiple banks of issue? Creation of a home market for industry was not a factor in the drive for Italian unification.[27] Indeed, one of the first measures taken after unification was the lowering of tariff barriers to foreign imports. United Italy was largely agricultural, and its southern and northern portions were embedded in the international economy in very different ways. Rightist governments did

---

and Michele Fratianni and Franco Spinelli, *A Monetary History of Italy* (Cambridge: Cambridge University Press, 1997), 61–64.

[23] De Rosa, "Unity or Plurality?" 463.

[24] Fratianni and Spinelli, *Monetary History*, 80.

[25] Broz has described such arrangements between banks of issue and governments as a trade of "cartel for credit." Lawrence Broz, *The International Origins of the Federal Reserve System* (Ithaca: Cornell University Press, 1997), 228.

[26] Ibid., 81; De Rosa, "Unity or Plurality?" 466.

[27] Toniolo, *Economic History*, 48; Frank J. Coppa, "The Italian Tariff and the Conflict between Agriculture and Industry: The Commercial Policy of Liberal Italy, 1860–1922," *Journal of Economic History* 30 (December 1970): 742–769, at 743.

pursue a program of railroad building in the decade after unification, but one that was only able to give a relatively weak contribution to market integration and virtually no stimulus to domestic heavy industry.[28] As one Italian economist wrote in 1866, "if we did not know that 22 million people have for some years been united in society and government, there would be very little in the economic order to show the observer that a great nation has been formed, that a great community of civilized men has been united by their own will."[29] It was not until 1871 that anything approaching a program for national market integration with real industrial backing began to be formulated, and not until 1877 that the first substantial protective tariffs were passed.[30] Though these were opposed by the banks of issue, they nevertheless conceded to the changes in return for a continuation of their privileged position.[31]

James Kurth has argued that Italian development typifies a "Southern pattern" of late development in which the light-industrial interests that stood for the integration of the domestic market were relatively weak due to the rapid development of heavy industry that needed an external market.[32] In a similar vein, Luigi De Rosa writes that by the late 1880s, "it became evident that there was a growing awareness that the Italian market was quite inadequate for the needs of Italian industry."[33] It matters little whether the BNR's failed attempt to become an exclusive bank of issue in these years stemmed from localist protection against it or from its own inability to adapt to unfamiliar financial practices in southern Italy.[34] The point was that in neither case was the drive to integrate the national market sufficient to propel the creation of a fully unified monetary system. Nor were state fiscal or administrative interests enough to push a thoroughgoing monetary consolidation. Instead, the state compromised with the multiple banks of issue system in order to bridge fiscal difficulties, and was able to rely on the banks jointly for Treasury services.

[28] Gino Luzzato, "The Italian Economy in the First Decade after Unification," in *Essays in European Economic History, 1789–1914*, ed. Francois Crouzet, William H. Chaloner, and Walter M. Stern (London: Edward Arnold, 1969), 203–225, at 213–215; Stefano Fenoaltea, "Italy," in *Railways and the Economic Development of Western Europe, 1830–1914*, ed. Patrick O'Brien (London: Macmillan, 1983), 49–120.

[29] Quoted in Luzzato, "Italian Economy," 203.

[30] Luigi De Rosa, "Economics and Nationalism in Italy (1861–1914)," *Journal of European Economic History* 11 (Winter 1982): 537–574, at 544.

[31] Toniolo, *Economic History*, 81.

[32] James R. Kurth, "Industrial Change and Political Change: A European Perspective," in *The New Authoritiarianism in Latin America*, ed. David Collier (Princeton: Princeton University Press, 1979), 319–362.

[33] De Rosa, "Economics and Nationalism," 554.

[34] For the first position, see De Rosa, "Unity or Plurality?" and Howell, *Capitalism*, 233; for the second, Sannucci, "Establishment."

The development of banks of issue in America followed a quite differ-ent path. From the passage of the Constitution to the Civil War, there was continuing controversy over whether the country should have a national bank of issue. The country had a national bank from 1791 to 1811, and again from 1817 to 1833.[35] Bank supporters squarely framed their support for a national bank of issue in the context of programs for the develop-ment and the integration of the internal market. Alexander Hamilton, in proposing the establishment of the First Bank of the United States in 1790, noted how it would facilitate payment and transmission of tax receipts; in his famous "Report on Manufactures" of 1791 he added that

> [t]he facilitating of pecuniary remittance from place to place is a point of considerable moment to trade in general, and to manufacturers in particu-lar, by rendering more easy the purchase of raw materials and provisions, and the payment for manufacturers' supplies. A general circulation of bank paper, which is to be expected from the institution lately established, will be a most valuable means to this end.[36]

Although the First Bank certainly had aspects of what Lawrence Broz has called a "cartel for credit" bargain limiting entry into the banknote issue market in return for loans to the government, this market integration com-ponent cannot be ignored. The Italian variant of licensing separate banks with regional monopolies would have served as well if loans to government were the only aim.

The market-integration political import of a national note-issuing bank was underscored in the formation of the Second Bank of the United States in 1816. As Charles Sellers has convincingly argued, the period following the War of 1812 saw the rise of a program for "national developmental-ism" that sought to concentrate key economic powers on the federal level. The foundation of the Second Bank was only one such measure. In these years, the Supreme Court also asserted the right of federal authorities to regulate corporations and ensure the sanctity of contract. A campaign was launched to build a nationwide transportation system. Finally, tariffs were increased to protect domestic industry.[37] These measures, very much in the Hamiltonian mold, once again demonstrated the close link between a

[35] Actually, the Second Bank of the United States lasted somewhat longer than this, but it had lost meaningful status as a federal bank by 1833.

[36] Alexander Hamilton, *Alexander Hamilton's Papers on Public Credit, Commerce, and Finance*, ed. Samuel McKee (New York: Liberal Arts Press, 1957), 245.

[37] Charles Grier Sellers, *The Market Revolution: Jacksonian America, 1815–1846* (New York: Ox-ford University Press, 1991), 70–102; Merrill D. Petersen, *The Great Triumvirate: Webster, Clay, and Calhoun* (Oxford: Oxford University Press, 1987), 48–49.

program for internal development and the support of a national note-issuing bank.

The national developmental program embodied by the Second Bank of the United States was not without enemies among the partisans of a variety of localisms. State governments, eager to charter their own banks as a source of tax revenue, were enemies of both banks.[38] (When out of Congress, Henry Clay worked as a lawyer for the Second Bank of the United States and brought suit against Ohio for an exorbitant tax it had assessed the bank.)[39] Agrarian localism, suspicious of banks and centralization in general, found a champion on the national level in Andrew Jackson, whose presidency saw the dismantling of national monetary institutions and the defeat of the campaign to have the federal government spearhead construction of a national transportation infrastructure.[40]

The national developmentalist program came to fruition in the period of the Civil War. The Republican Party used its dominance in a Congress shrunk by secession to implement long-standing developmentalist plans on tariffs and transport as well as money. Wartime monetary policy was complex, involving both the printing of an essentially unbacked fiat currency (the greenbacks) and laying the foundation for a new system of gold-backed federal currency after the war. In particular, wartime legislation established a National Bank system, under which the federal government would print the notes to be issued by a limited number of licensed banks. Although no national note issue bank was set up, a congressman was certainly justified in describing national banking legislation as "a centralization of power, such as Hamilton might have eulogized as magnificent."[41] Legislation introduced prohibitive taxes on the issue of notes by state banks, essentially eliminating this activity. Furthermore, at the insistence of representatives of western states whose state-regulated banks had collapsed at the war's outset, the redemption of notes was centered in New York, which was felt to have the most reliable banks.[42]

In both Italy and America, then, monetary consolidation (again, in the specific sense of control over banknote issue) took the form of government authorization of banknote issue by a limited number of banks. Monetary consolidation as the project of a single bank of issue closely linked to the national state was thus forestalled. However, in the United States, mone-

---

[38] Broz, *International Origins*, 232–240.

[39] Petersen, *Great Triumvirate*, 67.

[40] Sellers, *Market Revolution*, 301–331.

[41] Quoted in Heather Cox Richardson, *The Greatest Nation of the Earth: Republican Economic Policies During the Civil War* (Cambridge: Harvard University Press, 1997), 66.

[42] Richardson, *Greatest Nation*, 66–102; see also William Gerald Shade, *Banks or No Banks: The Money Issue in Western Politics, 1832–1865* (Detroit: Wayne State University, 1972).

tary consolidation was nevertheless brought about on a template created by a long-standing movement for market unification and powerful national economic institutions. The National Bank Act involved a compromise with the private banks that were to issue the notes, but the resulting monetary system was clearly national in scope, even if its center was in New York, not Washington. The more tenuous monetary consolidation in Italy from 1874 onward also represented a compromise of mutual interest between the fisc and banks of issue, but unlike the American version, this compromise was entirely detached from a larger project of building an integrated internal market. Indeed, the Italian compromise was with banks embedded in local markets and ways of doing business. The link of the project of monetary consolidation to market integration in the American case, like the lack of such a link in the Italian case, was to have important long-term implications for the structure of political forces. These implications can be seen in a brief investigation of the origins of central banking in the two countries. In Italy, a would-be central bank finally achieved that status only because its competitors collapsed. Central banking was never a political priority of a regionally fragmented, export-oriented business elite. America, by contrast, acquired a central bank as the result of a political movement that built a nationwide business coalition of enduring significance.

In Italy, the 1893 Banca Romano scandal occasioned the collapse of major northern banks and, shortly thereafter, the creation of two new "mixed banks" in Milan funded in substantial part by German capital. The crisis also led to the formation of the Banca d'Italia, a would-be central bank formed from several of the old issuing banks. The authority of this embryonic central bank was shaky, however. As Douglas Forsyth writes, "The major Milanese banks essentially created their own autonomous monetary system by holding the reserves and rediscounting the commercial paper of smaller banks that moved in their orbits . . . the directors of the Milanese banks apparently resisted the idea that the Italian issue banks should actively regulate the credit market at all."[43] The Milanese mixed banks' indifference to national banking institutions probably had its roots in their role as the core of a northern Italian industrial system focused heavily on exports and quite separate from the southern economy.[44]

It was decades before the BI gained full control over monetary policy after 1930, and even this was the result of what was essentially a collapse of

[43] Douglas J. Forsyth, *The Crisis of Liberal Italy: Monetary and Financial Policy, 1914–1922* (Cambridge: Cambridge University Press, 1993), 40.
[44] Alfredo G. Esposto, "Italian Industrialization and the Gerschenkronian 'Great Spurt': A Regional Analysis," *Journal of Economic History* 52 (June 1992): 353–362.

the Milanese banks.[45] The long-term weakness of the internal monetary system was presumably possible because it was not a major focus for the lobbying of business groups, which were oriented toward imperialism-secured export markets. The BI's lonely efforts to act as a central bank had no broad business support, and it is no surprise that this led it "to cooperate with the more speculative and corrupt banks in their efforts to gain greater control over the financial markets, thereby further destabilizing the financial system."[46] This is not the sort of constituency likely to be tied to nonfinancial business groups seeking a unified internal market.

The origins of modern central banking in America were sharply different. There are competing explanations for the origins of the political movement to create the Federal Reserve in the United States. But whether it was begun as the effort of a narrow group of international bankers to create institutions allowing the dollar to be profitably traded, or as the effort of a broad nationwide business coalition seeking monetary institutions that would be reliable without being excessively deflationary, the important thing about this movement is that it was thoroughly national in scope and brought together businesspeople from various sectors.[47] Livingston may choose to refer to this movement as an example of a class-in-itself becoming a class-for-itself; Broz may choose to refer to it an Olsonian privileged group discovering that its private interest will allow it to build a coalition for a public interest. Whatever the truth in these formulations, either one demonstrates how successfully the monetary consolidation of the Civil War cast politics in a national frame. Italy's monetary consolidation, by contrast, institutionalized regional financial fragmentation and did not provoke the formation of a nationally integrated business movement.

The cases presented in such summary form here are not intended to test a "theory of monetary consolidation"—as already suggested, the persistence of monetary innovation and the varying political-economic contexts into which monetary consolidation can be inserted make such a theory either unattainable or else so general as to be uninteresting. Certainly, these two cases do share some general features with the politics of Russian monetary consolidation as described in this book. In particular, politics is material politics—regions, government, and firms fight for their economic interests. It is even, at times, a politics of rent seeking. Yet it is not thereby

[45] Douglas J. Forsyth, "The Rise and Fall of German-inspired Mixed Banking in Italy, 1894–1936," in *The Role of Banks in the Interwar Economy*, ed. Harold James, Hakan Lindgren, and Alice Teichova (Cambridge: Cambridge University Press, 1991), 179–205, 196–200.
[46] Forsyth, *Crisis*, 11.
[47] For these interpretations, see, respectively, Broz, *International Origins* and James Livingston, *Origins of the Federal Reserve System: Money, Class, and Corporate Capitalism, 1890–1913* (Ithaca: Cornell University Press, 1986).

merely an allocation of preexisting resources. Rather, politics centers around the creation of new kinds of resources for distribution through new mechanisms. Politics is also not a bilateral relationship between a distant state and an atomized society, as the example of private note-issue banks vested with state functions demonstrates. Economic actors' own efforts to produce institutions, such as the agreements that stabilized banking communities in Milan and New York, offer challenges to and opportunities for projects of national monetary unification. And none of this is froth on the waves of history. The cases demonstrate that monetary consolidation is implicated in the processes that determine how—and the extent to which—politics becomes cast in a national frame and thus conditions the formation of key political forces. Long-term differences in the regional cohesion of business groups and the character of central banking demonstrate that monetary consolidation is not just more or less rapid movement to a single, known end point.

We may be sure that in Russia, too, the path by which monetary consolidation is achieved will have an enduring impact. But the contrast between Italy and America has one more direct implication for Russia's prospects. In Italy, banknotes were not convertible into gold for fifteen years, from 1866 to 1881. This amounted to a policy of a weak exchange rate. Certainly this had the effect of providing some protection for domestic producers.[48] But given the weak internal integration of the Italian market after unification, and the previous focus of both the southern and the northern economies on export opportunities, it is not outlandish to suggest another effect as well. The weak exchange rate made it harder for the domestic market to offer opportunities that could compete with those available on the foreign market. In these crucial years shortly after the country was formed, it was likely much easier and more profitable for exporters to focus on existing markets abroad than trying to overcome poor communications and the fragmentation of financial practices at home.

A similar argument applies to Russia. Unless monetary consolidation is to take the form of a passive central ratification of local money issue, bringing it to a conclusion will be an expensive and time-consuming project. It will require political backing from an economic force with nationwide interests. What monetary consolidation would offer to such a force—whether Gazprom or bank-led industrial groups—would be customers who could pay not in kind, and not in surrogate monies, but in rubles. If rubles are worthless, monetary consolidation will not be attractive. It may be that Russia's chance to overcome its nonmonetary economy depends on its ability to stabilize its monetary economy.

[48] Coppa, "Italian Tariff," 743.

A P P E N D I X

Internet Sources

For many of the following publications, I have drawn some issues from print sources and some from electronic sources. When a publication is cited without a page number, this means it is cited to its electronic version. The following are either the best sources for the electronic publications mentioned as of April 1998 or the site at which information cited in the text was collected.

Delo (Samara), 195.209.67.6/press/index.asp
Delovaia Sibir' (Novosibirsk), now off-line; some back issues at www.securities.com
Delovoi Ekspress, www.securities.com
Delovoi Iuridicheskii Zhurnal, www.dux.ru/koi8/koi8/enpp/EnppHome.html
Ekonomika i Zhizn' (Moscow), solar.rtd.utk.edu/friends/economics/el/Economics.html
Ekspert (Moscow), www.securities.com, www.park.ru, or www.expert.ru
Federal News Service (Washington), Dow Jones Information Service Text Library
Inforis Legal Database (Nizhnii Novgorod), www.inforis.ru:8001/home.html
Ispolnitel'naia Vlast', Den' za dnem, (Sverdlovsk), csp.mplik.ru/govpress/bulleten/BUL9701.HTM
Kommersant [renamed *Kommersant Vlast'*] (Moscow), www.securities.com
Kommersant-Daily (Moscow), www.securities.com.
Nauchnyi Park, www.park.ru
New in Russian Legislation, www.securities.com

Predpriiatie (Tomsk), www.tomsk.net:8001/Enterprise/

Rossiiskaia Aziia (Novosibirsk), www.park.ru

Rossiiskie Regiony (Moscow), www.transport.ru

Rossiiskii Neftianoi Biulleten', www.securities.com

Russian Economic Trends, www.securities.com

Segodnia (Moscow), www.securities.com

State Tax Service Website, http://is.park.ru/

V Mire Finansov, prilozhenie k gazete "Respublika Sakha,"
    srv.yacc.yakutia.su/~resp/mirfin/

Vestnik Upravleniia Pravitel'stvennoi Informatsiei, www.online.ru/rproducts/vestnik-upi/

WPS Regional Press Survey, www.securities.com

Index

Deflation, 113, 129–30
  monetary payment and, 191–92
De Rosa, Luigi, 212
Diakov, Anatolii, 197
Directors' corpus, 84, 93, 203
Discounting, 30, 36. *See also* Wechsel
Double movement (Polanyi), 112. *See also* Triple movement
Douglas, Mary, 11, 12, 22

Economic crisis, changing meaning of, 56–60
Economies of scope, 126
Economists' approaches to money, 15–16
Economy. *See also* Command economy; Substantive economy
  controls over, 24–25
  disintegration of, 73–76
  feudalism in, 206
  formal vs. substantive, 146
  political power and, 1–2
  political struggles and crises in, 56–60
  regionalization of, 5
  virtual, 174–75
Electric power companies. *See* Power industry; United Energy System
Emergency Tax Commission, 182, 198
Energy sectors, 146, 203–4. *See also* Gazprom; Power industry
Enterprise directors. *See* Directors' corpus
Enterprise money, 12
  partitioning of, 66
Enterprises, 61. *See also* Giro-wechsels; Ministries; Power industry; Provinces
  battle for barter by, 68–73
  electric power payment by, 128–29
  exit from money economy, 133
  extortionate relationship to, 67–68
  government response to nonpayment by, 131–37
  horizontal and vertical exchange and, 61–64
  in-enterprise distribution of goods and, 69
  interenterprise relations and, 102–7
  Party relations with, 63
  prepayment by, 96n52
  price liberalization and, 115
  special accounts for, 98
Equation of exchange, 32
Exchange fund, interregional barter and, 70
Exchange rate
  Gazprom and, 192
  metal industry and, 162–163

Far East Association of Economic Cooperation, 75
Federal Bankruptcy Commission, 187
Federal government. *See* Central government
Federal Reserve (U.S.), 216
Feudal economy, 206, 207, 208
Financial industrial groups, 189–90
Firms. *See* Enterprises

First Bank of the United States, 213
Fiscal federalism, nonmonetary taxation and, 169–73
Five-Year Plan, 24, 27–28
Fixed prices, 88
FKTsB (Federal Commission on the Securities Market), 184–85, 186
Float on payments, 45, 106
Fondy system, 47, 53
Foreign trade, 67, 163, 206
Formal economy, substantive economy and, 146
Forsyth, Douglas, 215
Free banking system, 89n35, 204
Frye, Timothy, 184–85

Gaddy, Clifford, 175
Gaidar, Yegor, 13, 82–84, 86, 87–88, 92, 93–94, 95, 103, 108, 110–11
Gazprom, 116, 152–53, 191, 197, 199. *See also* Power industry
  monetary payment and, 192–94
Gerashchenko, Viktor, 84–85, 97–98, 99, 101
Giros, 151–52, 179
Giro-wechsels, 183–84. *See also* Wechsel
  bank issuance of, 155–58
  barter and, 153–55
  federal government issuance of, 165–66
  local government issuance of, 158–61
Gold standard, 28–30, 32–33, 205
Goods famine, 29, 34–35
Gorbachev, Mikhail, 56–58, 77, 115
  barter and, 62
  failure of, 60
  perestroika, command economy, and, 64–68
Gosbank, 35–43, 54
  money creation and, 43–45
Goszakazy (state purchase orders), 67
Gourevitch, Peter, 144
Great Transformation, The (Polanyi), 4, 111, 143
Green, Roy, 30
Gresham's law, 151–52, 153, 156, 159, 167–68, 176
Grossman, Gregory, 59, 63
Gusev, Vladimir, 135

Hamilton, Alexander, 213, 214
Hanson, Philip, 144
Hard-state liberalism, 181–82, 187–90, 199, 201, 204
Heating companies. *See* Gazprom; Power industry
Hecksher, Eli F., 207
Home market (conciliationist) approach to monetary consolidation, 181–82, 200
Horizontal exchange relations in command economy, 59, 61–64
  economic and political unification and, 76
Hydropower plants, 138, 139
Hyperinflation, 25–26, 27

Ickes, Barry, 175
Ilf, Ilya (satirist), 11, 12, 79
IMF. *See* International Monetary Fund (IMF)
Industrialization, 35, 46, 51
   forced, 51
Industrial lobby, 94, 99. *See also* Directors'
   corpus
Industry. *See also* Power industry
   opposition to reform by, 84
   political representation of, 115–16
   sectors of, 115–16
Inflation, 58, 92, 105–6, 203
   accommodation paper and, 41
   Bolshevik analysis of, 25–28
   control over, 66
   Gerashchenko and, 101n77
   mechanisms for repressing, 63–64
   monetarist theories of, 13
   monetization and, 82
   rent-seeking and, 86
Inflation tax, 26–27, 34
Infrastructure, enterprise nonpayment issues
   and, 132–33
In-kind payments, 119–20, 138, 153, 166
   as price concession, 124–30
In-kind taxation, 20, 70–71, 135–37, 166–67
   local government giro-wechsels and,
     158–59
   payment reform and, 197–98
   provincial, 70–71
Institutions. *See also* Monetary institutions
   definition and functions of, 22–23
   development of, 45–46
Instructive bankruptcies, 92
Interenterprise relations
   central subsidies and, 102–7
   credit, 122n33
   debt, 89, 94
Interest rates, 100
   on cash and wechsel loans, 158
International Monetary Fund (IMF), 168, 188
   natural monopoly reform and, 191–92
Interregional alliances, 75, 87, 184
Interregional barter, 59–61, 70–71, 87
Intimidation approach, to monetary consoli-
   dation, 90, 91, 92–97, 180–181
Italy, monetary system of, 209–12, 215–16

Jackson, Andrew, 214
Jepperson, Ronald, 22

Kaznacheistvo (treasury office), 106n89
Knapp, Georg Friedrich, 16, 147
KNOs. *See* Treasury tax offsets (KNOs)
Kornai, János, 10, 104
Krasnoyarsk Province, 70, 72, 107, 117,
   120n29, 127, 133, 135, 138, 139. *See also*
   Power industry
   wechsels in, 159
Krotov, Pavel, 61, 206

Kulaks, 28
Kurth, James, 212

Latynina, Yuliya, 206
Law on Cooperatives, 65
Left (political) in 1920s, 33, 35
   money creation and, 43
Legal institutions, money defined by, 17–18
Lewin, Moshe, 46
Liberalism, hard-state, 181–82, 187–90
Ligachev, Yegor, 56–57, 69, 77
Liquidity, of wechsels, 150
Livshits, F. D., 31
Loans. *See* Credits
Local governments, 76, 143–45. *See also* Re-
   gional cooperation
   barter and, 147
   center-regional tax competition and,
     169–73
   vs. central control, 114–15
   giro-wechsels issued by, 158–61
   power company lobbying for payment and,
     138–42
   responses to barter of the bankrupt,
     130–37
Logic of Collective Action (Olson), 132. *See also*
   Olson, Mancur

Macroeconomic control, 58
   vs. production, 53
Macroeconomy
   disintegration in, 73–76
   imbalance in, 67
Manorial system, 207, 208
Market(s)
   barter of the bankrupt and, 111–17
   control of, 4
   for electric power, 197
   international, 67
   in Italy and United States, 209
   Soviet economy and, 201
   wechsels and, 40
Market economy, 2, 6–7, 61
Market forces, reaction against, 111
Market integration, in United States, 213
Market reform, 184
   economic argument for, 9
   limitations of concept, 7–8
   monetary consolidation and, 6–15
   as public good, 9
Markups, for profitability, 126
Matiukhin, Georgii, 66, 96
Media of exchange, metal-based, 205–6
Menger, Carl, 15
   on evolution of barter into money,
     149–51, 156
Mercantilism, Schmoller on, 113n7
Metallurgy committee, 191
Mezhfilialnyi oborot (MFO) (Soviet bank trans-
   fer system), 66–67

Nonmonetary exchange (*continued*)
  monetary expression of, 149
  national policy on, 164–69
  rate of exchange for, 161–64
Nonmonetary payment, 178–79
Nonmonetary taxation, and fiscal federalism.
  See In-kind taxation
Nonpayments, 47, 89, 93, 94–96, 103–4
  to power companies, 119–23, 128, 129, 130–37
Nonpayments commission, 164–66, 187
Nonpayments crisis, 102–3
"Not-in-My-Backyard Stabilization," 144

Offe, Claus, 97
Offset(s) (*zachet* or *vzaimozachet*), as political
  demand of directors' corpus, 93
  bank records system and, 97–107
  federal taxation and, 167–168
  by Gazprom, 152–153
  in 1992, 97–99
  in Soviet period, 47
  local taxation and, 135
Olson, Mancur, 132
Olsonian privileged group, 216
Organization for Economic Co-operation and
  Development, 169
Overvalued goods, 126

Paperless wechsel, 184, 185–86. *See also* Wechsel
Partitioned money, 25, 45–52, 53–54
Payment. *See also* Money; Nonpayments
  automatic for production, 46–47
  barter of the bankrupt and, 111
  credit and, 40
  delinquency in, 119
  methods of, 206
  to power companies, 118–19, 138–42
  system of, 96–97
  transactions, 17
  wechsels as, 150
Payment in kind, 113–14, 119–20
Payment order system, 88
Perestroika, 77
  and disintegration of command econ-
    omy, 64–68
Petrov, Yevgeni (satirist), 11, 12, 79
Philosophy of Money, The (Simmel), 16, 137
Piatakov, Grigorii, 37, 38, 41, 45
Planned economy
  Credit Reform and, 38
  disintegration of, 80
Plan-replacement barter, 75
Pochinok, Alexander, 199
Pocket banks, 105
Polanyi, Karl, 4, 5, 19, 107–8, 111–13,
  129–30, 143–44, 206
Politics
  barter of the bankrupt and, 110–11
  cash register or allocation vs. rule and con-
    trol images, 7–8, 111
  economic disintegration and, 74–76
  hard-state liberalism and, 189

Left vs. Right in 1920s, 33
market reform approach assumptions
  about, 11
monetization and, 83–88
power company debt collection and, 140
of price flexibility, 128
of stabilization, 114
Popov, Vladimir, 63
Potanin, Vladimir, 189
Power industry
  barter, giro-wechsels, and, 153–55
  collection problems of, 116–30
  local and federal responses to collection
    problems, 130–37
  natural monopolies, monetization, and, 190–98
  tax debts and, 146–47
Preobrazhensky, Yevgeni, 26, 33
Price(s). *See* Monetization; specific "price"
  entries
Price concessions (power industry), 121–23
  difficulty of making, 123–24
  in-kind payment as, 124–30
  and overvalued goods, 126
Price discrimination, 122–23
Price freezes, 191
Price liberalization, 2, 13, 108, 110, 113
  Gaidar and, 82–84
  monetization and, 80–88
  payment order system and, 88
Price policy, 28–29
Price-ratification barter, 127
Price regulation, 125
Price rigidity, 125, 175
  nonmonetary exchange and, 165
Price-setting markets, 161
Pricing
  cost-plus 127, 130
  of nonmonetary payments, 161–64
Primorye Province, 71, 72, 74, 117, 120n23,
  126, 132, 139, 140. *See also* Power industry
Private business, 58
Privatization, 189
  electric power companies and, 138–39
  of electric power systems, 195
Prodnalog, 26
Production
  classes of, 53
  control of, 24–25, 41–42
  credit and, 40–41, 46–47
  macroeconomic control and, 53–54
  money as lubricant of, 49, 101
  organization of, 12, 13
  role of money in, 23–24
  after Soviet breakup, 2
Production cycle, 50
Productivism, 99–100, 181–82, 183–87, 199, 201
Profit, price regulation and, 125–26
Provinces. *See also* Enterprises; Interregional
  barter; Ministries; Regional cooperation
  barter within, 59–61
  battling for barter and, 68–73
  as currency community, 69

governments of, 18
taxes in wechsels accepted by, 160
Provincial governments, 203–4. *See also* Local
governments; Power industry; Regional co-
operation; specific provinces
power sector and, 143–45
Public good, market reform as, 9
Public vs. private infrastructure, 19
Purchasing power, 25, 53n107
Pynchon, Thomas, 110

Quantity theory of money, 28–29, 32–33, 205
Quasi monies, 147

Rabkrin, 37
Rail sector, 116n12, 118n17, 190–91
Rate of exchange, for nonmonetary exchange, 161–64
Ratifying and regulation of credit, 90
Rational expectations program, 10
Rationing, 12, 47–48, 49, 51
avoiding, 69
in provinces, 73
Real Bills doctrine, 28–31, 33, 35, 37, 38, 53,
90, 91, 183
Redistribution, 87
Reforms. *See also* Credit Reform; Gorbachev,
Mikhail
cooperatives and, 65
debt, 177–78
industrial opposition to, 84
of natural monopolies, 190–98
by Yeltsin, 115
Regional cooperation, 184. *See also* Local governments
center-regional tax competition and, 169–73
interprovincial barter and, 58, 59–61
monetary consolidation and, 4, 17–20
power industries and, 138–42
Regionalization, wechsel programs and, 159
Regional power systems, 196–97
Regions. *See* Provinces; Regional cooperation;
Regionalization
Regulation
by Central Bank, 96
of power industry prices, 125–28
self-regulating markets and, 112
of taxes, 134–35
of wechsels, 184
Regulators, 178, 198
Rent-seeking, 9, 86, 216
"Report on Manufactures" (Hamilton), 213
Repressive mechanisms, for inflation, 63–64
Republics, post-Soviet, 81n4
Right (political) in 1920s, 33, 35
money creation and, 43
Risorgimento (Italy), 209, 210
Ruble, value of, 162–64
"Ruble zone," 81n4
Russia. *See also* Central government
competition with Soviet Union by, 73–76
after Soviet breakup, 1–2

Russian Congress of People's Deputies, 73
Russian Council of Ministers, 115

Samara Province, 133, 135, 138, 139, 152n10.
See also Power industry
banks in, 106
electric power companies in, 117, 120n23
in-kind tax in, 71–72
Sapir, Jacques, 95n48
Schmoller, Gustav von, 207
Schumpeter, Joseph, 6, 111, 130, 207
Scissors crisis (1921–1923), 26
Second Bank of the United States, 213, 214
Sectoral elites, 148
Seigniorage, 25–26, 98
Self-regulating markets, 112–13
Sellers, Charles, 213–14
Shadow economy, 63. *See also* Barter; Ex-
change; Horizontal exchange relations in
command economy; Vertical exchange re-
lations in command economy
Shafranik, Yuri, 141
Shanin, Lev, 42
Shays' Rebellion, 177–78, 179–80, 198
Shearer, David, 45
Shmelev, Nikolai, 63
Shortages, 29, 59
direction of, 67
money and, 64
provincial governments and, 72–73
Sibenergo, 153–54
Siberian Agreement, 59, 75, 87, 184, 185–87
Simmel, Georg, 1, 4, 16, 18, 52, 56, 137, 201
Smychka (worker-peasant alliance), 26, 28–35
Socialist production, 40
Social unit, 113
Society
misunderstood as assemblage of individuals, 10
monetary consolidation view of, 14–15
Polanyi on, 206
protection of, 143–45
Simmel on, 52, 201–2
Soviet, 52–53
Sociological-institutional approaches to
money, 15–17
Soft budget constraint, 10, 104–5
Sokolnikov, Grigorii, 27, 28, 32, 40, 53
Soskovets, Oleg, 165
Sovereignty
monetary consolidation and, 4, 6, 18
monetization and, 86
politics of, 7
Soviet Union
disintegration of, 1, 80
monetary system and society of, 52–53
Russian competition with, 73–76
Stalin, Iosif, 21
left and, 28
on role of money, 50–51
State (nation)
economic role of, 181–82
monetary consolidation and, 4, 14–15

State (nation) (*continued*)
   money and power of, 110–11
   paternalistic nature of, 105
   voluntarist vision of, 9–10
State Bank, 32–33, 37
   cash funds and, 66
State-building, 81–82
State Theory of Money, The (Knapp), 16, 147
Subsidies, 106
   central, 102–7
Substantive economy, 19, 20
   formal economy and, 146
Surrogate monies, 147, 149
Sverdlovskenergo, 195
Sylla, Richard, 209
Szatmary, David, 177

Tatarstan, 159
Tax arrears, 168, 171
Taxation in kind. *See* In-kind taxation
Tax code revisions, 125
Tax debts and debtors, 146–47, 168, 171, 187–90
Tax devolution, 172–73
Taxes and taxation, 2–3, 75. *See also* In-kind
      taxation
   central credits and, 100n69
   central vs. local control of, 114
   character of, 181
   collection of, 134–35, 170
   emission tax, 26–27
   of Gazprom, 192
   hard-state liberalism and, 187–90
   monetary and nonmonetary forms of pay-
      ment and, 178–79
   nonmonetary, 169–73
   nonmonetary exchange and, 162
   payment arrears, 134–35
   prodnalog, 26
   seigniorage as, 25–26
   in wechsels, 160
Tax evasion, 125, 200
Tax income, 166–67n61
Tax state, of Schumpeter, 207
Tiumen Province, 141, 172
Token money, 130
Tomsk province, 154
Treasury obligations, financing expenditures
   with, 165–66, 167

Treasury tax offsets (KNOs), 167, 168
Triple movement, 113–15, 129, 142, 143–45,
   148, 200–1. *See also* Power industry
   politics of, 203
Tveruniversalbank, 155

United Energy System (UES), 154–55,
   194–95, 196, 197. *See also* Power industry
United States, monetary system of, 209–10,
   213–15

Value
   consumer-driven theory of, 40
   disorganized by nonmonetary
      exchange, 175
   money as unit of, 15–17
   nature of, 40
   production-driven theory of, 40
Vecheka, 189
Vekselia. See Wechsel
Verdery, Katherine, 206
Vertical exchange relations in command
   economy, 59, 61–64, 67
   economic and political unification and, 76
Vesenkha, 35, 36, 39–40, 43
Viakhirev, Rem, 193
Virtual economy thesis, 174–75
Vzaimozachet. See Offset(s)

Wages
   cash payments of, 50
   in-kind, 138
War Communism, 25–26
Weber, Max, 3n3, 4n4, 137, 207, 208
Wechsel, 30, 31–33, 36, 40, 150–51, 183–87.
   See also Giro-wechsels
   cash controls and, 50
   elimination of, 43
   UES and, 196

Yanov, Alexander, 62, 77
Yasin, Yevgeni, 101–2, 199
Yeltsin, Boris, 1, 60, 69, 73, 74–76, 80, 81, 86,
   87, 115, 139. *See also* Russia
   barter and, 62
   Gorbachev and, 77–78

Zachet. See Offset(s)